MYERS+
CHANG
AT HOME

MYERS+ CHANG
AT HOME
YUM ME YUM YOU

JOANNE CHANG
WITH KAREN
AKUNOWICZ

Recipes from the Beloved Boston Eatery

Photography by Kristin Teig

Preface by Christopher Myers

HOUGHTON MIFFLIN HARCOURT
Boston • New York

To the tireless and amazing collection
of servers, cooks, dishwashers, and managers
who have allowed us to throw this party
every night for the last ten years.

—Joanne & Christopher

To LJ—
"Nothing else will do. I've gotta have you."

—Karen

CONTENTS

9 *Acknowledgments*

13 *Preface*

25 INTRODUCTION

75 DIM SUM

105 SALADS

129 AND THEN SOME

157 DUMPLINGS

181 WOK

199 NOODLES

227 RICE AND GRAINS

243 SIDES

267 FAMILY MEAL

285 DESSERTS

303 SAUCES, CONDIMENTS, AND BASICS

317 *Index*

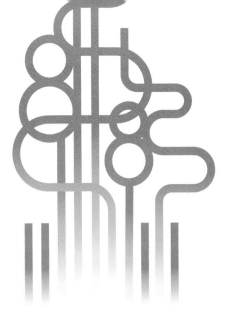

ACKNOWLEDGMENTS

I have always been a reader, and books have been a huge part of my life, so when Joanne and Christopher invited me to write this book with them it was the greatest gift someone could have given me. Thank you both for inviting me into your home and kitchen.

Thank you, Christopher, for over fifteen years of guidance, friendship, and mentorship. Thank you for geese and hats and the knowledge that you would always be my wingman (should I ever need one again). Working for you at Via Matta was a joy and an education I can never repay.

Joanne, you are not only as nice as everyone says but funny, gracious, and fierce in a way only you could manage. You are genuine in everything you do, and writing this book together was an amazing experience. There is no one I would rather split a spring roll with.

Thanks to all of the "Chang Gang," especially supreme recipe testers Ashley Lujares and Tessa Bristol, as well as Mari, Marvin, Dina, Lupe, Gabriel, José, Jesse, Jesus, and Veo who run the restaurant so well that I was able to take time to write this book.

Thank you Ashley Lucas for your friendship and all of your hard work on Team Cupcake Productions. To Rachel and Hannah, you are the best femmes a girl could ask for.

To Adam Halberg for sending me to Italy and Cassie Piuma for being the most talented and hardworking chef I have ever worked for, thank you both for the lessons you taught me.

To my mom, dad, and Jenn, thank you for giving me roots so I could have wings.

To my sweetheart, LJ, thank you for holding my hand and walking through this world with me. It is only because of your support that I was able to write this book. xx

—Chef Karen

When you get engaged, friends and family immediately start asking when the wedding is; once you get married the question changes to, "When are you having kids?" For Christopher and me, Myers+Chang served as our answer to both. We opened the restaurant to celebrate our love of Asian cooking and each other. Rather than a big wedding, we had an opening party for M+C (and then we eloped a few months later). Instead of 2.5 kids, we have forty (+/-) staff members at the restaurant at any one time who feel an awful lot like a rowdy, lovable gaggle of kids. This book is a culmination of a decade of working together, tasting together, eating together, laughing together, and once in a blue moon maybe disagreeing a bit . . . together.

It's hard to write an acknowledgment when you are a neighborhood restaurant, because everyone who comes in and gives us feedback has helped us morph our food into something better. I'll cast the net wide right off the bat and thank the neighborhood of the South End for embracing us on this lonely corner back in 2007 and supporting us day in and day out.

Thank you to our opening chef, Alison Hearn, for sharing your obsession with Asian food and sharing your vast talents with us our first few years and for creating dishes that are so addictive, they remain on the menu to this day. Thank you to Matt Barros for bravely carrying the torch after Alison left until Chef Karen arrived. And to our restaurant managers, Cheri, Scott, Alexandra, Heather, and

Kristi, you all kept our guests happy and eager to come back, allowing us to keep cooking, tasting, developing, and perfecting these recipes over the last decade.

To Esti Parsons for being the model of hospitality for everyone at the restaurant, the genuine warmth and goodness you bring to us makes us all better at what we do. You've been our number-one recipe taster (and our number-one fan) since way before we opened, and we are thankful for your pitch-perfect palate and for your hot and sour soup! That soup! Probably among the most complimented of our dishes.

We really cannot thank the cooks and servers who have come through the doors of M+C enough for their immense dedication and love and heart. This book is a testament to each one of you who worked your butts off to make sure our food constantly got better and our service was continuously viewed as the warmest and friendliest in Boston. Special shout-outs to our chefs and cooks in the kitchen: Kevin, Mari, Marvin, Ashley, Gabriel, Tessa, and Veo, for your help with these recipes over the years and with the testing for this book.

To our spectacular group of recipe testers, thank you! Each of you gave such detailed feedback on multiple iterations of the recipes that I'm convinced these are the best-tested recipes in any cookbook out there. Our readers will all delight in making these dishes successfully for their friends and family because of your careful testing. We are incredibly grateful.

I have known our editor, Justin Schwartz, for almost a decade and always hoped for a chance to work with him. Thank you, Justin, for your eagle-eye editing, your enthusiasm for our food, and your exacting guidance on how to make the recipes sing. I've learned a tremendous amount working with you, and I am very appreciative of your support and teachings. Simply put, this book is awesome because you pushed me from day one.

Kristin Teig, our photographer, first took pictures of me for a local magazine, and after watching her play Twister with her camera, arms, and legs to get just the right shot, I knew she was the one to nail down the heart and soul of our food. Kristin, your gorgeous pictures will be the reason readers will have drool stains on these recipes; you brought our food and our team to life and captured the vibrancy of M+C.

Stacey Glick, my agent, is not just a brilliant book agent but also a dear friend. Her annual pilgrimages to Myers+Chang with her adorable kids and sweetheart of a husband are among the visits we most look forward to all year. They proclaim each dish better than the last, which is really the whole reason we do this in the first place. Stacey, your steady counsel and sound business sense always lead me down the right path. Thank you for guiding me to make the best books I can.

Chef Karen, you waltzed into Myers+Chang over six years ago, and we have never looked back. You took on the herculean task of wrangling the recipes into a useable format not just for this book but also for our kitchen team. Our kitchen is stronger and better because of YOU. Our food is amazing because of YOU. Christopher and I thank you for your determination, charm, loyalty, and constant pursuit of excellence. You are a force to be reckoned with, and writing this book with you was actually, dare I say it, fun?! Yes, it was fun!

To Mama and Papa Chang, this book is my gift to you. While most of the staff call ME Mama Chang, the original Mama Chang is the inspiration for so many of our favorite recipes. And Papa Chang is the OG recipe taster. You both have always been my biggest fans, and every single success I have is due to the never-ending love and support you give me. I love you.

Finally, this book, this restaurant, and this amazing life I have would simply not be without Christopher. Christopher, I wish Bette Midler had never sung "You are the wind beneath my wings," because now the phrase is a cliché; if I could think of a better way to say this, I would be a music star. I am so unbelievably lucky to have my best friend, my husband, and my business partner all rolled up in one. Thank you for constantly pushing and sharing your vision of excellence for the restaurant, the bakeries, and this book. You are my world.

—Joanne

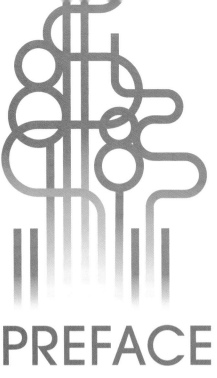

PREFACE

Myers+Chang opened at dusk on a pristine fall night in 2007. The temperature was about sixty-eight degrees. The sun was fading in Boston's storied South End but still dotting the corner of Washington and Berkeley Streets with tangerine and honeyed hues. Birds chirped, flowers bloomed, and kids played safely in the street. Okay, kids didn't play safely in the street, but there were a few colorful locals splayed out horizontal at the bus stop [*cue sound of bagged Cossack vodka bottle falling onto the sidewalk*]. The reality was that we were about to open a restaurant one short block away from Boston's largest homeless shelter and across the street from the city's most active pawnshop. Maybe not what the brokers would call prime retail, but we had deemed it prime for us. Equidistant from traditional Chinatown and the gentrifying South End, this lively corner felt like the best bit of old and the right bit of new. Our restaurant, years in gestation, months and months in planning and execution and build-out, weeks upon weeks of training with a bright-eyed collection of servers and fired-up tatted cooks, was finally ready. We were going to be afire with trend-setting and craveable food, fast and funky, full of spice and sass, altogether original yet echoing with throwback flavors of Taiwanese soul-cooking. An electric-pink dragon stretching seventy-five feet along the storefront and around the corner screamed to passersby that excitements were held within. Who wasn't going to love the food that my wife made for me every Sunday night while we were dating? Technicolor dishes from her Taiwanese parents' playbook, foods that mean as much to a first-generation Asian-American girl growing up in Dallas, of all places, as BBQ does to pretty much everyone else in Texas. A personal, idiosyncratic cuisine touched with a mother's love. Our service would be relaxed yet wise and warm, exact but without pomp, informed but without long speeches about the provenance of the carrots or the pedigree of the chef. And the music—whoa, the music! Everything from The Zombies to the Stooges, The Pretenders to the Pixies, The Beatles to the Beastie Boys. Rock and punk and loud. Electricity for all the senses: sight, sound, smell, taste. We were going to hit you with everything we had.

I wasn't entirely sure what to expect from our audience that opening night. Who was coming? I'd never done business in this part of Boston before, but this was Joanne's backyard. She had long ago captured the hearts of this neighborhood with a darling and original bakery, Flour. She had been a pioneer in this area, braving the perimeters and staking out the breakfast and lunch crowds with reasonably priced pastries and handmade delicacies and sandwiches. She painted an optimistic picture to me of an up-and-coming, chic enclave of skyrocketing realty, stylish shops, twee eateries, and a vibrant and seemingly starving dining public. On the other end of the market—and of town—I had done okay, creating and co-owning some of Boston's most highly acclaimed and appreciated restaurants. Rialto, Radius, Via Matta, and Great Bay were all critical successes and instrumental in the emergence of Boston as a serious dining destination. So here we were. I was certain that I had the high-end foodies spellbound with twenty-five years in the Boston scene, Joanne had the South End romanced with seven years of helping people to wake up and catch their trains, and we were collaborating on this culinary love child. What did we expect? My experience told me that openings were always glammy and chic and all abuzz with look-at-me fashionistas. Joanne may have had baser expectations that she kept to herself, not wanting to burst my bubble. Whatever. In my mind, this train was heading for fame and fortune.

The spastic energy and calamities of opening night originate months in advance and are uncontainable. Our home, mere blocks away, was a second terminus for this oncoming train. Home had ceased to be home months earlier, having morphed into a test kitchen, meeting hall, sewing circle, and war room. Our ridiculously long dining table, fifteen years old and in near mint condition, was at long last called into use as we conducted one tasting dinner after another, hosting gaggles of our best and most fussy friends. It's Boston, so we weren't short on invitees. This restaurant opening, every restaurant opening for that matter, requires that one uses all available resources. So if friends are put upon, you can only imagine what is required of family. Hence, Joanne's mother visited. And stayed, cooked, and stayed some more. Watching Joanne and her mother making dumplings, elbow to elbow, as silent and focused as two chatterers have ever been, is a memory as good as it gets from that opening fog. Mama Chang's Pork and Chive Dumplings (page 171) remain to this day my favorite dish on our menu, and the dipping sauce is my one true love.

Joanne's mother's sister, Auntie Mia, made the trip from Taipei with her husband and daughters. Joanne hadn't seen her cousins in a decade. They cooked and giggled endlessly; Uncle slept, a lot, and Auntie Mia, at seventy, without breaking a sweat, casually and elegantly pulled off the wildest most fragrant spring rolls I'd ever had, an inebriatingly seductive congee, and a *cong xin cai furu*, water spinach with fermented tofu, that was funky and marvelous. This immersive stew of food, culture, and family, the takeover of our home, the fusion of work and play, is simply the reason just about every restaurant person is in this business. It's overwhelming, but it is really hard to describe as anything other than awesome. And it always passes too fast. Thankfully, Joanne's parents visit the restaurant as often as possible to vigilantly defend the original flavors and traditions of our genesis.

To be clear, though, it wasn't solely family and tradition that created Myers+Chang. Traditional Asian fare wasn't really what we were aiming for. If you ask what we do at Myers+Chang, I'd humbly say we're interpreting traditional Asian fare and adding our own personality. Therefore, looking for our first chef required that we find someone with more than a soupçon of personality. Our opening chef, Alison Hearn, was a full portion, a thoroughbred talent with the disposition of an unbroken Montana colt. I'm not precisely sure what I mean by this not having spent much time as a cowpoke or ranch hand. I do know that each time we tried to throw a saddle on her, we ended up with fewer teeth in our collective mouths. She had worked for Daniel Boulud, Barbara Lynch, Tony Maws, and Susie Regis, quite simply four of my favorite chefs on the planet. Alison's passion was Southeast Asia, and she had the energy and creativity to open a dozen restaurants. Thankfully, we were only opening this one, because it almost killed her. Off to the races we were, bareback!

Back to our opening night: The doors are just about to open. HOLY SHIT, premeal! I'd forgotten. Premeal, or "preshift" or "briefing," is a restaurant personnel gathering—all hands on deck—before the doors are opened for service. Premeal runs the gamut from the sacred to the profane, and more likely the sanctimonious to the silly. In the right hands, a premeal can be delivered with all the gravity of a Billy Graham homily. This is where the general manager, the owner, the chef, or whoever is so inspired delivers a sermon on specials, guests to arrive, birthdays to celebrate, and all the razzmatazz of how this night, the most important night in history, is going to proceed. The "BREAK!" before leaving the huddle. No one makes a move without hearing it. So, here I am, thirty years of experience, and I hadn't planned a word. I'd all but forgotten.

Forgetting premeal on the opening night of an eagerly awaited urban restaurant is just wrong. It's tantamount to the groom grabbing his new bride and bolting from the altar, passing all invitees without a wink, nixing the dancing, the toasts, the dinner, the cake, and ultimately sprinting directly to the bridal suite and bouncing up and down on the bed all the while the bride is waiting at the door to be carried over the threshold. In other words, it's not wrong—it's unimaginable.

I did that.

At that moment, I had a legit epiphany: I realized nothing I said was going to matter a whit anyway. We were either prepared or we weren't. We'd tasted every wine, cocktail, and dish over and over again. The staff, a randy lot, had more than likely all tasted one another. Such is restaurant life. We were ready to open the doors. It was actually kind of a relief to have the pressure of that moment dissolve. I took a breath and presented my one word premeal sermon: "SMILE!!!"

Here we go. Step to the door. Take a big deep breath. Touch lips and heart two times, sign of the cross, and just like Big Papi, a final kiss to the heavens. I unlock the doors, bracing for the pushing and shoving, shoulders down, head up, and HERE WE GO! And the doors open. A nattily clad Boston ginger enters, hair pulled back in a tight bun, sweet smile. She's pushing a baby carriage. Maybe she needs directions to the doggie park around the way? Should I warn her of the impending ravelike crowd about to descend? She offers that her husband was parking the minivan and would be right behind her, but she was ready to sit. I'm not sure if anyone else's world stopped for a beat at that moment. Mine did. Parking the mini what? Wasn't there a caravan of Benzes and limos out there? I look over her shoulder for either her husband scrambling to not lose his place in line, or any other A-list types desperate to get a seat and dig our florescent fuchsia chopsticks into mind-blowing Asian grub. And over that shoulder, what do I see? Another couple pushing another baby carriage. This pair looks slightly desperate, and the woman confesses, "We haven't been out of the house in months. Are you open?" I greet them and move the carriage aside to create some space to move. I seat them with care. Rushing back to the door, was it Keith Lockhart, Lisa Hughes, surely one of the Wahlbergs was invited, J. Soroff with band of lovelies? Nope. Next up: another couple . . . pushing another baby carriage. What the . . . ? Wasn't this the Myers+Chang opening night? I had to admit, though, this carriage was gorgeous. A Silver Cross Balmoral Classic, I've since Googled. If nothing else, this was the Benz of baby carriages.

At this point, exhausted from the interminable planning and designing, the wrestling with the city about this and that, the innumerable changes and compromises that occur, and this dizzying procession of wearied but handsome newly formed families . . . I was so dazed and confused, I wanted to get in that cushy pink pram and tuck myself alongside their resting baby boy and just sleep. Our host area had become a parking garage for prams. Boston had survived the Big Dig, $14 billion, and ten years as a full-blown construction zone to avoid blockages just like this. Our host stand, a gorgeous artifact, a fifties hand-painted Indochine home bar found in Palm Springs of all places after a tireless months-long hunt by a drove of obsessed designers from our architect David Hacin's talented bench, was now fully camouflaged, lost to all. Forget the forest, forget the trees—it was just baby carriages.

Do I have a point in detailing any of this? I do: That the best laid plans . . . ain't crap. Throughout all our late-night strategy sessions, the endless tastings, the pinch of sriracha here and a bit more dragon there, the creation of the "recipe" that would ultimately become Myers+Chang—none of it readies you for what you will become, and nothing can ever be fully anticipated. The restaurant ultimately isn't ours, and it never was. It's yours. It's Boston's, to do with as it will. I was anticipating late nights, a scene, the occasional rumble. Instead, those first guests, those fertile yet sleep-deprived couples, turned out to be a real slice of what Myers+Chang is today. A true neighborhood restaurant. We have watched those kids grow up on our dumplings and scallion pies, weaned from mother's milk to our sleep-inducing, sugary Thai iced teas. Mother's little helper. Look out into the dining room on a random Friday night, and you'll see the most variegated cross section of hunger

you can imagine. The passionate foodies are Instagramming alongside suburban retirees who are beside young college kids who crowd around the communal table, bumping up against a decked-out couple on a first date; or two professors, we thought colleagues, are blowing out candles on a cake to celebrate an anniversary. They are shoulder to chopstick against tourists from Montreal or Australia or Indonesia asking questions of two Dominican kids and their parents after their little league game concludes next door. Ten years later, you still see those families with babies and carriages. Maybe Stella will be here that night. Her mom and dad own Stella restaurant down the street. She's been coming to the restaurant for as long as we've been open, and I have a pile of her crumpled and grease-streaked comment cards on my desk to prove it. Nine years' worth. I've witnessed her penmanship change from illegible Crayola scratchings of "YUM" to "This is my happy place!" to, ahh, the first set of teeth tinged with sarcasm: "I love Myers+Chang! But mostly Chang!!" A shot at me, God love her. Along with her little brother, Max, no one at Myers+Chang feels any less fully that they're part of our family. We hope that we're a bitty part of theirs. We're not just a neighborhood restaurant . . . we are *her* neighborhood restaurant.

Why a Myers+Chang cookbook? For the same reason you open a restaurant: to share. To share our chef and partner, Karen Akunowicz, and her ebullient approach to Asian cooking and bring her into your kitchen. She's the crouching tiger and the pink dragon of Myers+Chang incarnate. Hidden? NEVER! To become the fabric of something of which you're not quite yet sure. We aim to bring Myers+Chang into your home. Yet, as I hope I've shown, plans ain't always all that. So this cookbook might just sit in your baby carriage for a while, until you get some time . . . and sleep. It's not going to be anything without you, without your creativity, your personality, your new kitchen, or your beloved old paint-chipped Cuisinart. Your full participation is required. When you do find time to open this and begin your exploration and experiments, after you nail a few of the recipes, or many of them, we hope you'll throw a party. Aim high. Dig in and extend yourself. Go all out. Assemble an overly ambitious guest list and include your chef friends. Everyone has a chef friend these days. Invite, of course, those you want to impress, and a few people you're not sure will take you up on your invitation. Invite your closest friends and those you haven't seen in years. Fill the room with hungry lovely people. When you open your doors to your first arrivals, take a deep breath. Smile. If you're as off as I was, then you'll see that it's not your boss's impossibly hip wife but rather your next door neighbor, and he's wearing that crazy sweater, you know the one, that Cosby sweater, and right behind him is Esther Bensonovitch from down the street—oy, does she know Chinese food!—she's from New York, as she constantly tells you. And then here come the Parsons from your garden co-op, and they're with their drooly Great Dane who is dribbling all over your new Jimmy Choos. Plans, ha! Nonetheless, open that door wide, wider still, open your arms and give them the biggest and sincerest hug of appreciation, and then feed them. Share with them your creations and welcome them into your home. As we do every single day. It's a thrill and a privilege. You'll see.

—Christopher Myers

INTRODUCTION

I grew up eating only Chinese food. My mom cooked for my dad, brother, and me every night, and we had rice and stir-fries and noodles. I was around six or seven playing at my best friend Linda's house when her mom invited me to stay and have dinner. I don't think I'd ever not eaten with my family at that point. We sat at the dinner table, Linda's mom passed me a plate of meat loaf and some mashed potatoes and peas, and I sat waiting patiently. "Are you okay? Do you need anything else?" she asked. I was baffled, and it showed. "Where's the rice?" I didn't know you could have dinner and not have rice. She asked me if I always ate Chinese food at home, and again I was confused. "Nope, I just eat food." Because to me, that's all it was: regular yummy food.

By the time I entered my teens, I had learned to love pizza and hamburgers, mostly from hanging out with my friends. At that point, I was helping Mom with dinner every day when I got home from school and before she got home from work. She called me every afternoon around four p.m. to check in on my brother and me and give me a list of tasks—my first prep lists. "Chop the scallions and make sure the white parts are chopped up fine. Press the tofu so the water comes out so it fries up better. Dice up the chicken—be careful with the cleaver—and mix it with some ginger and egg whites and soy sauce before I get home." For a while, my grandparents lived with us, and my grandma joined in. She didn't speak any English, and I didn't speak any of her dialect of Chinese, *Hakka*, but we both loved being in the kitchen. She taught me her tricks, like how to add fried shallots to my mom's stir-fried noodles for extra crunch and flavor and how best to use pickled mustard greens in stews and sauces, and we bonded over perfectly braised chicken thighs.

I left for college, studied math and economics at Harvard, and spent two years as a management consultant after graduation before realizing that I was at my happiest when I was in the kitchen. Mom and Dad were more than a little shocked when I called them to tell them I was quitting my stable, lucrative office job to go work as a line cook at one of the top restaurants in Boston. "Just for a year," I promised them. I wanted to see what cooking professionally was all about. My first day at work as a cook, I walked into the kitchen, breathed in the eye-watering sharpness of diced onions, dodged a prep cook swinging a stockpot onto the stove, watched as a swarm of servers descended upon a makeshift table set up with a tasting of the day's specials, and knew I was home.

The first decade and a half of my culinary career was focused, however, not on cooking but on baking. After that pivotal first cooking job as a garde-manger or appetizer cook, I segued into the pastry side of the kitchen where I fell head over heels in love with sugar, butter, flour, and magic. My first pastry chef job was at Rialto restaurant in Cambridge, MA, where I met Christopher, who was one of the owners. (Yes, I married my boss, but I swear it was long after I worked for him.) We became fast friends. He has a knack for corny food jokes that I loved (and still do): "Why did the apple turnover? Because it saw the jelly roll!" He shares my insatiable sweet tooth, which led him to my pastry station several times a day. And he became a valued mentor, guiding me with food and management and life advice.

Our friendship continued to grow even after Christopher left Rialto to open first Radius, then Via Matta, then Great Bay, all restaurants in Boston, and I moved to NYC to be part of the opening team of Payard Pâtisserie. I eventually returned to Boston to open my dream bakery. Christopher suggested the name "Flour," and I was smitten: both with the perfect suggestion and with him. By this time our longtime friendship had morphed for me into a full-blown crush. I confessed to him while sitting on the benches outside Flour one morning, "Christopher, I LIKE-like you." Thankfully he like-liked me back, and we started dating.

I spent most evenings at his place where I made dinner for us when he was not working. I cooked the food I grew up with: Mom's dumplings, spicy tofu stews, lots of garlicky wokked greens, simple gingery chicken stir-fries, and of course, rice. Unbeknownst to me, he kept waiting for a lasagna or a pot roast or a leg of lamb to show up on the dinner table. I had never roasted a chicken or braised a short rib in my life. To me, it was perfectly normal to eat this way seven days a week.

This wasn't the type of Chinese food he was used to, though. He grew up eating Polynesian-style, sweet-and-sour, moo-goo-gai-pan takeout. It's the type of Americanized Chinese food that occupies its own category. He brought it home once for me to try, and it made me understand why my cooking was not quite registering as Chinese food to him. "THIS is Chinese food," I announced when I glazed pan-roasted salmon with ginger, soy, and scallion broth and sautéed my mom's pork and cabbage noodles. Where was this kind of cooking in the restaurant world we were a part of?

We were getting more serious about each other, but our schedules were imperfect. Most days I was getting ready to go to work in the wee hours of the morning to open the bakery when Christopher was coming home after a long night at one of his restaurants. We barely had time for a "have a good day/have a good night" kiss. We started brainstorming how we could do a project together, despite the fact that we were already both incredibly busy, as a way to spend more time together. It was daydream talk, the stuff of late night musings as you're falling asleep coming up with whatever pops into your head: We'd create a bistro and connect it to the bakery! Flour would start wholesale baking, and we'd help with the dessert program at his restaurants! We'd sell everything and move to Hawaii to open a little cafe together!

At that time I was on the board of directors of a local nonprofit, Project Place, that works with the homeless. They were getting ready to move into a brand-new building that had a retail space on the ground floor. They asked Christopher and me, as the resident restaurant experts, to help design the space so that they could rent it out as a restaurant. One of the "what-if-we" scenarios Christopher and I shared was opening a little Asian joint to mesh our mutual infatuation with Chinese food. After going over the floor plans at home, we looked at each other and said, "Why don't WE take this and open something?"

We knew what we wanted. Christopher had spent his career at that point on high-end restaurants and wanted a place that was more casual and neighborhood focused. I had been cooking Chinese food all my life but had never really seen the type of food I loved to eat at the restaurants we frequented. If you wanted Chinese

food, you went to Chinatown. Period. Why couldn't you go out on a date, meet a gaggle of friends, celebrate a promotion or birthday, have a dinner with a nice bottle of wine and fabulous service . . . and eat Asian food? It seems obvious now, but back then restaurants were mostly Italian, Mediterranean, French, American . . . but never Asian.

So I resigned from the board, and we signed a lease. At that point, we had been engaged for about a year. We had every intention of getting married the traditional way with a ceremony, dancing, cake—the whole shebang. In between endless redrafting of guest lists and figuring out which hors d'oeuvres we might serve at a wedding, we turned our attentions to deciding on kitchen equipment, selecting server uniforms, and picking out logos and menu paper. We were both way better at making decisions about how to make a great restaurant. We hired our first chef, Alison Hearn, who had worked in some of the top kitchens in Boston and was as obsessed with Asian food as we were. Alison, Christopher, and I spoke the same food language, and we spent weeks testing and testing some more, on one another and on friends and family. We ate out a lot. We pored over recipe books and magazines. We invited my mom from Dallas and my aunt from Taiwan to come to Boston and give us lessons. I finally got to make and share the food I grew up with. The restaurant opened in September 2007. (And Christopher and I eloped the following year.)

The restaurant was around four years old and on its way to becoming a neighborhood staple when I first considered writing this book to share our recipes. I had just published my first book, *Flour*, a baking book with my best pastry recipes, and we were hitting our stride at Myers+Chang. My publisher was sniffing around for the next project, and this book seemed a natural suggestion. In hindsight, we were nowhere near ready. Alison had moved on, her sous-chef Matthew Barros had taken her place, and we were getting ready to find his replacement when he got another opportunity. We were lying in bed one evening when Christopher, out of nowhere, blurted out, "Chainsaw!" He started furiously texting with someone, and by the next day we had a new chef. Karen Akunowicz had formerly worked for Christopher at Via Matta, first as a bartender and then as the sous-chef. She had earned her nickname, "Chainsaw," by her willful determination to work her way through any problem until it was solved. After working for Christopher, she was a sous-chef and then a chef for a few other restaurants, and she had spent the past year teaching cooking and life skills to at-risk youth. Karen entered the restaurant like a force of nature: strong willed, passionate, gorgeous, and powerful. I felt that the restaurant had been doing well up to that point; she whipped us into shape. She immediately refocused our menu and our training, and in so doing she helped get these recipes foolproof and ready so that we could teach them to you.

During the first many months Karen and I were working together, I shared the when and why and how of every dish, and she absorbed the pedigree and spirit of the entire menu. We talked food philosophy and phobias (she doesn't do squash, I dislike fatty pork); and she brought her Italian and Mediterranean training to our kitchen; and I coached her on how to use a wok and why rice is important with every meal. She was initially hesitant about learning how to cook a style of food she had never formally trained in; preparing Asian food seemed inaccessible, mysterious, and foreign. I assured her that Myers+Chang was everything she knew how to do already but simply looked at through a different lens. Sichuan dan dan (page 217) is traditionally a righteous mess of spicy noodles dressed with pork ragu; in Chef Karen's hands, she takes the classic Italian Bolognese that she learned to cook as a chef in Modena, Italy, and shifts it our direction with star anise, pork belly, and a four-hour braise (streamlined to fifty minutes for you). If it uses ingredients in our fridge and pantry and it tastes amazing, then we want to share it with our guests.

And that is how our menu has developed. We are not tied to any purely authentic or formal style of cooking. Instead, we are constantly looking for the best, most delicious dishes we can create. Sometimes we veer into southern cooking with an Indonesian version of chicken and waffles, or we might head back into your childhood with a sloppy joe made with Korean BBQ beef and kimchi pickles that rivals Mom's. After trying greasy chewy scallion pancakes from a late-night Chinatown binge, I knew we could recreate this classic with a yeasted dough that fries up fluffy and light like fried dough at the state fair. As Christopher says, "We take various Asian styles as our starting-off point, and we apply our own whatchamacallit to it."

The restaurant reflects the Zeitgeist not just in the food but in the atmosphere. The walls are lined with mirrors that are sometimes decorated in handwritten slogans that sound like a fortune cookie on acid: "Confucius was here (and thought our food rocked)." "He who laughs at himself never runs out of material." "Dragons make great pets . . . in bed." Other times they are painted with a long snaking tiger winding its way into the kitchen. Still other times they might show hashtags of recent events to stir up conversation among the staff and the guests. At each pre meal (the twenty-minute daily info session we have with our servers before we open for dinner service), we often end with the rally cry, "MORE YELLING!" We shout out enthusiastic greetings to our guests when they walk in the door, yell our thank-yous and goodbyes as they are leaving (we've been compared to the von Trapp family), and belt out which items we've run out of and which are back on the menu. In as many ways as we can, we share with everyone who enters Myers+Chang our buzzy, upbeat energy.

Here we share this infectious spirit and eighty of our top recipes with you to replicate in your home. We are all about fresh products, exotic herbs, and redolent spices. Chef Karen and I teach you how to navigate your way through unfamiliar foods and pick out the best shrimp to create our mouth-numbing Sichuan Shrimp Lettuce Wraps (page 93) that will convince you to eat shrimp with the head, tail, shell, and all. You'll learn a modern take on the familiar lemon chicken; our version is made crispy with panko crumbs and bright with candied citrus and pickled red cabbage. Our Spicy Silky Tofu (page 193) with kimchi and pork will make even tofu doubters into tofu lovers—we've seen it happen time and time again at the restaurant, and it's one of our staff's favorite dishes. Mama Chang will be by your side instructing you on the proper way to fold dumplings, starting with her traditional Pork and Chive and ending with Chef Karen's Juicy Duck and Ginger Dumplings (page 167). Wield a wok and recreate our Wild Mushroom Lo Mein (page 200), an umami bomb of shiitakes, soy, noodles, butter, and miso. Experiment with using tamarind paste to flavor a roasted-cod dish served alongside Vietnamese mint, jicama, and grapefruit slaw.

These recipes are rarely traditional: We are deeply inspired by the flavors of Asia while committed to making our dishes personal to us. For the last decade, we've been feeding our fantastically loyal neighbors and far-flung visitors to Boston with the foods we ourselves are in love with. We make these dishes every day in our open kitchen, and we are thrilled to share them with you to make at home. #yummeyumyou

HOW TO SHOP

When you walk into an Asian grocery store, how do you know what's what? The aisles are not always clearly marked, and even if you are fluent in Chinese, navigating your way through an Asian market can be challenging. You can easily spend a whole afternoon exploring the endless bottles and jars and sauces and greens and barely make a dent. We have an Asian market conveniently across the street from the restaurant that we visit several times a day. We love it so much that we named one of our dishes after it: Ming's Market Greens are whatever fresh vegetables we find at the grocery cooked *furu*-style (try the recipe on page 249). Here are the ingredients we use the most.

Asian pears

Asian pears are typically bulbous with crisp, white flesh similar to an apple. They have a refreshing pear flavor and are both juicy and firm at the same time. Even when they are really ripe, they don't mush out like a Bartlett pear. They have a long storage life, lasting up to 2 weeks at room temperature and 3 to 4 weeks in the refrigerator. We love them for snacking (they're Chef's favorite afternoon snack), and they add crunch and sweetness to salads. If you can't find Asian pears, substitute Bosc pears or Granny Smith apples.

Bean sprouts

The bean sprouts we use are mung bean sprouts (not the skinny little alfalfa sprouts that come on sandwiches). They are thick and resemble a short noodle. Crisp and refreshing, they are great in stir-fries, salads, and soups. Make sure the bag they come in is very dry; this ensures that your sprouts are fresh. Abundant in Asian markets, bean sprouts have become mainstream, and you can now often find them in the produce section of regular grocery stores as well. If completely dry and stored in plastic, bean sprouts should last up to 5 days in the refrigerator. Give a quick rinse right before using.

Black Chinkiang vinegar

This is our favorite vinegar. Made from fermented sweet rice from the Chinkiang region of China, this vinegar has low, smoky, malty tones. It gives a boost of acidity without being too sharp and is fantastic with everything from vegetables to grilled

meats, especially pork or lamb. We liken this to balsamic vinegar, with less viscosity and a much lower price tag. In fact, substitute balsamic if you don't have any black vinegar at your house. You can typically find a bottle for under two bucks, often with a telltale bright yellow label. Keep it in your cabinet indefinitely after opening, as there is no need to refrigerate.

Bok choy

Bok choy is a member of the *Brassica* (broccoli, cauliflower, cabbage) family and is sometimes called Chinese cabbage. They don't form heads like many brassicas, but instead have smooth dark green leaves with a pale, thick, crunchy base. They are mild and crispy and refreshing. You can find bok choy in most grocery stores now, as it has become pretty mainstream. Store it in the crisper of your refrigerator, and it should last about a week.

Chili oil

This ruby red condiment is made from vegetable oil that has been infused with chili peppers and is very hot. It is commonly used in all Asian cooking, especially Sichuan cuisine, where it is used not just as a condiment but an ingredient in characteristically incendiary dishes. We like Roland brand, which comes in a small glass bottle. It will last you quite a while, as a little goes a long way. We love to mix it with black vinegar as a quick dipping sauce for dumplings.

Chinese five-spice powder

Star anise, Sichuan peppercorn, fennel, Chinese cinnamon, and clove make up the five spices in Chinese five-spice. We make our own blend, carefully toasting and grinding each one, but you can easily buy it at the store. It is an important ingredient in traditional red braises and the secret ingredient in our Sichuan Dan Dan Noodles (page 217). While folks often think that Chinese five-spice is sweet, we find it more deep and savory, making it ideal with roasted and braised meats.

Chinese mustard powder

Not quite the same as regular mustard powder, this mustard powder often comes in a medium-size plastic bag at your local Asian supermarket or online. It has a distinct "nose spice" (like wasabi or horseradish) that clears out your sinuses if you ingest too much. We turn this powder into our Chinese Hot Mustard Sauce (page 304) and like it so much that we use it for more than just a dipping condiment; we add spoonfuls of it to various stir-fries for additional oomph and flavor. If you cannot find it, you can substitute regular mustard powder, but you might want to add a bit of powdered wasabi to give it that extra kick.

Chinese sausage

When we call for Chinese sausage, we mean the sweet, firm sausage also known by its Cantonese name, *lap chong*. It is a dried, hard, cured sausage usually made from pork with a high fat content. It is normally smoked, sweetened, and seasoned with soy sauce. Sausages typically come six to eight links in a vacuum-sealed pack. They are intense in flavor, and we chop them up and use them for seasoning and flavoring dishes. We like to use Chinese sausage with really savory dishes to add a sweet component.

Cilantro

Early morning at the restaurant, you can smell the unmistakable scent of fresh cilantro throughout the whole kitchen as the cooks wash and stem cases of this ubiquitous herb. Cilantro, also known as coriander or Chinese parsley, has a distinctive fragrance and flavor that you either love or hate. For those who dislike it, it tastes rotten or soapy. We even put a warning on our menu that if you can't stomach it, we will remove it from any dish we can. We are among the lovers, and we can't get enough of the clean, herby flavor it lends to many of our dishes. It comes in bunches that will keep for about a week if stored in a plastic bag in the crisper of your refrigerator.

Coconut milk

Different from coconut cream or coconut water, coconut milk is the liquid that comes from the grated meat of a ripe coconut. It is a popular ingredient in both Southeast Asia and southern China. In the can, the milk separates so that the richest part is on the bottom. We open the cans from the bottom to save the time of scraping out the thick cream with a spoon. We use Aroy-D brand at the restaurant. Once opened, store any unused coconut milk in an airtight container for up to 2 days, or better yet, freeze it in ice cube trays for longer, fresher life.

Dried flat wheat noodles

We love to use fresh noodles since we are right next to an Asian market where they are readily available, but if you can't find fresh Shanghai noodles, dried flat wheat noodles are a great substitute. These are made with wheat flour, salt, and water and are pale cream in color. Often sold in bundles sealed in plastic or in a box, they are flat and about the same size as linguine. Cook these in boiling water for 8 to 10 minutes, until they are soft and springy, then drain and run cold water over them to keep them from sticking together. Unlike Italian pasta, Chinese noodles tend to be softer and less toothsome.

Dried red Thai chili

We use whole dried red Thai chilies in many of our recipes. We throw them into stocks and braises like you would a bay leaf; we rehydrate and grind them up for a potent chili paste; we infuse them in canola oil to make our own chili oil. They are the base for our Surprising Sauce (page 144) and Nam Prik Pao (page 259). They are a reddish-brown color and about 2 inches long, and they offer a pungent and long-lasting heat. You can find them in most Asian markets. If you need to substitute, use dried árbol chili, which will be a bit smokier and not as spicy.

Dried scallops

These umami bombs are actually the dried adductor muscle from a scallop. They are made from cooking scallops and then drying them, and they range from golden in color to orangy. They are highly prized in China and often pretty pricey. You can find them in well-stocked Asian markets behind the counter in a big glass jar (for high-quality expensive ones) or in plastic bags along with the dried shrimp in the refrigerator section (for more reasonably priced ones). If you can't find them, you can substitute dried shrimp in any recipe.

Dried shrimp

Little packaged dried shrimp are intense and sweet and release their oceany flavor when heated in oil. They are used frequently in many Asian cuisines, especially Malaysian. They are super tiny, about the size of your thumbnail, and range in color from bright pink to salmon colored. Find them in sealed plastic bags in the refrigerated section of all Asian markets.

Dumpling wrappers

You can make these by hand, but at Myers+Chang, we simply couldn't keep up with the hundreds of dumplings we fold and sell every day. We tried! Our kitchen is tiny and space is limited. So we march across the street to Ming's, the Asian market we visit several times a day, and buy the wrappers they have there. There are pale white wrappers made of wheat and golden yellow ones made with egg. We use the wheat wrappers made by Twin Marquis, which are really consistent. They are pliable but they do dry out easily like fresh pasta, so cover them with a damp tea towel when you are working with them. You can store them in an airtight container for a week in the refrigerator or freeze them for up to a month.

Fermented black beans

These are tiny salted soybeans that have been fermented for a long time and are packed with intense, deep flavor and lingering musk. They add a rich depth to meatless dishes, and they are often combined with garlic and cooked into a sauce.

Find these in lumpy plastic bags in most Asian markets, and store them indefinitely, tightly wrapped, in a cool dark place in the pantry. Once you master a basic black bean sauce, you will want to try using it on everything. It pairs well with tofu, chicken, seafood, pork, beef, vegetables . . . pretty much everything.

Fermented tofu paste

This is one of our favorite ingredients ever. It is funky, earthy, salty, and rich. It gives the distinct mouthfeel of dairy while being completely vegan. This liquid gold comes in little jars often with a yellow label. Sometimes it's labeled "soybean in sesame oil" or "soybean in chili oil." It also goes by *jiang dofu* or *furu*. It looks like little cubes of tofu floating in oil. We puree this with water to turn it into a sauce for vegetables and stir-fries, and we also use it to thicken and flavor our tofu noodle soup at lunch. Once opened, store jars in the refrigerator tightly sealed for up to 6 months.

Fish sauce

The first time I smelled fish sauce, I couldn't believe it was something you cooked with. But it's true—what stinks in the bottle makes magic in your mouth. Now I can't imagine cooking without it. In the way that a few chopped-up anchovies give depth to Caesar dressing, fish sauce provides an elusive, compelling underlying note for sauces and stir-fries. It is also the base for *nuoc cham*, a condiment so bright and addictive, we put it on almost anything. Fish sauce is made from fermented dried anchovies and is a rich amber color. In Chinese cooking, it is often used as an ingredient, and in Southeast Asian cuisine, it is mostly used raw to create a condiment or dipping sauce. We use it both ways. We like Red Boat fish sauce or 3 Crabs brand (you'll see three crabs on the label). Find it in the bottle section of your Asian grocery store or in the Asian section of most supermarkets.

Galangal

Galangal is often referred to as "young ginger." However, although they are from the same family (rhizome) and look similar (galangal is lighter with tighter skin), they taste quite different. Galangal tastes more like pepper than ginger and has a spicy, zingy taste. Ginger is much milder. Galangal can, however, be prepared much the same way as ginger: grated, sliced, or pickled. Find it in the frozen section of most Asian markets. You can occasionally find it fresh as well. Substitute fresh ginger if you can't find galangal, and add a bit of white pepper to the recipe.

Garlic

Garlic is a member of the allium family and is related to onions, chives, leeks, and scallions. It is an ingredient in many, many of our dishes at the restaurant. We grate, slice, dice, puree, roast, pickle, and wok char it. The second G in the Asian trinity, GGS (ginger, garlic, scallion), it can be subtle or bold, sweet or pungent, depending on how you use it. Buy garlic cloves by the head; the skin on the outside should feel tight and full. When you peel it, the garlic should be a little sticky—that's how you know it's nice and fresh. Store garlic in a cool dark area in your pantry with plenty of air circulation around it and it will last for at least 2 months.

Garlic chives

You can always tell when we are using these in the kitchen by their heady, earthy, garlicky smell. They are also known as chive grass, but they are much more garlic than chive. They can be overwhelming for folks who are not familiar with them, but we love to work with them. They give a distinct flavor to Auntie Mia's Spring Rolls (page 86) and Mama Chang's dumplings (page 171). We throw them into stir-fries along with all the other vegetables. They are about 2 feet long, thin, flat, and grasslike; they come in big bunches banded together in the produce section of Asian grocery stores. If you have to, you can substitute regular chives, but try to seek these out. They are really worth it.

Ginger

"When in doubt, add more ginger. Any time I am working on a new recipe that calls for ginger, I think about what Joanne will say when she tastes it, and I double it," says Chef. Ginger is a flowering plant whose rhizome (think: cluster of roots) is edible and fragrant. One of the Gs in the Asian trinity, GGS (ginger, garlic, scallion), it is spicy and fresh, whether grated, sliced, or juiced. Find it in the produce section of any grocery store. You can also find ginger juice at most juice bars. Ginger can be stored in the crisper of your refrigerator for up to 3 weeks. **Pro tip:** To peel ginger, use the edge of a metal spoon to scrape down the bumpy sides; the papery peel will rub right off.

Glass noodles

These noodles are texturally our favorite: slippery, chewy, slurpy, and totally fun to eat. They are made of sweet potato starch, and when cooked, they are translucent and a bit grayish in color. Sometimes called cellophane noodles, they come dried, in various lengths. They are often used in Korean cooking, and they shine in both soups and stir-fries. Parcook them ahead of time for stir-fries, or add them directly to your soup and they will thicken the broth as they cook. If you can't find them, substitute rice vermicelli noodles.

Hoisin sauce

This thick, sweet, strong sauce is used for dipping and roasting meats and as a component in many stir-fry sauces in Chinese cooking. It is typically made of soybeans, chilies, garlic, sesame, vinegar, and Chinese five-spice powder. It is often served with Peking duck and mushu dishes; we use it as a glaze for our braised pork belly buns. Lee Kum Kee is an easy-to-find brand that we like that comes in a small jar or bottle. Once opened, store hoisin tightly sealed in the refrigerator for up to 6 months.

Kimchi

Kimchi is a traditional Korean side dish that is such a staple in Korean life that people say "kimchi" instead of "cheese" when posing for pictures. Made of fermented vegetables (usually cabbage, radish, or scallions) seasoned with garlic, scallion, salt, sugar, vinegar, anchovy paste, dried shrimp, and Korean chili powder, it is eaten with almost every Korean meal. Originally, kimchi was fermented underground in clay pots to keep it cool in the summer and unfrozen in the winter. We don't do that. Instead, we purchase some of our kimchi and make others kinds from scratch, like our giardiniera kimchi and our kimchi cucumbers. We would kimchi the heck out of everything if we could. In the summer, we get cases of cool vegetables like broccoli leaves from Sparrow Arc Farm, and we turn them into kimchi. Buy it at any Asian market in glass jars in the refrigerated section. Nowadays, fancy grocery stores are selling expensive versions of "artisanal" kimchi. We say it's way better to make your own.

Korean chili paste (*gochujang*)

This popular Korean paste is made of fermented chilies, glutinous rice, soybeans, and salt. The consistency is a bit similar to miso but stickier. *Gochujang* is sweet and unctuous but only sometimes spicy, even though it is a deep red color. Our friend Mary Rhei makes our *gochujang*. Her family has been making Rhei-Maid *gochujang* for decades, and it is the best product we have tasted. You can tell how much love goes into making it. Buy *gochujang* in 16-ounce jars in most Asian markets. The jars are squat and typically have a picture of a chili on them. In a pinch, substitute miso paste and red pepper flakes.

Korean chili powder *(gochugaru)*

These beautiful, fine red flakes are the most important ingredient in kimchi. They vary in color from brick red to orangy red to orangish, and they are sometimes finely ground and sometimes coarsely ground. They are smoky and floral with a medium heat. Find them in small plastic bags in Korean markets and some general Asian markets. If you can't find *gochugaru*, substitute Aleppo pepper or árbol chili.

Kosher salt

This is our standard salt at the restaurant. We use it exclusively unless we are using a special finishing salt for a dish. The grains are larger and the taste is cleaner than regular iodized table salt. It's easier to season with kosher salt as well since it's not as, well, salty. Instead, kosher salt helps bring out the flavors of whatever you sprinkle it on rather than just making the whole thing taste like salt. The measure for kosher salt and table salt is different, so be careful if you are not using kosher! Table salt is a lot finer, and you typically need about half as much as kosher.

Lemongrass

Lemongrass grows in sturdy stalks and looks like a big, stemmy weed. If you crossed a lemon with an herb, you would have the aroma of lemongrass. Used in many of our Southeast Asian–inspired dishes, it needs a bit of work to process. The top dry part and the outer papery part are not useful. Instead, we peel the outer layers from the stalk and bruise the pale core with the back of a knife to use in stocks, braises, or soups. We sometimes use a sharp knife to slice the core into very fine rings, then mince it even finer, and then sometimes we put it in the food processor to break it down even further. However you use it, it is worth the trouble. There is nothing quite like it. If you can't find lemongrass, try to find lemongrass paste, substituting 1½ teaspoons of the paste for every 1 stalk of lemongrass. You could also substitute the grated zest of 1 lemon for every 1 stalk of lemongrass, although the flavor will be very different.

Lo mein noodles

Sometimes labeled "Hong Kong noodles" or "pan-fried noodles," lo mein noodles are sold both dried and parcooked. They are thin and made of wheat and sometimes egg, which gives them a yellowish color. *Lo mein* translates to the general dish of tossed stir-fried noodles as well as the actual noodle. If you can't find lo mein noodles, substitute spaghetti.

Madras curry

We love Madras curry. It gets its name from a city in southern India called (you guessed it) Madras, which was a frequent stop for English merchants in the 1600s. The funny thing is that the curry was actually invented by restaurants in Great Britain. It's a bit spicier than regular curry powder due to its higher chili content. It adds heat and richness that you won't get from a standard curry powder. Find it in spice shops as well as most grocery stores.

Makrut lime leaves

Makrut limes are a citrus fruit found in tropical Southeast Asian countries. (They are also called kaffir limes, but the word *kaffir* is offensive in some cultures, so we call them by their less common but more acceptable name, makrut.) The leaves are incredibly fragrant and full of essential oils. They are dark green and leathery and always come in a little pair. They are used to perfume curries and are almost always used in conjunction with lemongrass. You can usually find them frozen. They are really expensive, but a little goes a long way and they will keep in your freezer for up to 6 months.

Michiu

Michiu is a Chinese cooking wine fermented from rice. It is softer and rounder than Shaoxing cooking wine and less sweet. Substitute mirin or even dry sherry if you can't find it. It doesn't have the sharpness that cooking wine often has and is great in soups and stir-fried with meats and vegetables. My mom always had a bottle of this in the cabinet, as it is very common in Taiwanese cooking.

Mint

Mint is one of the herbs in what we call the Thai Trio (Thai basil, mint, cilantro). You want to buy mint that is bright green and not wilted. Store it wrapped in a damp paper towel in a plastic bag in the refrigerator. We love using it to accent anything earthy and green (think: asparagus, artichokes), and it is magic with mushrooms. In many of our Thai- and Vietnamese-inspired recipes, we use big handfuls of it; don't be shy with this big, bright herb.

Mirin

Different from Shaoxing cooking wine, mirin is a Japanese sweet rice wine that lends a mild acidity to a dish. It's a useful ingredient to have on hand because so many Asian recipes call for it. If you don't have mirin, you can mimic its sweet-tangy flavor by substituting dry sherry or dry white wine with about ½ teaspoon of sugar mixed into every tablespoon of sherry or white wine.

Miso paste

Most of us know miso from Japanese sushi restaurants that serve warm bowls of miso soup as a starter. Miso paste is a thick salty-sweet fermented soybean paste that is used for so much more than flavoring soups. It can be used to glaze vegetables and fish, and we have even made desserts out of it (it makes a killer buttercream frosting). We use red miso, which is the most intense and flavorful. A little goes a long way. Store miso paste tightly wrapped in the refrigerator after opening.

Mung bean noodles

These guys are made from the starch of the mung bean, a little green legume that is a common filling in Chinese pastries. The noodles are also known as bean threads, bean thread noodles, glass noodles, or cellophane noodles. Similar to their Korean counterpart (which are almost always made from sweet potatoes), they are called cellophane noodles because they are translucent. Don't confuse these with vermicelli noodles, which are opaque white and made from rice (although you can often interchange them in most recipes). They are typically sold dried in 1-pound packages. We stuff them into spring rolls, simmer them in stock for soup, and cook them in boiling water to drop into stir-fries.

Napa cabbage

This beauty is widely available in Asian markets, and you can often find it at the grocery store as well. If not, substitute regular green cabbage and slice it a lot finer, since green cabbage is tougher. Spot napa cabbage by its crinkled, ruffled, pale green leaves and white slender base. It is very versatile: tender enough to eat as a salad but also hearty enough to be stir-fried. Napa is also used in a lot of dumpling and spring roll fillings. If you don't use the whole head, wrap it tightly in plastic wrap and store in your refrigerator for up to 5 days.

Nori

Nori is not just for sushi anymore. These dried seaweed sheets are typically about 8 inches square and come in plastic packs. They are deep green-black and have a bit of shine to them. We toast them in the oven for a few minutes to crisp them up before using. Try crumbling them on top of salads and noodles like we do. You can find these at all Asian markets, and they are now widely available at regular grocery stores with a decent Asian section.

Oyster sauce

Oyster sauce is made from sugar, salt, water, cornstarch, and oyster extract or "essence." The passed-down story of the invention of oyster sauce is that Lee Kam Sheung, who ran a small restaurant that specialized in oyster stew, lost track of time in the kitchen. He smelled something strong and when he looked in the pot, the normally clear soup had turned into a thick, brownish sauce. He tasted it and was surprised by how delicious and unique it was. He started to sell this new product, which turned out to be very popular in Chinese cooking. We like Maekrua brand oyster sauce—we call it infinity sauce, because on the bottle there is a picture of a woman pouring the oyster sauce from a bottle with her picture on it and so on and so forth for infinity. Vegetarian oyster sauce substitutes mushrooms for the oysters. Find oyster sauce in most Asian markets in the same aisle as sesame oil and fish sauce. It usually has a picture of an oyster somewhere on the bottle.

Panko

This Japanese wonder bread crumb is the only breading we use at Myers+Chang. It is puffed breading with large flakes and a light, airy texture. It fries to a feathery crispness that is hard to impart with any other bread crumb, even homemade. You can find it in most grocery stores now, as it has become very mainstream. Store it in an airtight container in a cool, dry place.

Rice

I love rice so much that my family calls me Rice Head. For me, a meal isn't complete unless I have a bowl of rice next to me. In Chinese cooking, the best kind of rice is medium or long grain. Long grain cooks off separate and fluffy and makes great rice the next day for fried rice. Medium grain cooks off moist and tender, and the grains have a little soft mush to them so that you can easily eat it with chopsticks. (This is my favorite type of rice.) Short-grain rice is used mostly for risotto and sushi and clumps a lot when cooked. Brown rice is rice that still retains some of the bran, giving it more nutrients and fiber. Once considered the poor person's rice, it has become more popular in recent years because of its health benefits. Brown rice takes more water and time to cook and has a nuttier flavor. Sweet or glutinous rice is mostly used in Thai cooking and desserts. Store uncooked rice indefinitely in an airtight container in a cool, dark area in your pantry. Store cooked rice in an airtight container in the refrigerator for up to 3 days or in the freezer for up to 6 months.

Rice noodles

Chef's favorite! Chewy, bright white, and slippery, these come in many shapes and sizes and are referred to as *fen* or *fun*. They are made from rice flour and water, and they come fresh and dried. We use the fresh ones, which we find in the refrigerated section of the Asian market near the tofu and dumpling wrappers. They come in a wide flat sheet that you can cut or slice to the size you want. Buy the ones that feel the softest; these are the freshest and will soak up sauce really well. If they feel hard, pry them apart gently and soak in a bit of hot water to soften before stir-frying. They can be refrigerated for up to a week or so, but will get progressively harder as the days go on. If you can't find fresh rice sheets or noodles, dried thick rice noodles (not rice vermicelli; see below) are a decent substitute. These are found in both Asian and regular supermarkets.

Rice vermicelli

Pretty much every Sunday while I was growing up, my mom would make two different stir-fries for lunch. One with a typical thin wheat noodle (see dried flat wheat noodles, page 36) for me and Dad, and one using these noodles that she called *mi fun* for her and my brother. *Mi fun* were my brother Chris's favorite; he was such a picky eater that when my mom found something he liked, she made sure to make it as often as possible. *Mi fun* or rice vermicelli are threadlike, chalky-white dried noodles made of rice flour and water. They often come in small bundles and can be labeled "maifun" or "rice sticks." The best way to cook rice vermicelli is to submerge it in boiling water for 5 to 8 minutes until tender. Dried rice vermicelli may be stored indefinitely at room temperature if wrapped well.

Rice vinegar

Unseasoned rice vinegar is not the same as rice wine. Both are fermented from sweet rice, but rice wine is cooking wine that has not been fermented into vinegar. It is also not seasoned rice vinegar, which has salt and sugar added to it. Rice vinegar adds a pop of brightness and acidity to a recipe without adding additional flavor as you would get from red wine vinegar or the like. It is pretty neutral, very versatile, and an important staple in our pantry. We get it by the case, but you can purchase it at any Asian market and pretty much any regular grocery store by the bottle. Stored in a cool, dry place, it has a lengthy shelf life of at least 6 months.

Sambal oelek

"I will choose sambal oelek over sriracha any day of the week. Don't get me wrong, I know how people love their rooster sauce, and I have used plenty of it in my day, but I reach past it every time for Sambal," says Chef. An Indonesian fresh chili paste made with chilies, a little salt, and vinegar, sambal oelek is chunky and textural, packs more fresh-chili heat, and has less sweetness and acidity than sriracha. Many different versions of sambal are made all over Indonesia (the *oelek* refers to the mortar and pestle used to make it). It is an important part of our Nasi Goreng (page 236). Huy Fong makes a version in a jar with a green cap, and it can usually be found next to its smooth sister, sriracha.

Scallions

Also called green onions, scallions are part of the Asian food trinity, GGS (ginger, garlic, scallion). We use scallions in almost everything. When used raw, they add a bright onion taste that isn't so sharp that they leave your mouth burning for hours; stir-fried, they get a little sweet while still imparting a lot of mild onion flavor to your cooking. They come in bunches of eight or nine scallions, and you can use the whole stalk, white and green parts both. Sometimes we specify green parts only for greater visual impact, but you can always use the whole thing. They will keep in the crisper in your refrigerator for about 5 days.

Sesame oil

Growing up, we always had a small bottle of Kadoya sesame oil in our pantry. Mom would add a few drops to stir-fries or soups when she wanted to add richness and flavor. Once a specialty item found only in Asian grocery stores, sesame oil is now easily found in most supermarkets. Not all sesame oils are the same. Light sesame oils tend to be used more as a cooking oil, whereas toasted (darker) sesame oils are used more often for flavoring. We use toasted sesame oil, which is made from toasted sesame seeds and is amber colored and stronger smelling than light sesame oil.

Shanghai fresh wheat noodles

Found in the refrigerated sections of your Asian market, Shanghai fresh wheat noodles are often sold in 1-pound pouches of thin or thick noodles. We use Twin Marquis brand and cook hundreds of pounds of them a week. You can cook these ahead of time by lowering them into boiling water for 6 minutes, shocking them

in ice water, and then tossing with a bit of vegetable or sesame oil to keep them from sticking together. Or boil them and add them right to your wok or soup bowl while they are nice and hot.

Shaoxing cooking wine

The most well-known Chinese cooking wine, Shaoxing is fermented from rice and is deep amber in color. There are what seems like a million different brands at your Asian market, but almost all will have a distinctive red label. We use Shaoxing in almost all our braises, especially for ribs and pork belly. If you don't have it readily available, you can substitute white wine or even a bit of Madeira or dry sherry.

Shrimp paste

There are many different types of shrimp paste, each for a different use. It's made of fermented ground-up shrimp and salt. This funky condiment amps up any dish with umami and deep oceany flavor. We use a light shrimp paste in bean oil that comes in a small glass jar with a yellow top for our different kimchi pickles and sauces. The paste is bright orange and the oil is almost red. We also use a dark toasted shrimp paste that is bricklike in color and very earthy; it resembles brown clay and we use this one for the Terasi (page 239) that goes in our Nasi Goreng (page 236). Refrigerate it after opening; it will keep for up to 2 weeks.

Sichuan bean paste

This magic sauce is also known as *doubanjiang* and is often considered the heart and soul of Sichuan cuisine. It comes in small jars or cans in hot and sweet varieties, and it is also labeled "hot bean paste," "chili bean sauce," or "hot Sichuan bean sauce." It's made with fermented broad beans, soybeans, rice, salt, and chilies. I always have a jar in my refrigerator at home; I'm addicted to its hot, spicy, salty, earthy flavor. You can use it simply by frying it in a bit of oil and tossing with noodles or vegetables or as the base for more complex sauces as we do at the restaurant.

Sichuan peppercorns

Trick question: What is called a peppercorn but is not a peppercorn? You guessed it: Sichuan peppercorns. Often called prickly ash in the market, these are dried berries from the Chinese prickly ash plant. They possess a crazy mouth-numbing quality and a floral, heady nose. While not spicy, they are often paired with bean paste and chili oil, which are hot, hot, hot. Find these in small plastic bags at the market; toast them in a dry skillet for 4 to 5 minutes, then grind them up. Use these sparingly, since too much will literally make you not able to taste your food for the rest of the meal.

Soy sauce

Walk into any Asian market and head toward the bottled-sauces aisle, and you'll be struck by how many different kinds of soy sauce are lining the shelves. If you thought all soy sauces were alike, that's like saying all vinegars are the same. We use all of them!

REGULAR: One of the oldest condiments in the world (it's the OG seasoning agent), soy sauce is a by-product of fermented soybeans and wheat that have been mixed with brine. Dark, thin, and salty, it is also earthy and full of umami. Find it everywhere.

It is as ubiquitous as kosher salt. Kikkoman is our brand of choice; we just get it in huge buckets instead of small bottles. Store it away from heat and light and refrigerate after opening.

LOW SODIUM: You know, this is the kind with the green top at your neighborhood sushi joint. (We call it Green Soy at the restaurant.) Low-sodium soy sauce is brewed exactly the same way as regular; however, after the fermentation process is completed, about 40 percent of the salt is removed. Just magically sucked out somehow. We don't ask questions—we just use it. In fact, we use it almost exclusively in our cooking because it gives us more control over the saltiness of a dish, similar to using unsalted butter when you bake. Store it away from heat and light and refrigerate after opening.

THICK SOY: This is definitely not your run-of-the-mill soy sauce. Thick soy sauce is made mostly of molasses and is super dark and viscous. We buy the one from Koon Chun, which is also the brand we use for hoisin sauce, but be sure to read the labels! All their jars have the same yellow labels and are written in the same red letters, so it's easy to buy the wrong thing if you are not being careful (we know this from experience). This soy sauce is less salty and definitely sweeter. It gives body to stir-fry sauces and adds a subtle sweetness without extra sugar. Can't find it? Stir a bit of regular soy sauce into the molasses. Refrigerate after opening.

KECAP MANIS: Also called Indonesian sweet soy, this is a sweet soy sauce made from fermented soybeans and flavored with palm sugar, galangal, and star anise. *Kecap manis* gets its name from the Malay fish sauce called *kecap* that is a distant cousin; *kecap* is twice removed from our tomato-based American ketchup. If you can't find a bottle, make your own with equal parts soy sauce and dark brown sugar stirred together. Store away from light and heat and refrigerate after opening.

TAMARI: Produced and fermented in the same way as soy sauce, but with rice instead of wheat grains, tamari is soy sauce's gluten-free sibling. It offers the same flavor as soy sauce but has more sodium; be careful when substituting it 1:1 for soy sauce, or you will wind up with a salt bomb. Tamari is sold in bottles wherever you buy soy sauce, and unopened bottles can be stored indefinitely in your cabinet. Refrigerate after opening.

Spring roll wrappers

These are made with wheat flour and are flexible and somewhat spongy looking. They can be kept in the freezer and thawed for an hour on your counter before using. They are about 8 inches square and come twenty-five sheets to a pack. These are great for spring rolls, egg rolls, *lumpia*, or even in place of phyllo dough. We use Spring Home brand at the restaurant. If your spring roll wrappers are old, they will dry out (even in the unopened package) and be frustrating to work with. It is best to keep them frozen until you are ready to use them. Likewise, while working with them, keep them under a damp tea towel so that they don't dry out.

Sriracha chili sauce

If you don't know it by the name "sriracha," then you probably know it as "rooster sauce." This spicy, smooth, piquant sauce is so popular, you could call it the new ketchup. It comes in a large clear squeeze bottle with a big rooster drawn on it and an unmistakable green top. There is some controversy about the name: who makes the best, where it originates from, and more. We stay out of the fray and focus on all the different ways we can use it: to add spice to sauces, blend into mayo, drizzle over pizza, or, Chef's favorite, squeeze onto hard-boiled eggs. Not just limited to Asian markets, sriracha can be found pretty much everywhere.

Tamarind

A brown pod with a sticky, fruity pulp, tamarind is a beloved ingredient in Southeast Asian cooking. It typically comes as a paste or concentrate in a jar or is cooked down into a square brick. If you find the brick, it has more true tamarind flavor but takes a bit more work to use. First soak it in hot water to soften the pulp until it dissolves, and then press it through a sieve to get the seeds out. Tamarind is sour and tart and has a distinct tropical flavor that is hard to replicate with anything else.

Thai basil

Sturdier than its Italian counterpart, Thai basil has a sharper bite, with firm pointed leaves and dark purple stems. The flavor is deeply herbaceous, sweet, and a touch peppery. It's part of our Thai Trio (Thai basil, cilantro, mint) that makes up our most loved and used herb combination. Use sweet Italian basil or opal basil as a

substitute. Thai basil comes in large leafy bunches or wrapped tightly in plastic and is available in most Asian markets. Store it on your countertop in a vase or glass of water like flowers and it should last at least a week, if not more.

Thai bird chilies

These little green and red heat bombs are adored by chili heads everywhere. They are smaller than your pinky, with a sharp point at one end and a small green stem. Their fresh, burning heat is how we turn up the volume in our Green Papaya Slaw (page 118) and our Tiger's Tears salad (page 126), and they are the base for our housemade sriracha (Dragon Sauce, page 305). The green ones are slightly milder, and the red ones are hotter and riper versions of the green. A little goes a long way. Please wear gloves when preparing them. (You're welcome.) They are readily available in Asian markets, but substitute Fresno, serrano, or jalapeño peppers if you can't find them.

Thai red curry paste

We have included a recipe for red curry paste on page 307, but if you want to purchase it to make life easy, we are not judging. Roland brand makes both red and green curry paste. Do whatever you can to keep this Thai staple in your pantry or freezer. It's typically made with lots of garlic, shallots, chili peppers, galangal, shrimp paste, salt, makrut (kaffir) lime peel, coriander root, coriander seeds, cumin seeds, peppercorns, and lemongrass. If you make it from scratch, cooking the curry paste methodically by stirring it for a long time and toasting it in a bit of oil really changes the dimensions of your dish. It gets deeper and more flavorful as it cooks. It is fantastic with shellfish and fish as well as poultry and veggies. Oh, and *rice*! Lots of *rice*! In a pinch, you could use curry powder rehydrated in a bit of coconut milk. (Here we might judge. Just a little.)

Tofu

Many people claim not to like tofu, which I find devastating. Tofu is not just a new health food but a valued commodity in China with a two-thousand-year-old history. Also called bean curd, tofu is made (much the same way mozzarella is) by mixing ground soybeans with water and turning it into soymilk and then curdling the milk. High in protein, it is not just for vegetarians. It is for anyone looking for a delicious, inexpensive, versatile ingredient that soaks up the flavor of whatever it is prepared with. Here are the various kinds we use at the restaurant.

SILKEN TOFU: This custardy tofu is a secret weapon in our vegan arsenal. It is how we make creamy dressings and sauces with no dairy, and it is the "ancient secret" in our amazing chocolate mousse. Also called soft, silk, or Japanese-style, this tofu has a softer consistency than regular tofu and will fall apart if not handled carefully. Sometimes silken tofu is packaged in aseptic boxes that do not require refrigeration. Because of this, it is sometimes sold in a different section of grocery stores than regular tofu, which is packed in water and requires refrigeration. The tofu in boxes doesn't taste quite as good as the refrigerated tofu, but it is great in a pinch. Make this your new best friend. If you find refrigerated silken tofu, change the water each day to ensure longer life and freshness.

FIRM TOFU: This tofu absorbs flavors well and is excellent for all kinds of cooking: roasting, pan searing, stir-frying, deep-frying. We cube it and use it in all our vegetarian stir-fries. Find it in the refrigerated section stored in water with a peel-away plastic top. Change the water each day after opening to keep it fresh. If you do this, it will last well over a week in your refrigerator.

PRESSED TOFU: Pressed tofu is dense and chewy and extremely versatile. You can fry it, slice it raw and add it to salads, stir-fry it, and marinate and bake it. We marinate it, dredge it in cornstarch, and fry it for our tofu buns. It comes packaged in unflavored little squares that are pale yellow or flavored with Chinese five-spice powder in dark chocolate brown squares. Find it in Asian grocery stores in the refrigerated section.

FRIED TOFU: You can purchase tofu that has been fried and packaged . . . or you can just make it yourself. You'll find yellow blocks of fried tofu in packages along with the fresh tofu. Honestly, though, we recommend that you simply purchase firm tofu and fry it on all sides in about 1 inch of vegetable oil until it is hot and crispy on the outside and creamy on the inside.

Udon noodles

This popular Japanese wheat noodle is thick, springy, and starchy. It is often used in soups in Japanese cuisine. We use it in our Wok-Charred Udon Noodles with Chicken and Bok Choy (page 207) as well as in pretty much every staff meal we make. Parcooked udon noodles are found in the refrigerated noodle section of most Asian markets. (We use Twin Marquis brand.) Cook them for 6 minutes in simmering water before using them in soups or stir-fries. You can also buy dried udon noodles in the packaged noodle section of Asian markets.

Wasabi

Sometimes called Japanese horseradish, most people know wasabi as the spicy green paste they get with their sushi alongside some pickled ginger. Fresh wasabi is actually a root that is pungent and spicy (in that nose-spice kind of way that clears out your sinuses). The fresh stuff is tough to come by, but the paste and powder are readily available in the Asian section of most supermarkets. Test it out first so that you know how strong it is; it varies greatly depending on age and brand.

White pepper

Known for its sharp, fragrant bite, white pepper is used to add extra flavor to Chinese soups and spicier stir-fries. Like black pepper, white pepper comes from the dried fruit of the pepper plant. For white pepper, the dark outer skin of the pepper fruit is removed by soaking before the seed is dried. White pepper is often used on fish, so as to not discolor the light flesh with black pepper. We don't use a lot of white pepper in our cooking, but we love it in our hot and sour soup (page 83) for the floral note it adds.

Wonton wrappers

Wonton, egg roll, dumpling, and gyoza wrappers all start from the same basic dough. Both the size (big for egg rolls, small for wontons) and shape (round or square) depend on what you are using them for. Wonton wrappers are typically square and a bit thinner than dumpling wrappers. Use them in soups where the thin skins make for delicate pretty wontons. They are also awesome fried; we slice them into strips, fry them, and use them on top of salads to give them extra crunch and love. We use Twin Marquis brand, found at most Asian markets, and you can freeze the leftovers in an airtight container.

HOW TO EQUIP YOUR KITCHEN

While you can certainly make many of these dishes with the equipment you already have in your kitchen, here are a few essential items to up your game when it comes to Asian cooking.

Bamboo steamer

Bamboo steamers are inexpensive and incredibly helpful in Asian cooking. You can use them for steaming whole fish, vegetables, or dumplings. Steaming gently cooks the food and locks in both moisture and nutrients. If you buy stackable steamers, you can also efficiently steam different ingredients at the same time. You need a large saucepan that is bigger than your steamer so you can place the steamer fully inside the saucepan; fill the pan up with water to just below the bottom of the steamer and place it on the stove. Heat just until the water simmers and steams. Use parchment paper to line the steamer for ease of cleaning.

If you don't have a bamboo steamer, you can rig one up with your wok. Fit a small wire rack on the bottom of the wok so that it rests a few inches above the bottom, and fill it up with water to just under the rack. Line the rack with parchment paper and place your food on the rack, turn on the heat so the water boils and steams, then turn off the heat and cover with a tight-fitting lid. But for a few bucks, a bamboo steamer is really the way to go.

Chef's knife

This is every cook's best friend. If you have one good chef's knife and one cleaver, you can easily make all the recipes in this book. A 7-inch blade is comfortable for most folks. Keep it sharp by honing it and sharpening it regularly.

Chopsticks

Chopsticks are not only for eating with! They are awesome for removing food from your wok or pan, as well as elegantly plating ingredients. Once you learn how to use them, you will use them interchangeably with your tongs.

Cleaver

Cleavers are an excellent addition to your home knife collection. A medium cleaver will work for both coarse chopping and fine slicing. It feels heavy (in a good way) in your hand. The heft makes it great for cutting lots of meats and vegetables into small pieces, which is the basic definition of how to prep for every stir-fry ever. Cleaver blades are typically made from steel, which will rust if you leave them wet. Take care to dry your cleaver after every use and oil it on a regular basis.

Fish spatula

A "fish spat" is a must-have for every kitchen. One of the first lessons Chef teaches her cooks is to make sure they each have one on their station. It is the only spatula she uses at home and at work. While it is called a fish spatula, you can use it for many different things such as flipping burgers, eggs, and pancakes. It has a short handle with a slotted thin flat blade, and it is very flexible. Like cooking with chopsticks, once you get used to using it, you'll never go back to a regular spatula again.

Rice cooker

While you certainly don't *need* a rice cooker, it is the easiest and fastest way to make perfect rice every time. My dad doesn't know how to cook a thing, but when I was a kid, his one job every day after he came home from work was to "cook the rice." In other words, he filled the rice cooker up with rice and water and pressed the button. (He was a really great cleaner!) If you invest in a rice cooker (they are not expensive, but they do take up space on your counter), you can "set it and forget it" while you prepare the rest of your meal. It also holds the rice and keeps it warm so you can make it in advance and not worry about timing the cooking of your rice to go with the rest of the meal.

Spider

A spider looks like a long stick with a shallow mesh basket attached to the end. These are very useful for lifting food from hot water when blanching or removing food from hot oil. They are inexpensive, and like the other items in this list, once you get comfortable with it, you will find multiple uses for it. We also use ours as a quick strainer when we are boiling small batches of noodles.

Tongs

A pair of tongs in your kitchen is invaluable. "For me, they are an extension of my hand. When I can't find them in my house, I feel like I can't cook," says Chef. They allow you to gently handle your food, carefully place food in a pan without

burning yourself, and lift larger items easily. You can take dumplings out of the steamer basket or pluck greens from blanching water. You can also lift the lid off a pot or stir with them as well. They play the same role as a pair of chopsticks would, but they are able to handle larger items (and are handy for if you have not quite mastered your chopstick game). Every home cook needs a pair. Go to a restaurant supply store and buy yourself a pair of metal Winco tongs for a few bucks; don't fuss with expensive ones from the fancy restaurant stores.

Wooden spoon

You never want to use metal on metal when you are stirring a pot, so use a wooden spoon, which is also nonreactive, important when you're working with acidic ingredients. A larger 10-inch spoon is most useful.

Wok

When buying a wok, you basically have three choices: Teflon-coated nonstick, thin stainless steel, and traditional heavy cast iron. We recommend the stainless steel with a 14-inch circumference for your home; it is the most useful, and the cast-iron can be incredibly heavy when you are just learning. It is fairly inexpensive, and when properly seasoned, it will act like a nonstick pan and last for years. It's a great investment for your kitchen.

If you have a gas stove, you can also purchase a "wok ring" to place over your stove burner. The ring stabilizes the round bottom of the wok and centers the heat on the bottom, while causing the flames to lick the sides so the whole pan is hot. This helps to create *wok hei* (see opposite).

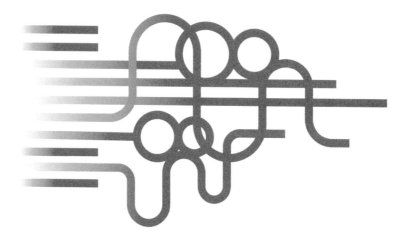

HOW TO WOK

A wok is the perfect all-purpose cooking pot, and its characteristic concave shape has not changed for years. The steel conducts heat almost instantaneously, and you can use it for stir-frying, deep-frying, braising, blanching, steaming, smoking, and sauce making. It really is an all-in-one essential piece of equipment for cooking Asian food.

What is so special about a wok? You cook with a wok to add *wok hei*, which translates to "breath of the wok" or "wok air." You simply can't achieve it without a wok. It is the magical char and fire-kissed flavor we crave. When you toss food in the wok, the air and the heat on all sides of the pan transform the food. Guests ask how our Wok-Roasted Lemongrass Mussels (page 189) or Wok-Charred Udon Noodles (page 207) get so delicious and smoky, and we tell them, "It is the wok and lots of love." They don't believe that there isn't a secret smoky ingredient. There is! It's called *wok hei*.

Buy a wok in any Asian market or well-stocked kitchen equipment store. For home use, we recommend a 14-inch stainless-steel wok, and if you want to go all-out and you have a gas stove, get a corresponding wok ring.

To clean and season your wok, submerge it in extremely hot, soapy water, and rub the inside all over with a sponge. Next scrub the outside with a steel wool, and rinse the wok well. Place it over high heat, and dry with a few paper towels (be careful not to burn yourself). Place 1 tablespoon vegetable oil on a paper towel, and rub the entire inside of wok off the heat. Repeat this process until there is no trace of black residue. The wok is now ready for making all the recipes in this book.

To maintain the wok, make sure you never, ever use detergent in the bowl. That will eat away at the patina that you are trying to build in the wok. Instead, clean the wok with extremely hot water and a stiff-bristled brush. Rinse it and dry it quickly with paper towels to prevent rusting.

Here are a few key tips to successful wokking.

- **The oil needs to get so hot it shimmers and smokes.** This will be the hottest stove cooking you have ever done. When you think you have waited long enough for the oil to heat up, count to fifteen. Very slowly.
- **Cut all your meat and vegetables in roughly equal sizes so they cook evenly.**

- **Have all your ingredients ready to go before you start cooking.** All of them. Once you start wokking, you can't stop. You want to cook quickly and sear in all the flavor and capture all the *wok hei* essence in your food.

- **Don't crowd the wok!** If you have a small wok or large recipe, split the ingredients in two to ensure that everything gets ample space in the wok. Overcrowding will lead to slow cooking and steaming, the enemy of *wok hei*.

- **Have fun!** It's breathtaking to see how fast and amazingly delicious your cooking can be with a wok. If you have fun, you will do it more, and the more you do it, the better you'll get.

MYERS+
CHANG
AT HOME

HOW TO COOK RICE

Cooking great rice is key to cooking great Asian food. You can get a rice cooker, but if you don't have one, use these tips to cook great rice. If you are used to rice pilaf or risotto, the concept of plain white (or brown) rice might seem boring. But that means you have not yet learned how to eat Chinese food (see page 70).

Rinse the rice first. I always rinse my rice three times because that is how my mom taught me. She says rinsing it washes off any loose starch, which makes it sticky. Our goal is light, fluffy, tender rice with distinctive grains. Use a sturdy pot with a flat bottom and a tight-fitting lid. The easiest method is to simmer the rice in a measured amount of water until it is almost but not quite done and then turn off the stove, cover the rice, and let the steam and any remaining water absorb into the grains and fluff them up. We offer specific measurements in our recipes for Perfect White Rice (page 315) and Perfect Brown Rice (page 316), but the exact amount of water does depend on how old the rice is. Older rice may need a bit more water, which you can simply stir in after it has steamed and let it continue to absorb.

HOW TO VELVET

Ever wonder how the chicken in your local takeout joint's chicken and broccoli can be so darn tender? It's called velveting. Velveting is a Chinese cooking technique used in stir-frying. It works on any meat and ups your wok game from average to expert.

First, marinate thinly sliced meat in cornstarch and egg white (rice wine or dry sherry are sometimes added for extra flavor). The longer you can marinate, the better; we marinate for at least a day, but you can successfully velvet with a quick 15-minute marinating. Then heat up what feels like an ungodly amount of oil in a wok or deep saucepan. (You can also velvet using water, although we much prefer the richness and flavor that velveting in oil brings.) Here is where your spider (see page 59) comes in handy. When the oil is hot, flash-fry (or flash-poach, if using water) the marinated meat in the oil, cooking it ever so briefly so that the outside barely cooks and seals in the juices of the meat.

The thin coating that the velveting creates on the meat (which you wouldn't even know is a coating at all, it's so thin) keeps it tender while making the meat surface a vehicle for sauce to stick to in a way that seared meat alone doesn't. Velveting helps prevent the meat from overcooking and becoming dry, and as the name implies, it also gives the meat a smooth, velvety texture.

HOW TO SHAPE DUMPLINGS

We have a prep cook from El Salvador, Maricella, who makes dumplings faster than anyone we have ever seen in Taiwan, China, or any Chinatown. She learned from me first and then from Chef Karen, and after making hundreds of dumplings a day for almost a decade, she's become the one in charge of training the team. Pretty much any time the restaurant is open, she or someone she trained is in our prep kitchen making dumplings.

The first step to folding dumplings is to grab a friend! Folding is a family affair and way more enjoyable when everyone is involved. Have a dumpling-making party with your friends, or have your kids join you (which is how I learned to make dumplings). One of our cookbook testers, Keith, said that learning to make dumplings with his spouse was so much fun that they asked each other, "Why don't we cook together more often?" and now they have regular date nights devoted to cooking. Try these out with someone you love.

HALF-MOON FOLD: This is the most basic dumpling fold; it is also the start of many other folds. It is the foundation for your dumpling education, so read carefully. Even if you only master this one fold, you will be a dumpling ninja. It is an easy, quick fold that works for most fillings. The shape looks like a Polish pierogi sans the crimped edges.

1. Fill a small bowl with water. Keep your wrappers under a damp cloth.
2. Place 1 tablespoon of the filling in the center of a round, thawed dumpling wrapper. **Pro tip:** Use a tiny ice cream scoop.
3. Using your finger, dampen the edges of the wrapper with a little water.
4. Carefully fold the wrapper in half, pushing out any air and sealing the edges together. At this point, it will look like a half-moon.

5. Pinch the edges together to seal tightly.

6. Place the dumplings on a tray and keep covered with a damp cloth until you are ready to cook them; or freeze the dumplings on the tray, then transfer to a zip-top bag or airtight container and freeze to cook at a later date.

BIG HUG FOLD: This fold is a continuation of the half-moon fold. When you pull together the ends of the dumpling and pinch them at the base, it creates a curve and a dimple that makes the filling pocket tight and dense. This gives it a nice snappy bite. The action of pulling the ends together looks like the dumpling is giving itself a big hug, which is how it got its name. Resembling an Italian cappelletti, this dumpling is terrific for steaming.

1. Fill a small bowl with water. Keep your wrappers under a damp cloth.

2. Place 1 tablespoon of the filling in the center of a round, thawed dumpling wrapper. **Pro tip:** Use a tiny ice cream scoop.

3. Using your finger, dampen the edges of the wrapper with a little water.

4. Carefully fold the wrapper in half, pushing out any air and touching the edges together. At this point, it will look like a half-moon.

5. Pinch the edges together to seal tightly.

6. Pull the corners around and together, pinching and sealing them at the bottom of the dumpling.

7. Place the dumplings on a tray and keep covered with a damp cloth until you are ready to cook them; or freeze the dumplings on the tray, then transfer to a zip-top bag or airtight container and freeze to cook at a later date.

BELLYBUTTON FOLD: This fold is almost the same as big hug fold, but you use a square wrapper and the finished dumpling looks like it has a little hat or kerchief on top. Much like the Italian tortellini (named for Venus's navel—hence bellybutton), these pretty ladies are great for catching sauce or broth in their folds. They also sit nicely so they can be steamed or cooked pot sticker–style.

1. Fill a small bowl with water. Keep your wrappers under a damp cloth.

2. Place a square wrapper on your work surface with one of the points facing your belly.

3. Place about 1 tablespoon of the filling in the center of the wrapper. **Pro tip:** Use a tiny ice cream scoop.

4. Using your finger, dampen the edges of the wrapper with a little water.

5. Fold the wrapper over, point to point, and seal the edges so you have a triangle.

6. Take the triangle and squish the filling upward with your thumb to fill the dumpling.

7. Folding toward you, join the "feet" of the triangle together while using your finger to press in the middle of the dumpling.

8. Place the dumplings on a tray and keep covered with a damp cloth until you are ready to cook them; or freeze the dumplings on the tray, then transfer to a zip-top bag or airtight container and freeze to cook at a later date.

CLASSIC PLEATED FOLD: This is the traditional method of folding dumplings. I learned this from my mom, who learned it from her mom, and so on. Mom and I would try to see who could out-pleat the other. The most pleats won. I remember we once had fourteen pleats total, but I don't remember who won. These take a little practice, but once you get it, you'll really get it. For me, these are the most fun to make.

1. Fill a small bowl with water. Keep your wrappers under a damp cloth.

2. Place 1 tablespoon of the filling in the center of a round, thawed dumpling wrapper. **Pro tip:** Use a tiny ice cream scoop.

3. Using your finger, dampen the edges of the wrapper with a little water.

4. Fold the wrapper in half like you are making a taco.

5. Press just the top of the taco together, and then starting from the top, pleat one side of the dumpling wrapper and press it into the opposite flat side. Repeat so that you have two pleats on one half of the dumpling.

6. Repeat on the other half so that the dumpling has four pleats total.

7. Place the dumplings on a tray and keep covered with a damp cloth until you are ready to cook them; or freeze the dumplings on the tray, then transfer to a zip-top bag or airtight container and freeze to cook at a later date.

CIGAR FOLD: We fold our Lemony Shrimp Dumplings (page 164) in this distinctive shape to differentiate them from our other pot stickers. Many of our guests have shellfish allergies, and having these shaped differently helps ensure we don't run them to the wrong table during a busy Saturday night. (This actually happened early on, which is why we immediately created this fold.) This fold uses a square wrapper and is pretty easy to master.

1. Fill a little bowl with water. Keep your wrappers under a damp cloth.
2. Place a square wrapper on your work surface with one of the straight sides facing your belly.
3. Place about 1 tablespoon of the filling in the center of the wrapper and spread it out a bit lengthwise so it is a bit longer.
4. Using your finger, dampen the edges of the wrapper with a little water.
5. Fold the side closest to you halfway up the filling, and fold the top side down to meet it and overlap slightly.
6. Seal with a bit of water and press gently.
7. Press down on the left and right sides of the wrapper to seal well. The finished dumpling will look like a cigar.
8. Place the dumplings on a tray and keep covered with a damp cloth until you are ready to cook them; or freeze the dumplings on the tray, then transfer to a zip-top bag or airtight container and freeze to cook at a later date.

HOW TO USE CHOPSTICKS

Christopher claims that the biggest life-changing aspect of marrying me was realizing that we should all use chopsticks for everything. He now eats salad, nuts, and even sometimes pasta with chopsticks. Just like Papa Chang! I am so much more comfortable with chopsticks that I carry a pair with me in my purse wherever I go. We recently started adding disposable wooden chopsticks to the utensil holders at our bakery, Flour, so people enjoying salads at the bakery can eat them like we do.

First, take one stick and hold it as if you are about to sign your name. Grip it firmly. Wave it around in the air. Conduct a few lines of Beethoven's Fifth. Then take the second stick and slide it under the first one so it's parallel. Now grab the top stick with your thumb, index, and third finger, and let the bottom stick rest against the first knuckle of your ring finger, wedged along the base of your thumb

knuckle. At this point, you want to separate the sticks so that the top stick is firmly controlled by your thumb, index finger, and the side of your middle finger. The bottom stick is held in place by the pressure of your ring finger pressing against your thumb knuckle via the chopstick. Your fingers should be about 3 or even 4 inches away from the tips of the chopsticks. Don't get too close to the tips, or it will be hard to control the movement of the sticks. As you slide your fingers farther from the tips and toward the end, you should be able to wave them around more.

Once you feel sort of comfortable holding the chopsticks like this, it's just a matter of practice. The more you use them, the easier it will be, and soon you'll be forgoing your fork and knife for these as well.

HOW TO EAT CHINESE FOOD

The first time I ever had a meal without rice, I was six or seven at my best friend's house for dinner. Until then, I had never had dinner without an endless mound of rice to eat everything with. There's a way to eat Chinese food that is lost on many people. Today when I am at the restaurant, if I see that someone has not ordered rice, I will often just send it. It makes me so sad to see it untouched on a table.

Hence, we need to make sure that all of you really know how to eat Chinese food. The most important thing to remember is that stir-fries are meant to be eaten with rice. Not having a little bowl of rice next to you when you are eating a stir-fried dish is like having a hamburger without the bun. One goes with the other. These dishes are strongly flavored assuming that you'll take a small bite of saucy pork or chicken along with a small bite of unseasoned rice to create a balanced bite.

If you have ever wondered how Chinese people can eat little bits of rice with chopsticks, the key is that we typically eat our rice from the bowl. Grab a bowl, fill it with a little rice, and then add some stir-fried Hakka Eggplant (page 244) or Rainbow Beef (page 196). With the bowl near your mouth, you can now create a bite-size mouthful of rice and eggplant or beef and scoop it with the chopsticks into your mouth. As you eat, you continually create little perfect bites of pungent, salty, spicy dishes tempered by the warm rice. Eating this way slows you down so you can appreciate and enjoy your food. It's a way of life. It's *our* way of life, and we can't wait to share it with you.

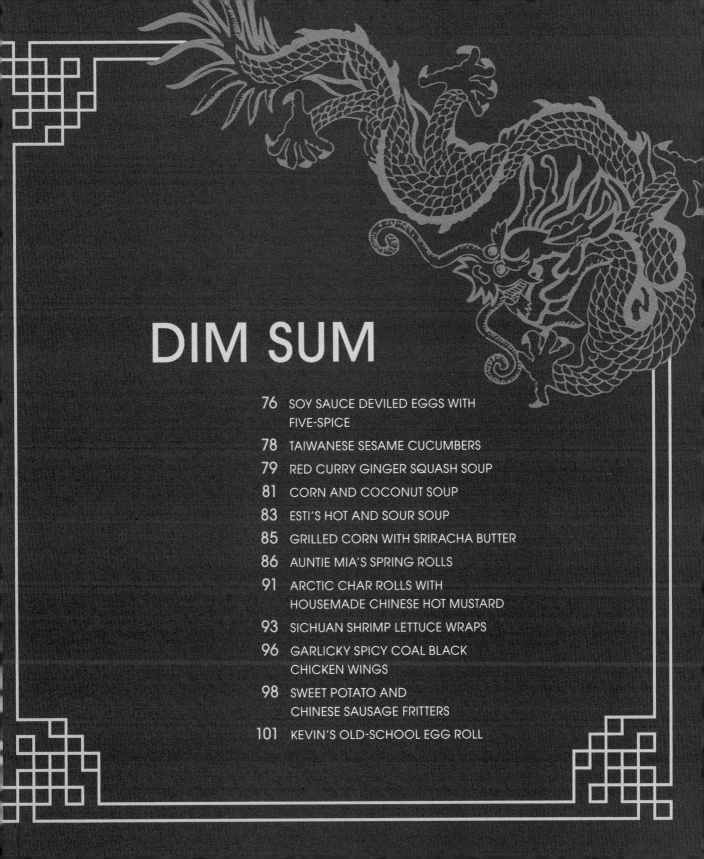

DIM SUM

76 SOY SAUCE DEVILED EGGS WITH FIVE-SPICE

78 TAIWANESE SESAME CUCUMBERS

79 RED CURRY GINGER SQUASH SOUP

81 CORN AND COCONUT SOUP

83 ESTI'S HOT AND SOUR SOUP

85 GRILLED CORN WITH SRIRACHA BUTTER

86 AUNTIE MIA'S SPRING ROLLS

91 ARCTIC CHAR ROLLS WITH HOUSEMADE CHINESE HOT MUSTARD

93 SICHUAN SHRIMP LETTUCE WRAPS

96 GARLICKY SPICY COAL BLACK CHICKEN WINGS

98 SWEET POTATO AND CHINESE SAUSAGE FRITTERS

101 KEVIN'S OLD-SCHOOL EGG ROLL

SOY SAUCE DEVILED EGGS WITH FIVE-SPICE

MAKES 16 DEVILED EGGS

We offer these at Myers+Chang on our weekend dim sum menu. My mom used to make soy sauce eggs for dinner. She would throw hard-boiled eggs into soy sauce–braised beef or chicken as a way to stretch the meal for four hungry mouths, and I would eat them all instead of the main dish. We've updated them here with a hot mustardy bite of wasabi at the end. Be careful! A little goes a long way.

8 large eggs

2 cups soy sauce

½ cup sweetened rice wine or mirin (not rice wine vinegar)

½ bunch scallions (4 or 5), white and green parts finely chopped (about ½ cup)

¼ cup sugar

¼ cup peeled and chopped fresh ginger (about 4-inch knob)

8 whole star anise

3 tablespoons finely minced fresh garlic chives or regular chives

2 tablespoons mayonnaise

2 tablespoons sriracha

2 to 3 teaspoons wasabi paste (start with the smaller amount and add more if you prefer more nose-clearing heat)

¼ teaspoon kosher salt

¼ teaspoon ground white pepper

¼ teaspoon Chinese five-spice powder, for garnish

Place the eggs in large saucepan and cover with cold water. Bring to a boil, turn down the heat, and simmer for 7 minutes. Remove from the heat and let the eggs sit in the hot water for 2 minutes. Drain and peel the eggs under cool running water.

In a separate saucepan, combine the soy sauce, rice wine, scallions, sugar, ginger, star anise, and 1 cup water and bring to a boil. Remove from the heat and let the mixture cool until it is warm to the touch. Place the peeled eggs in

the soy mixture and refrigerate for at least 4 hours and no more than 8 hours.

Remove the eggs from the soy mixture and carefully cut them in half lengthwise. Remove the yolks and place in a small bowl. Add 2 tablespoons of the garlic chives, the mayo, sriracha, wasabi, salt, and white pepper. Mush around till smooth, then taste a little bit; you want the yolks peppery and hot, so add more wasabi as needed to achieve this (different wasabis have different heat levels). Either spoon the yolks neatly back into the whites (dip your spoon in water for ease of scooping), or transfer them to a piping bag or a small plastic sandwich bag with a hole cut out of the corner and pipe the yolks back into the whites, filling the cavities. Top evenly with the remaining 1 tablespoon garlic chives and a pinch of five-spice powder. Serve immediately.

TAIWANESE SESAME CUCUMBERS

SERVES 4 TO 6

At Ippudo, a popular Japanese ramen restaurant with a location in New York City, Christopher and I had Japanese cucumbers dressed simply with sesame oil, salt, and sesame seeds. They were so delicious that we got a second order to go, which I then carried on the train all the way back to Boston to share with the Myers+Chang team. I wanted to replicate this crunchy fresh starter at Myers+Chang, and this dish fast became a customer favorite. What makes them Taiwanese? My mom and I worked together to develop our own version of this recipe, and we are both Taiwanese, so now these cucumbers are as well. English cucumbers are long and skinny and have very little to no seeds; they are especially crunchy and easy to eat, making them perfect for this quick snack.

2 English cucumbers

½ cup toasted sesame oil

3 tablespoons unseasoned rice vinegar

3 teaspoons kosher salt

½ cup white sesame seeds

2 teaspoons red pepper flakes

2 scallions, white and green parts finely chopped (about ¼ cup)

Freeze the cucumbers for 15 minutes to really get them cold. Cut the cucumbers into thirds, then cut each third into five or six spears and place them all in a large bowl.

In a small bowl, whisk together the sesame oil, vinegar, and 1 teaspoon of the salt until the salt has dissolved. Pour the dressing over the cucumbers. Using a spice grinder or a food processor, grind up the sesame seeds, the remaining 2 teaspoons salt, and

the red pepper flakes and process until the sesame seeds are mostly ground into a coarse powder. Set aside about a quarter of the ground seeds for garnish and add the remaining ground seeds to the cucumbers. Toss the cucumbers, dressing, and seeds until well mixed. Divide among four to six small bowls and sprinkle the reserved seeds on top of the cucumbers. Sprinkle each bowl evenly with the scallions. Serve immediately.

RED CURRY GINGER SQUASH SOUP |

SERVES 4

Kabocha squash, if you can find it, is one of the sweetest squashes there is. It looks a bit like a speckled green pumpkin, and the flesh is dense and creamy. It's a terrific base for this rich, warming soup. The lemongrass and lime leaf brighten up the coconut and curry flavors, which in turn balance the sweetness of the squash and spiciness of the ginger. This soup is easy to make and a boon to have in the freezer when you need a quick meal. Use olive oil instead of butter for a vegan version.

2 tablespoons unsalted butter

1 small yellow onion, chopped

2 tablespoons peeled and finely chopped fresh ginger (about 2-inch knob)

1 tablespoon Homemade Red Curry Paste (page 307) or jarred Thai red curry paste (we like Roland brand)

1½ pounds uchici kuri, kabocha, or butternut squash, peeled, seeded, and cut into 2-inch cubes

1 stalk lemongrass

One 13.5-ounce can coconut milk

2 makrut lime leaves or grated zest of 2 limes

2 tablespoons freshly squeezed lime juice, plus more to taste

1 tablespoon sugar, plus more to taste

2 teaspoons kosher salt, plus more to taste

In a large stockpot, melt the butter over medium heat. Add the onion and ginger and cook gently, stirring, until the onions turn translucent, 4 to 5 minutes. Add the curry paste and cook, stirring, until fragrant, about 1 minute. Add the squash and about 2 cups water and cook until mushy, about 15 minutes. Peel and discard the dry, papery outer layers of the lemongrass; trim off the top two-thirds of the stalk, which is also dry and papery, along with the very base and discard. Split the bottom third (5 to 6 inches) of the stalk, where it is pale and bendable, in half lengthwise and add it to the squash along with the coconut milk and lime leaves. Simmer for about 30 minutes. Fish out the lime leaves and lemongrass stalk and discard. Season with the lime juice, sugar, and salt.

Puree the soup in a blender or food processor until smooth. Always use caution when blending hot liquids, and be sure to vent your blender a bit so it doesn't explode. Pass the soup through a fine strainer. Taste and add more lime or sugar or salt as needed. Add more water to thin out the soup if needed; it should run off the back of a spoon. Serve immediately. The soup can be made up to 4 days in advance and stored in an airtight container in the refrigerator or in the freezer for up to 2 weeks.

CORN AND COCONUT SOUP

SERVES 4 TO 6

This is one of the most indulgent soups you'll ever eat. We make it every summer when corn is at its peak and serve it hot or chilled. We once had a server who loved it so much that he ordered it every day he worked, five days a week. We were a little worried for him because it is so very rich, but he countered that since we only offer it for a month or so, he had to get his fill. Touché! Get your fill when corn is so sweet that you can eat it raw and straight from the cob.

8 ears sweet corn, shucked

4 tablespoons (½ stick) unsalted butter

1 medium leek, cleaned and thinly sliced (about 1 cup)

4 medium shallots, thinly sliced (about 1 cup)

2 teaspoons kosher salt

1 teaspoon ground white pepper

Two 13.5-ounce cans coconut milk

2 makrut lime leaves or grated zest of 2 limes

4 to 6 teaspoons sambal oelek

4 to 6 fresh Thai basil leaves, thinly sliced, for garnish

The easiest way to remove the kernels from an ear of corn is to place a tea towel on a cutting board and hold the ear upright on the towel. Run a sharp knife down the cob to slice off the kernels. They will collect on the tea towel, and you can shake them out into a bowl. Continue with the rest of the corn. You should have about 6 cups kernels. Set aside.

In a large flat-bottomed saucepan, melt the butter over medium heat. Add the leeks and shallots and season with the salt and white pepper. Cook, stirring with a wooden spoon or rubber spatula, until the leeks and shallots are soft and translucent, about 5 minutes. Add the corn kernels and cook, stirring, for another 3 minutes. Pour in the coconut milk (be sure to scrape all of the cream from the cans) and add 1 cup water. Stir in the lime leaves. Simmer over low heat for 15 minutes, then remove from the heat.

Let cool just a bit (for safety reasons), remove the lime leaves, and puree the soup in small batches in a blender on high. Strain the soup through a fine sieve until it is perfectly smooth and deliciously creamy. You may need to strain it twice. Discard the pulp that remains in the sieve. Divide the soup

among four to six soup bowls and garnish each bowl with 1 teaspoon of the sambal and 1 thinly sliced Thai basil leaf. Serve immediately. The soup can be made up to 3 days in advance and stored in an airtight container in the refrigerator or in the freezer for up to 2 weeks. Reheat over medium-low heat for 6 to 8 minutes until hot, adding a bit of water if needed to loosen the soup.

ESTI'S HOT AND SOUR SOUP

SERVES 4

"Who is Esti?" is a question asked at M+C as much as "What is *gochujang*?" She is Christopher's muse, best friend, former business partner, spiritual sister, and simply the nicest and most beautiful person I know. She's a preternatural super sniffer with the best palate of anyone he's ever worked with, be it chef, sommelier, or otherwise. She comes from a crazy food family where her parents had dueling Wolf ranges back in the sixties. She is obsessed with hot and sour soup and orders it every time she eats Chinese food. This soup is an homage to her and her family of food-obsessed Jews from the old country of Brooklyn, by way of Russia. Find a better hot and sour. We dare ya.

2 tablespoons vegetable oil, such as canola

½ pound ground pork

6 scallions, white and green parts finely chopped (about ¾ cup)

1 tablespoon peeled and finely chopped fresh ginger (about 1-inch knob)

1 medium garlic clove, minced

4 cups Basic Chicken Stock (page 313) or canned low-sodium chicken broth

14 to 16 ounces soft or firm tofu, cut into ½-inch cubes

5 dried shiitake mushrooms, soaked in hot water until soft and thinly sliced

2 tablespoons dried wood ear mushrooms (also called cloud ear fungus), soaked in hot water until pliable and thinly sliced

½ cup unseasoned rice vinegar, plus more to taste

3 tablespoons soy sauce

2 tablespoons toasted sesame oil

2 teaspoons sugar

2 teaspoons sriracha, plus more to taste

1¼ teaspoons ground white pepper

2 large eggs, at room temperature

In a large flat-bottomed saucepan, heat the vegetable oil over medium-high heat until it shimmers. Add the pork, all but 2 tablespoons of the scallions, the ginger, and garlic and cook, stirring occasionally, for about 1 minute. Break up the pork into smaller pieces but don't worry about completely breaking it down. Add the stock, bring it to a boil, and then reduce the heat to maintain a simmer. Add the tofu and shiitake and wood ear mushrooms to the broth. Give the broth a stir and add the vinegar, soy sauce, 1 tablespoon of the sesame oil, the sugar, sriracha, and 1 teaspoon of the white pepper and bring it back up to a simmer. Taste and adjust the seasoning with more sriracha or vinegar if you want the soup hotter or more sour.

Whisk the eggs together in a small bowl and, with the soup at a steady simmer, whisk them slowly into the broth. Bring back up to a simmer. Divide among four bowls and garnish each bowl evenly with the remaining 2 tablespoons scallions, 1 tablespoon sesame oil, and ¼ teaspoon white pepper. Serve immediately. The soup, minus the eggs, can be stored in an airtight container in the refrigerator for up to 3 days. Bring the soup back up to a boil, add the eggs, and garnish as directed.

GRILLED CORN WITH SRIRACHA BUTTER

SERVES 3 TO 6

We originally made this corn as a component of a popular dish, Wok-Charred Octopus with Sriracha Grilled Corn. One of our favorite regulars, David, would order just the sriracha sauce that we toss the octopus with. He asked if we would bottle the sauce for him so that he could pour it on everything at home. "But David, it's just butter and sriracha and scallions!" He didn't believe us, so here's the proof. We grill the corn with the husk off so that the sweet kernels char and then slather it with this spicy butter. It is summer personified. This recipe makes six ears, but we have found that it only serves two or three people because no one can eat just one ear.

½ cup (1 stick) unsalted butter, cubed, at room temperature

5 tablespoons sriracha

3 teaspoons kosher salt

6 ears corn (we like bicolor or Silver Queen)

2 tablespoons extra-virgin olive oil

½ teaspoon freshly ground black pepper

2 scallions, white and green parts finely chopped (about ¼ cup)

In a medium bowl using a wooden spoon or in the bowl of a stand mixer fitted with the paddle attachment, beat the butter with the sriracha and 2 teaspoons of the salt until the butter is orange and has a whipped texture. Set aside.

If you have a grill, preheat the grill.

Shuck the ears of corn and place them on a plate or baking sheet. Drizzle with the olive oil and season with the remaining 1 teaspoon salt and the pepper, rolling the corn around until

evenly covered. Place the corn directly on the grill over medium-high heat. If you don't have a grill, cook the corn in a large flat-bottomed skillet on the stove over medium-high heat. Turn the corn every minute or so until it picks up some color and char and the ears are grilled evenly, 12 to 15 minutes.

Remove the corn from the grill, cut the ears in half, and roll them around in the butter. Place them on a serving platter, sprinkle the scallions evenly over the corn, and dig in.

AUNTIE MIA'S SPRING ROLLS

MAKES ABOUT 12 ROLLS

Before Myers+Chang opened, my Auntie Mia traveled to Boston from Taiwan to pay me a visit. She heard that Christopher and I were opening a Chinese restaurant, and she wanted to make sure my family's recipes were well represented. Cooking truly transcends language. Despite the fact that Auntie Mia speaks not a word of English, and Christopher and I know about three Taiwanese words between us, her detailed hands-on lesson on how to make these savory, earthy rolls was better than any cooking class at the Cordon Bleu. When Chef Karen joined the team, she upped the ante by adding glass noodles and Swiss chard to the filling, making them even more appealing. We all held our breath the next time Auntie Mia came to town and tried our updated version of her classic. Her wide grin was all we needed to know that she approved. At the start of pretty much every dinner service, Chef and I split a spring roll to check the seasoning and, well, because we are almost always hungry.

A few notes about the ingredients. We use sweet potato glass noodles, which are made from potato starch and are somewhat translucent. You can also use mung bean noodles or rice vermicelli. All are found in the dried noodle section of Asian grocery stores or online. The glass and mung bean noodles usually come in a big package, and the rice vermicelli are often sold in small bundles about the size of your clenched fist. Don't confuse the wheat spring roll wrappers for this recipe with dried rice spring roll wrappers. The ones you want here are found in the refrigerated section of an Asian grocery store; they are square shaped, flexible, and somewhat spongy looking.

5 to 6 ounces uncooked sweet potato glass noodles, mung bean noodles, or rice vermicelli

2 tablespoons vegetable oil, such as canola

4 cups lightly packed Swiss chard or other leafy green, such as spinach

1 tablespoon plus 1 teaspoon kosher salt

½ teaspoon freshly ground black pepper

1½ cups minced fresh garlic chives or regular chives

2 medium carrots, coarsely shredded on the large holes of a box grater or using the grating blade of a food processor (about 1 cup)

1 cup crumbled firm tofu, placed in cheesecloth and squeezed dry (about 8 ounces)

½ cup shredded bamboo shoots (see Note; use the large holes of a box grater or the grating blade of a food processor)

6 whole dried shiitake mushrooms, soaked in hot water until soft and finely chopped

1 tablespoon toasted sesame oil

2 tablespoons all-purpose flour

12 refrigerated 8-inch-square wheat spring roll wrappers

5 to 6 cups vegetable oil, such as canola, for frying

½ cup Rhubarb Duck Sauce (recipe follows), for serving

In a large pot, bring about a gallon of water up to a rolling boil and add the glass noodles. (See Note. If you are using rice vermicelli noodles, follow instructions at the end of the paragraph.) Cook for 7 minutes, drain in a colander, and immediately pour ice water over the noodles to stop them from overcooking and cool them down so you can handle them. Toss lightly with 1 tablespoon of the vegetable oil to keep them from sticking and set aside. (If using rice vermicelli, place the noodles in a large bowl and pour boiling water over them to cover. Let sit for 4 minutes, until soft, and then drain. Toss with 1 tablespoon of the vegetable oil to keep them from sticking and set aside.)

In a large flat-bottomed saucepan, heat the remaining 1 tablespoon vegetable oil over high heat. Strip the leaves off the stems of the chard,

discard the stems, and add the leaves to the saucepan along with 1 teaspoon of the salt and the pepper. Cook, stirring, until just wilted, about 2 minutes. Remove from the pan, let cool, and squeeze the liquid out of the chard with your hands. Chop the chard into small pieces so you don't have long stringy greens when you bite into the rolls.

In a large bowl, mix together the noodles, chard, chives, carrots, tofu, bamboo shoots, and mushrooms. Give the filling a squeeze with your hands to remove excess liquid. You want the filling to be cool and on the dry side. Soggy filling will make sad, soggy spring rolls. Season the mixture with the remaining 1 tablespoon salt and the sesame oil and mix well. The filling can be made up to 1 day in advance and stored in an airtight container in the refrigerator.

continued
↓

In a small bowl, make a slurry by whisking together the flour and 2 tablespoons water with a fork. Lay a spring roll wrapper on a clean, dry surface with one of the points facing your belly. Place 3 to 4 tablespoons of the filling in the corner closest to you. (It may seem like a lot, but you want the rolls to be full of filling.) Start rolling the bottom corner up and over the filling until it is rolled halfway up away from you. Fold over the left side and then the right side tightly toward the center. You should have an envelope shape. Dip your finger into the slurry and paint it onto the remaining edge of the spring roll wrapper (like the glue on an envelope). Continue rolling away from you with a tuck-and-roll motion. You want nice, tight, beautiful spring

rolls. Repeat with love. Uncooked spring rolls can be made up to 8 hours in advance and stored in an airtight container in the refrigerator.

To fry the rolls, fill a large deep saucepan with 2 inches of vegetable oil. Heat the oil to 350°F or until a cube of bread fries to a nice golden brown in 10 seconds. Working in batches of four, gently slide the rolls into the oil and fry, turning them over to make sure all sides are crispy and golden, for about 2 minutes (see Note, page 92). Place on a wire rack to cool just a bit before you bite into them (or just burn your mouth because they are so darn good!). Serve immediately with the Rhubarb Duck Sauce.

Notes: Use whole bamboo shoots in vacuum-sealed bags if you can find them for best flavor; otherwise, use canned whole bamboo shoots.

We recommend that you cook off the entire bag of noodles. Then you can keep them in the fridge and eat them for lunch during the week. Otherwise, you will have an opened, half-bag of noodles lurking in your cabinet for a year.

Rhubarb Duck Sauce

MAKES ABOUT 1½ CUPS

Christopher and Karen love to reimagine new versions of their favorite Chinese takeout dishes from growing up. Nothing says "takeout Chinese" more than those packets of duck sauce that are always thrown into the bag by the handful. We created a fresh version of this sauce that has tang and body without all the gloppy-ness. When it's springtime and early vegetables are begging to be used, Chef poaches rhubarb in a very light simple syrup and purees it into a vinegary sauce with a little kick. We swap out the rhubarb for stone fruits in the summer, quince in the fall, and Asian pear and cranberries in the winter. Freeze any extra and use it on grilled meats and fish.

2 large stalks rhubarb

⅓ cup plus 3 tablespoons sugar, plus more to taste

½ cup unseasoned rice vinegar, plus more to taste

2 tablespoons low-sodium soy sauce

1 teaspoon sriracha

1 tablespoon peeled and chopped fresh ginger (about 1-inch knob)

1 teaspoon Korean chili powder

TRIM the rhubarb (the leaves are poisonous, so be sure to discard them) and cut the stalks into 2-inch sections. In a medium saucepan, combine ⅓ cup of the sugar with 1½ cups water and simmer over medium-high heat until the sugar has dissolved. Add the rhubarb and poach over medium heat until the rhubarb is very soft and loses its shape, 6 to 8 minutes. Using a slotted spoon, remove the rhubarb from the syrup and transfer to a blender. Discard the syrup (or let cool and combine with seltzer water and ice for a refreshing drink).

ADD the vinegar, the remaining 3 tablespoons sugar, the soy sauce, sriracha, ginger, and chili powder to the blender and blend on high until smooth. Taste and adjust the seasoning, adding more sugar or vinegar as needed to make the sauce sweeter or more sour. The Rhubarb Duck Sauce can be stored in an airtight container in the refrigerator for up to 3 days or in the freezer for up to 3 weeks.

ARCTIC CHAR ROLLS WITH HOUSEMADE CHINESE HOT MUSTARD

MAKES 6 ROLLS

Every great dish, restaurant, menu, or cookbook is an assemblage of creativity, collaboration, inspiration . . . and theft. This Arctic char dish was theft. With a twist. Christopher and I were doing what we do when we travel: something we borrowed from my parents called *wang yi wang*, which basically means "to wander." We were in San Francisco, walking around aimlessly, no reservations, no plan; we didn't Yelp or Google or tweet. We decided where to eat when our feet hurt beyond belief. We happened upon The House in North Beach. We ordered and devoured this dish. They used salmon. We came back to Boston and made it utterly ours by using char. Ahem. Ain't we clever. Thank you, Angela and Larry Tse, owners of The House. We think your food is terrific. xxx

12-ounce skinless Arctic char fillet (use salmon or rainbow trout if you cannot find Arctic char)

1½ teaspoons kosher salt, plus more for seasoning

½ teaspoon freshly ground black pepper

1 tablespoon all-purpose flour

6 refrigerated 8-inch-square spring roll wrappers

6 (8-inch-square) sheets unseasoned toasted nori (dried seaweed)

5 to 6 cups vegetable oil, such as canola, for frying

1 recipe Chinese Hot Mustard Sauce (page 304)

Using a sharp chef's knife, divide the Arctic char fillet into six pieces, each a rectangular "brick" about 3 inches long, 1 inch thick, and 2 ounces in weight. If you can't cut the fillet into evenly sized rectangles, don't fret; cut them into long, thin pieces and you will piece them together when making the rolls.

Sprinkle the fish evenly with the salt and pepper and set aside.

In a small bowl, make a slurry by whisking together the flour and 2 tablespoons water with a fork. Lay a spring roll wrapper on a clean, dry surface with one of the points

continued
↓

ARCTIC CHAR
ROLLS WITH
HOUSEMADE
CHINESE
HOT MUSTARD

continued

facing your belly. Lay a sheet of nori directly on top of the spring roll sheet but turned 90 degrees so the nori is oriented left to right; the wrapper and nori together will form a star shape. Place about 2 ounces of fish on the nori near the bottom of the nori sheet close to you. (If you were able to cut your fillet evenly into six rectangles, you will use one piece per roll. If you cut your fillet into smaller pieces, combine two or three pieces together to get about 2 ounces and lay these on the nori.) Lift up the corner of the wrapper closest to you and fold it over the fish. Roll halfway up the wrapper away from you. Fold over the left side and then the right side tightly toward the center so you have an envelope shape. The nori is sturdier than you might think, so don't be afraid to roll tightly. Dip your finger into the slurry and paint it onto the top edge of the spring roll wrapper (like the glue on an envelope). Continue rolling with a tuck-and-roll motion until you have completely sealed the fish in a little roll. Repeat with the remaining

fish, wrappers, and nori to make six rolls. The rolls can be made up to 1 day in advance and stored in an airtight container in the refrigerator.

Fill a large deep saucepan with the vegetable oil to a depth of about 2 inches. Heat the oil to 350°F or until a cube of bread fries to a nice golden brown in 10 seconds. Gently slide the rolls into the oil, turning them over every now and then, until all sides are crispy and light golden, 2 to 3 minutes (see Note).

Let the rolls rest for 1 minute on a wire rack or paper towel–lined plate so that the fish can "carryover cook." (It will continue to cook as it rests and the fish will be cooked to a lovely medium/medium-rare this way.) Slice the rolls lengthwise on an angle with a sharp serrated knife so that you can see the juicy fish inside. Season the cut fish with a pinch of salt and serve immediately with Chinese Hot Mustard Sauce.

Note: Don't dispose of your cooking oil by pouring it down the sink or it will clog your pipes. Instead, let the oil cool completely, then transfer it to a disposable airtight container, seal, and throw it away in the garbage.

SICHUAN SHRIMP LETTUCE WRAPS

SERVES 2 ENTHUSIASTIC SHRIMP EATERS

One lucky summer day, our seafood purveyors sent us a sample of some lovely head-on shrimp. I immediately remembered eating peel-and-eat shrimp for the first time with my uncle John when visiting him in Florida years ago. I wanted to re-create that moment, sitting by the ocean, and give them a salt and pepper finish. I thought of Sichuan peppercorns. Really a berry, Sichuan peppercorns have a special mouth-numbing tingling quality that is like nothing else. Combined with chili oil and grilled lemon, these shrimp really sing. Sichuan food is known for its heavy use of chili and garlic, and these live up to their name. The herbs keep it fresh, and the caramelized lemon picks everything up, adding a sweet, almost buttery component. If you have everything cleaned and prepped in advance, the meal comes together in minutes. Joanne likes to tuck the shrimp into lettuce cups, fill them with herbs, and eat the shrimp, crunchy shells and all. Go ahead, get messy and eat the head! —*Chef Karen*

12 head-on, shell-on jumbo shrimp or prawns (about 1 pound), or 12 headless deveined shell-on jumbo shrimp (about ¾ pound)	2 tablespoons vegetable oil, such as canola (for cooking if you do not have a grill) 1 lemon, quartered ¼ cup Sichuan Dressing (recipe follows)	6 to 8 Bibb lettuce leaves ½ cup fresh cilantro leaves (about ¼ bunch) ½ cup fresh Thai basil leaves (5 to 6 stems)

If you are using head-on, shell-on shrimp, start by deveining them: Using the tip of a small, sharp paring knife and starting from the base of the head, pierce through the back of the shrimp shell and slice down to the tail. You want to cut just deep enough to split the back of the shell in half and cut into the shrimp just enough to pierce the surface and expose the black vein that runs along the back of the shrimp. Run your finger along the pierced shrimp to remove the vein.

If using a grill, heat up your grill. Place the shrimp and the lemon wedges on a hot spot. If you don't have a grill, in a large flat-bottomed skillet, heat the vegetable oil over medium-high heat until it shimmers, about 1 minute. Carefully add the shrimp and the lemon wedges.

continued
↓

SICHUAN
SHRIMP
LETTUCE
WRAPS

---

continued

Cook the shrimp until one side starts to turn pink and the lemon begins to char, 2 to 3 minutes. (Charring the lemon will make it juicy and caramelize its flavor.) Flip the shrimp and lemon wedges over. Shrimp basically have their own built-in thermometer: When their tails curl up, they are done. Wait for the shrimp tails to curl and the shrimp to turn entirely pink, 2 to 3 minutes. Remove both the shrimp and lemon wedges from the grill or skillet and place them all in a large bowl. At this point, if you do not want to eat the shells (although we encourage you to try them, for extra flavor and crunch), peel the shrimp and discard the shells. Otherwise, leave them with the shell and head on. Add the Sichuan Dressing and toss until well coated.

Divide the Bibb lettuce between two serving plates and arrange the fresh herbs on the lettuce. Divide the shrimp evenly between the plates, arranging them on the lettuce and herbs. Place the lemon wedges alongside. The best way to eat these is to squeeze the caramelized lemon onto the shrimp, roll up the shrimp in a lettuce leaf and herbs, and eat it like a taco. If you are adventurous and left the shrimp unpeeled, eat the whole crunchy zingy package: head, tail, shell, and all. Be sure to serve with a lot of napkins!

Sichuan Dressing

MAKES ABOUT 1 CUP

This recipe is a uniquely flavorful and versatile sauce to have on hand. Toss leftover dressing with cooked chicken or beef and add it to a salad, or use it as a spicy sauce for a stir-fry of your favorite protein and vegetables. I often add a spoonful to steamed vegetables and rice for a late-night snack when I come home from work.

2 tablespoons Sichuan peppercorns

¼ cup vegetable oil, such as canola oil

2 tablespoons hot Sichuan bean paste

2 tablespoons unseasoned rice vinegar

1½ teaspoons red pepper flakes

2 medium garlic cloves

1 medium shallot, halved

½ cup chili oil

IN A SMALL skillet, toast the peppercorns over medium-low heat until they start to become fragrant and floral and pop a bit, 4 to 6 minutes. Transfer them to a food processor and add the vegetable oil, bean paste, vinegar, red pepper flakes, garlic, and shallot. Process on low speed until the garlic and shallot are very finely chopped, scraping down the sides of the bowl a few times with a rubber spatula or wooden spoon. Add the chili oil and continue to blend on low speed to fully blend the dressing. (If you don't have a food processor, crush the peppercorns in a spice grinder or with the back of a knife and place in a medium bowl. Mince the garlic and shallot very fine and add to the bowl. Whisk in the vegetable oil, bean paste, vinegar, and red pepper flakes until combined. Add the chili oil last and whisk vigorously until well combined.) The dressing will be a bit lumpy from the bean paste, shallot, and ginger, and it will be characteristically oily. It can be made up to 1 week in advance and stored in an airtight container in the refrigerator or in the freezer for up to 2 months.

GARLICKY SPICY COAL BLACK CHICKEN WINGS

SERVES 3 TO 4 ENTHUSIASTIC CHICKEN WING EATERS OR 6 TO 8 REGULAR PEOPLE

What's in a name? Turns out a lot. **These wings are wildly flavorful, addictive . . . and ugly.** When this dish was first on our menu as General Myers' Chicken Wings, they would arrive at the table, and guests were horrified. The honey in the chicken marinade caramelizes and turns the wings jet black, and guest after guest would send them back, turned off and thinking they were burnt to a crisp. But when we renamed them Coal Black Wings, we took away the alarming unexpected eye shock, and, well, a wing by any other name should taste this sweet. This is one of Christopher's favorite dishes, and when they are on the menu, he has them six times a week. No joke. Plate these on something pretty. It'll help.

5 pounds chicken wings

12 medium garlic cloves, smashed

1 bunch (8 or 9) scallions, white and green parts coarsely chopped (about 1 cup)

¾ cup toasted sesame oil

¾ cup sambal oelek

2 cups low-sodium soy sauce

¾ cup honey

2½ to 3 quarts vegetable oil, such as canola, for frying

1 recipe Dragon Sauce (page 305; optional)

1 cup crumbled blue cheese (optional)

In a large plastic container or a metal or glass baking dish, place the wings in a single layer and set aside. In a medium bowl, add the garlic, scallions, sesame oil, sambal oelek, and soy sauce and whisk to combine. Warm up the honey either in the microwave for 15 seconds or in a small saucepan over medium heat for a few seconds to make it nice and runny. (This will allow it to more easily mix into the marinade.) Whisk the honey into the soy marinade. Pour over the wings and massage into the skin with your hands. Cover the wings and refrigerate overnight. Don't skip the overnight marinating step! The wings need time to really soak up the soy and honey and all the other great flavors.

The next day, preheat the oven to 350°F and place a rack in the center of the oven. Line a rimmed baking sheet with aluminum foil or parchment paper.

Remove the chicken wings from the marinade and place them on the prepared baking sheet. Strain the marinade directly into a medium heavy-bottomed saucepan and discard the solids. Bake the wings until they are cooked through (test by pulling apart a wing and making sure the chicken is opaque and no blood remains), 30 to 35 minutes. Remove from the oven and set aside. The wings may be parbaked up to 2 days in advance and stored in an airtight container in the refrigerator.

While the wings are baking, bring the marinade to a boil over high heat; reduce the heat to medium and simmer for 40 to 45 minutes, until it thickens a bit and becomes syrupy like warm honey. Set aside. The wing sauce can be made up to 2 days in advance and stored in an airtight container in the refrigerator. Reheat in a small saucepan before using.

Fill a large, heavy, flat-bottomed pot with vegetable oil to a depth of 3 inches. Heat the oil to 375°F, using a candy thermometer for accuracy. Give the wings a bit of a shake to remove any excess marinade and fry them in batches of eight or so until they are dark and crispy, about 3 minutes (see Note, page 92). Watch out! The oil bubbles and sputters like crazy when you first put in the wings. And they turn *black* due to the honey and soy, so don't be alarmed when this happens. Remove them from the oil and place on a plate or baking sheet lined with paper towels to soak up the excess oil. When you have fried all the wings, put them in a large bowl, pour over enough of the reduced marinade to cover the wings, and toss well to coat. Serve with the Dragon Sauce and blue cheese crumbles. You just upped your Sunday Funday snack game.

SWEET POTATO AND CHINESE SAUSAGE FRITTERS

MAKES 7 TO 8 FRITTERS

An addictive treat, these fritters are creamy and soft inside and super crunchy on the outside. They get their exceptional crunch from the panko crust. Panko is a Japanese bread crumb that is puffed so that it fries up light and crispy. You can find panko in most grocery stores, along with small cans of red curry paste (often labeled "Thai") and plastic jars of sambal oelek. You'll likely have to visit an Asian grocery store to find Chinese sausage, sometimes labeled "*lap cheong.*" It is a firm, cured sausage that is reddish in color like salami with a distinctive sweet flavor. Feel free to substitute chopped-up chorizo, bacon, or ham, or leave it out altogether for a vegetarian version. If you can find Japanese sweet potatoes, which have a purple skin and are especially sweet, definitely use those; otherwise, regular sweet potatoes or even yams work well here.

2 medium sweet potatoes (about 1½ pounds), scrubbed clean

⅓ cup finely chopped Chinese sausage

2 scallions, white and green parts finely chopped (about ¼ cup)

2 tablespoons unsalted butter, melted

1 tablespoon Homemade Red Curry Paste (page 307) or jarred Thai red curry paste (we like Roland brand)

1½ teaspoons kosher salt

1 large egg

¾ cup panko bread crumbs

¼ cup vegetable oil, such as canola, plus more as needed

½ cup Sriracha Aioli (page 308), or ½ cup mayonnaise mixed with 2 tablespoons sriracha

Preheat the oven to 350°F and place a rack in the center of the oven.

Place the sweet potatoes directly on the oven rack and roast for about 1 hour, until they are completely cooked through. You should be able to easily poke a small knife directly into the middle of the potatoes when they are done. Remove from the oven and let cool. When they are cool enough to handle, peel the skin off with a small paring knife and place the flesh in a medium bowl. Mash the potato with a fork until smooth. Add the sausage, scallions, butter, curry paste, and salt. Mash with a fork or wooden spoon until well combined.

continued ↓

98

SWEET
POTATO AND
CHINESE
SAUSAGE
FRITTERS

continued

In a shallow bowl, whisk the egg with a fork and pour the panko crumbs onto a large plate. Shape the sweet potato mixture into small cakes, 2 to 3 inches in diameter and 1 inch thick. Dip the sweet potato cakes in the egg to coat both sides, then in the panko crumbs, covering them completely.

In a large, heavy, flat-bottomed skillet, heat the vegetable oil over medium heat. Carefully place the fritters a few at a time in the hot oil and fry them until they are golden brown on both sides, about 3 minutes per side. Drain them on a plate lined with paper towels. Serve the hot fritters with the Sriracha Aioli.

KEVIN'S OLD-SCHOOL EGG ROLL

MAKES 4 LARGE ROLLS

This dish is full-on Americana. It's inspired by the tradition of Chinese-Polynesian cooking that Christopher remembers from his youth and that you can still find pretty much everywhere on the North Shore of Boston. The Kevin of the recipe title is Kevin Rafferty, our dear friend and our sous chef for too short a time. Creating this dish was a force of his culinary will. His will was, let's say, strongly encouraged by abundant cheerleading from Christopher. Christopher longed desperately for something, anything, on the menu that was a real-deal replica of the type of campy food he ate as an overserved high school sneak-drinker. This thing is stuffed and rolled out to the thickness of a baseball bat. Okay, not that thick, but thhhhhiiiick. It is crackly and crunchy but with a slight chewiness from being double wrapped, and it's served with a piquant and "wicked" apricot dipping sauce. Note that the egg roll wrappers will dry out if left uncovered, so place a damp towel on top of the ones you are not working with when rolling these up.

2 cups shredded red cabbage (about ½ medium head)

1 cup shredded napa cabbage (2 to 3 large leaves)

1 medium carrot, shredded on the large holes of a box grater (about ½ cup)

1 bunch scallions (8 or 9), white and green parts thinly sliced (about 1 cup)

2 tablespoons sugar

2 tablespoons black Chinkiang vinegar (substitute balsamic vinegar if necessary)

1 tablespoon kosher salt

½ pound ground pork

2 teaspoons peeled and finely chopped fresh ginger (about ¾-inch knob)

2 teaspoons soy sauce

½ teaspoon sesame oil

1 medium garlic clove, finely chopped

1 tablespoon vegetable oil, such as canola

1 tablespoon fish sauce

1 tablespoon all-purpose flour

One 8-ounce package 8-inch-square wheat egg roll wrappers

5 to 6 cups vegetable oil, such as canola, for frying

Spicy Apricot Dipping Sauce (recipe follows)

Place the red cabbage, napa cabbage, carrot, and scallions in a large bowl and stir in the sugar, vinegar, and salt. Let sit for 1 hour at room temperature, or up to overnight in an airtight container in the refrigerator.

continued
↓

In a separate medium bowl, mix the pork, ginger, soy sauce, sesame oil, and garlic. Get in there and use your hands to mix very well. In a medium skillet, heat the vegetable oil over medium-high heat. Add the pork mixture and stir continuously with a wooden spoon for 3 minutes, until the pork is cooked through. Turn the heat off and stir in the fish sauce. Set aside and let the mixture cool. The pork can be made up to 1 day in advance and stored in an airtight container in the refrigerator.

Using a large piece of cheesecloth (if you don't have cheesecloth, use a large coffee filter or a thin, clean dishtowel), place the cabbage mixture in the center and squeeze the cabbage to get out as much moisture as possible. Let rest for 5 minutes, then squeeze again. Be sure to squeeze out as much liquid as possible. Squeeze, squeeze, squeeze! (You will be surprised how much comes out; the mixture goes from 4 to 5 cups down to 1½ cups.)

In a large bowl, combine the cabbage mixture and pork mixture. Use your hands to mix until the filling is homogenous.

In a small bowl, make a slurry by whisking together the flour and 2 tablespoons water with a fork. The eggroll wrappers are thin and the filling is hefty, so you are going to double up and place one wrapper directly on top of another when rolling. Stack two wrappers on a clean, dry surface with one of the points facing your belly. Dip your finger into the slurry and paint it onto the edge of the wrapper. Place about a quarter of the filling in the corner closest to you (it may seem like a lot, but you want the rolls to be very full). Fold the bottom corner over the filling and away from you and tuck it under. Fold over the left side and then the right side tightly toward the center. You should have an envelope shape. Continue rolling away from you with a tuck-and-roll motion. You want nice, tight, beautiful egg rolls or they will fall apart when you cook them. Repeat with the rest of the filling to make three more rolls. The egg rolls are best fried within a few hours after you roll them.

Fill a large deep saucepan with about 2 inches of vegetable oil. Heat the oil to 350°F or until a cube of bread fries to a nice golden brown in 10 seconds. Working with two at a time, gently slide the rolls into the oil and fry, turning them over to make sure all sides are crispy and golden, for about 4 minutes (see Note, page 92). Transfer to a wire rack to cool just a bit before slicing in half and digging in. Serve immediately with the Spicy Apricot Dipping Sauce.

Spicy Apricot Dipping Sauce

MAKES ABOUT ½ CUP

¼ cup apricot puree (see Note)

¼ cup sugar

1 tablespoon unseasoned rice vinegar

2 teaspoons grated lime zest (from about 1 small lime)

1 red Thai bird chili, stemmed and finely minced (see Note)

IN A SMALL bowl, combine the apricot puree, sugar, vinegar, lime zest, chili, and 2 tablespoons water. Stir to dissolve the sugar and combine all the ingredients. This sauce gets spicier as it sits. Store in an airtight container in the refrigerator for up to 1 week or in the freezer for up to 1 month.

Notes: Totally weird, but if you can't find puree, use no-sugar-added apricot or even peach baby food.

While handling the Thai bird chili, wear gloves and don't touch your eyes, or anywhere else.

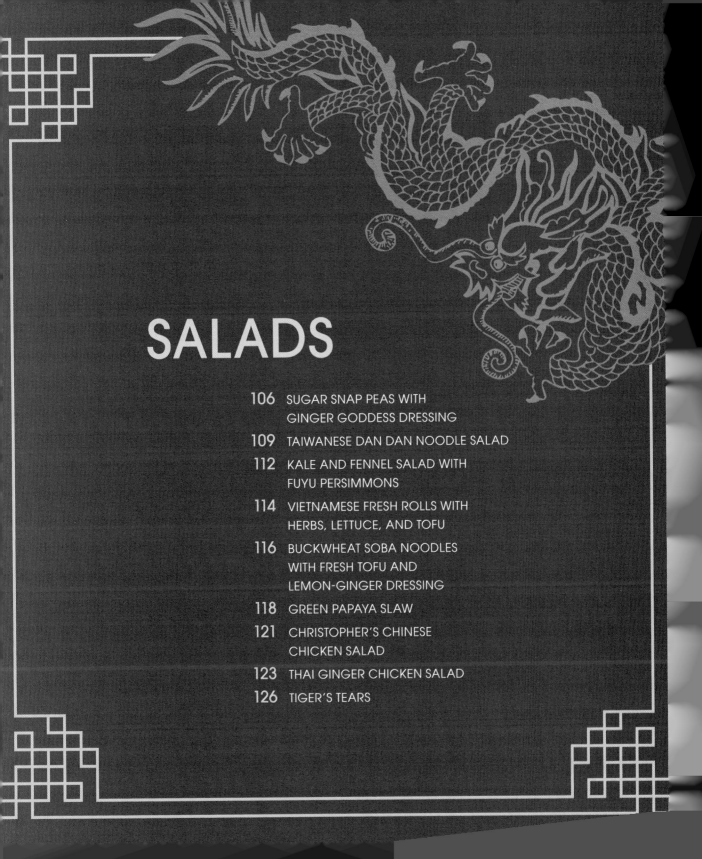

SALADS

106 SUGAR SNAP PEAS WITH
GINGER GODDESS DRESSING

109 TAIWANESE DAN DAN NOODLE SALAD

112 KALE AND FENNEL SALAD WITH
FUYU PERSIMMONS

114 VIETNAMESE FRESH ROLLS WITH
HERBS, LETTUCE, AND TOFU

116 BUCKWHEAT SOBA NOODLES
WITH FRESH TOFU AND
LEMON-GINGER DRESSING

118 GREEN PAPAYA SLAW

121 CHRISTOPHER'S CHINESE
CHICKEN SALAD

123 THAI GINGER CHICKEN SALAD

126 TIGER'S TEARS

SUGAR SNAP PEAS WITH GINGER GODDESS DRESSING

SERVES 4 TO 6

At Myers+Chang, we love taking something retro or iconic and making it new again. Green Goddess dressing originated at the Palace Hotel in San Francisco in 1923. The chef at the hotel wanted to pay tribute to the director George Arliss and his new play *The Green Goddess*. Typically, it contains mayonnaise, sour cream, chervil, tarragon, and other soft herbs. We lighten it up here by removing the mayo and using sunflower seeds instead to thicken it, and by adding lots of ginger juice and cilantro. Take crunchy sugar snap peas and toss with the creamy dressing, tart pickled shallots, and more sweet-and-salty sunflower seeds for a perfect way to welcome spring.

2 tablespoons unsalted butter

1 tablespoon sugar

2 teaspoons kosher salt

½ cup raw sunflower seeds

2 pounds sugar snap peas

1 recipe Pickled Shallots (page 312)

¾ cup Ginger Goddess Dressing (recipe follows)

8 fresh mint leaves

In a small saucepan, melt the butter over low heat. Add the sugar and 1 teaspoon of the salt and stir with a wooden spoon until combined. Add the sunflower seeds and toss until coated and candied, 2 to 3 minutes. Spoon out onto a plate to cool. The sunflower seeds can be made up to 1 week in advance and stored in an airtight container at room temperature.

Trim the sugar snap peas by using a sharp paring knife to remove the "string" from the top and along the spine. Slice the peas lengthwise on an angle and place them in a large bowl. Drain the pickled shallots and add them to the peas. Add ¾ cup of the Ginger Goddess Dressing and the remaining 1 teaspoon salt. Toss well to combine and divide among four to six serving bowls. Tear the mint leaves into small pieces and sprinkle evenly on top of the salads, along with the candied sunflower seeds. Serve immediately. Use the remaining dressing on tomorrow's salad or eat with baby carrots.

Ginger Goddess Dressing

MAKES ABOUT 1¼ CUPS

¼ cup raw sunflower seeds

¼ cup ginger juice (see Note)

¼ cup freshly squeezed lime juice

¼ cup fresh tarragon leaves

½ cup fresh cilantro leaves (about ¼ bunch)

½ cup fresh parsley leaves (about ¼ bunch)

2 teaspoons honey

2 teaspoons kosher salt

½ cup sour cream or whole-milk Greek yogurt

PLACE the sunflower seeds, ginger juice, lime juice, tarragon, cilantro, parsley, honey, and salt in a blender. Puree on high until very smooth, adding a few drops of water as needed to get the mixture moving. Pour into a bowl and fold in the sour cream. The Ginger Goddess Dressing can be made up to 5 days in advance and stored in an airtight container in the refrigerator.

Note: To make ginger juice, peel and slice fresh ginger into coins, place in a blender with enough water to cover the coins and get the mixture to move in the blender, and puree the ginger. Squeeze the ginger puree through a cheesecloth into a bowl for a powerful bright juice that you'll want to add to everything. We do! Alternatively, you can purchase ginger juice in small bottles at some specialty grocery stores, or if you live near a juice bar, they often will juice ginger for you.

TAIWANESE DAN DAN NOODLE SALAD

SERVES 4 TO 6

Dan Dan was nearly our name at Myers+Chang. Or Bang Bang, or Yoko Chang, or Rice, and about a hundred more. Name a child, and everyone raves over your wonderful choice. Name a restaurant, and everyone has an eye roll, a vociferous opinion, or a suggestion based on their recent trip to Myanmar. *Dan dan refers to the over-the-shoulder pole with hanging pots or baskets that we've all seen in every old Chinese movie.* Peddlers sold their lunch wares in the village streets with one pot filled with noodles and another with spicy sauce. The key was making the sauce so strong that you didn't need a lot to flavor the noodles; it was a cheap and filling lunch. Taiwanese *dan dan* often differs from its Sichuan roots by using peanuts and/or sesame seeds and is often vegetarian. Raw peanuts are not as common as roasted, but they are worth seeking out. Cooking the peanuts in peanut oil adds a depth of peanutty flavor that takes these to another level.

2 tablespoons unseasoned rice vinegar

1 tablespoon sugar

1 teaspoon kosher salt

½ teaspoon freshly ground black pepper

1 English cucumber, cut into thirds and each third cut into 5 or 6 spears

One 16-ounce package thin wheat Shanghai-style fresh noodles, or 12 ounces dried spaghetti or linguine

2 tablespoons chili oil

1 recipe Dan Dan Sauce (recipe follows)

¼ cup roasted peanuts (from making Dan Dan Sauce)

1 cup fresh cilantro leaves (about ½ bunch)

In a small saucepan, heat the vinegar, sugar, salt, and pepper over medium heat, stirring to melt the sugar. Remove from the stove and let it cool all the way down until it is no longer warm to the touch. Add the cucumber spears to the pan to marinate in the dressing. Set aside.

Fill a large pot with about a gallon of water and bring it to a boil. Add the noodles. If using fresh noodles, boil for 3 to 4 minutes; if using dried spaghetti noodles, boil until the noodles are just past al dente and soft when you bite into them, about 10 minutes. Drain the noodles in a colander and immediately

continued
↓

rinse with cold water to stop them from cooking. Asian noodles are a lot softer than what you might be used to for al dente Italian noodle dishes, so adjust your cooking time accordingly.

Transfer the noodles to a large bowl. Sprinkle with the chili oil and toss to coat. Add the Dan Dan Sauce and

mix to coat the noodles evenly. Divide among four to six serving bowls. Coarsely chop the reserved roasted peanuts from making the Dan Dan Sauce and sprinkle them evenly over the noodles. Mix the cilantro into the marinated cucumbers. Top the noodles evenly with the dressed cucumbers. Serve immediately.

Dan Dan Sauce

MAKES ABOUT 2 CUPS

1 cup peanut oil

1¼ cups raw peanuts

⅓ cup unseasoned rice vinegar

⅓ cup sugar

2 medium garlic cloves, smashed

One 2-inch knob fresh ginger, peeled and thinly sliced

2 fresh Thai bird chilies, or 1 jalapeño, stemmed and halved

2 tablespoons toasted sesame oil

2 tablespoons soy sauce

2 tablespoons sriracha

POUR the peanut oil into a medium saucepan and slowly bring it up to a gentle simmer over medium heat. It won't actually bubble up but instead it will start to shimmer a bit. Carefully add the peanuts to the hot oil and simmer, stirring continuously to avoid scorching them, until they are just barely golden brown, 3 to 4 minutes. You'll know when they are close to ready when you start to smell them roasting; they become quite fragrant and nutty. As soon as you smell them and see that they are just starting to color, carefully pour the peanuts and oil into a glass or metal bowl (it will melt plastic) and let cool until just warm. The peanuts will continue to pick up color as they cool in the hot oil, so take them off the heat the moment you see them start to brown. Using a slotted spoon, remove about ¼ cup of the cooled roasted peanuts from the oil and set aside to use as a garnish. Set aside the remaining peanuts and oil.

WHEN the peanuts and oil are warm and no longer dangerously hot, pour them into a blender or food processor. (A blender is best since it will grind the peanuts the smoothest, but if you only have a food processor, that will work as well.) Add the vinegar, sugar, garlic, ginger, chilies, sesame oil, soy sauce, sriracha, and 2 tablespoons hot water. Puree on high until the mixture is smooth. Add a bit more hot water if needed to get the mixture moving. Be patient with this—and careful, please! Baby this mixture and give it a lot of love. Any time you make a nut-based sauce, be prepared to work with it a little bit; hum your favorite song and give your blender a workout. When the sauce is smooth and all the ingredients well combined, transfer it to an airtight container. The Dan Dan Sauce can be made up to 1 week in advance and stored in the refrigerator. Remove from the refrigerator a few hours before using and whisk vigorously to mix the oil back into the sauce. Store the reserved peanut garnish in a covered container at room temperature.

KALE AND FENNEL SALAD WITH FUYU PERSIMMONS

SERVES 6

When kale salads hit the food-trend circuit, they hit hard. Our friends at the popular Cambridge restaurant Alden & Harlow even named theirs the Ubiquitous Kale Salad. Most people might not think "salad" when they get a Chinese food craving, but this one will change that. Kale's sturdy leaves stand up well to the bold flavors we love to mess around with. We make an Asian version of chimichurri, a popular Argentinian condiment for grilled meats that you'll want to dip everything in, to dress the leaves. Fuyu persimmons look a bit like squat small orange tomatoes; they are firm when ripe, slice well, and add sweet crunch.

1 bunch Tuscan, curly green, or red Russian kale, thick stems removed, leaves chopped (about 4 cups)

¼ teaspoon kosher salt

¼ teaspoon freshly ground black pepper

1 recipe Thai Basil Chimichurri (recipe follows)

1 medium head fennel, trimmed and thinly sliced (about 2 cups)

2 Fuyu persimmons, thinly sliced (or substitute 2 thinly sliced apples, pears, firm peaches, or firm nectarines)

½ cup Lemon-Ginger Dressing (page 308)

1 recipe Crispy Shallots (page 312)

Place the kale in a large bowl, season with the salt and pepper, and add the Thai Basil Chimichurri. Mix well to coat the kale and let it soften for about 15 minutes. The oil in the chimichurri will help break down the kale so it is easy to eat. Add the fennel and persimmons and dress with the Lemon-Ginger Dressing. Toss well to combine and divide among six plates. Garnish with the Crispy Shallots. Serve immediately.

Thai Basil Chimichurri

MAKES ⅓ CUP

This recipe is easily doubled or tripled. It's fantastic spooned liberally over grilled meats, or add a few spoonfuls to soup for extra spice and huge amounts of flavor.

¼ cup fresh Thai basil leaves (from 2 or 3 stems), finely minced

¼ cup extra-virgin olive oil

1 tablespoon peeled and finely chopped fresh ginger (about 1-inch knob)

1 medium shallot, finely minced

1 medium garlic clove, finely minced

1½ teaspoons black Chinkiang vinegar

¼ teaspoon kosher salt

¼ teaspoon freshly ground black pepper

IN A MEDIUM bowl, combine the basil, olive oil, ginger, shallot, garlic, vinegar, salt, and pepper and whisk well. Store in an airtight container in the refrigerator for up to 5 days.

VIETNAMESE FRESH ROLLS WITH HERBS, LETTUCE, AND TOFU

MAKES 6 ROLLS

Our guests love these. Love. Why? Because they're fresh. As advertised. Rolled to order. All night long at the restaurant you can hear Chef calling out "Fresh rolls!" to the prep team in the back kitchen who stop what they are doing to carefully assemble these as the orders flow in. Many places roll and stack, or roll and refrigerate, which is terrible for the rice wrapper. Cold air and time are no friends of this dish, as it is prone to getting dry and chewy, which distracts from the crispy collection of veggies hidden within. We serve them with a lively piquant satay sauce that makes them rich and satisfying. If you're going to call it fresh, it better be fresh.

2 ounces dried thin vermicelli rice noodles

1 tablespoon vegetable oil, such as canola

6 dried rice paper wrappers (8 to 9 inches in diameter)

½ cup fresh Thai basil leaves (about ¼ bunch)

½ cup fresh cilantro leaves (about ¼ bunch)

½ cup fresh mint leaves (about ½ bunch)

1 cup shredded romaine lettuce

1 medium carrot, coarsely shredded on the large holes of a box grater or using the grating blade of a food processor (about ½ cup)

½ English cucumber, cut into thirds and each third cut into 5 or 6 spears

½ cup pressed tofu or extra-firm tofu, thinly sliced

1 recipe Peanut Satay Sauce (recipe follows)

Rice vermicelli noodles are best cooked by steeping them in boiling hot water instead of plunging them into boiling water, like you would pasta. Place the rice vermicelli noodles in a large metal, glass, or durable plastic bowl. Boil a kettle or saucepan full of water and pour the water over the noodles to cover. Help them soften by pushing them into the water with a wooden spoon or rubber spatula. Let sit for 5 to 6 minutes, until soft, and then drain. Toss with the vegetable oil to keep the noodles from sticking together and set aside.

Fill a large bowl with warm water and dip one rice paper wrapper into the water for 5 to 10 seconds. It will lose its stiffness and soften. Do not oversoak the rice paper or it will fold back onto itself and be hard to handle. Carefully remove the wrapper from the water and place it flat on a dry work surface. Gently wipe off any excess water.

On the bottom third of the wrapper closest to you, lay one-sixth of the basil, cilantro, mint, lettuce, carrots, cucumbers, tofu, and rice noodles in a row in that order, piling upward as much as possible. Leave about 2 inches uncovered on each side. Fold the bottom edge of the wrapper over the filling, tucking tightly and pulling toward you. Now fold in both sides and continue to roll upward away from you, tightly pressing and sealing the fresh roll as you finish. Roll and tuck firmly so your fresh roll is tight and doesn't fall apart. Repeat with the remaining fresh roll wrappers and filling. Serve immediately with Peanut Satay Sauce.

Peanut Satay Sauce

MAKES ABOUT 1 CUP

½ cup smooth peanut butter

5 tablespoons unseasoned rice vinegar

3 tablespoons sriracha

1 tablespoon sugar

1 tablespoon soy sauce

1 tablespoon hoisin sauce

IN A MEDIUM bowl, combine all the ingredients and whisk together vigorously. The sauce can be made up to 1 month in advance and stored in an airtight container in the refrigerator. Whisk in 1 tablespoon water to loosen if necessary before serving.

BUCKWHEAT SOBA NOODLES WITH FRESH TOFU AND LEMON-GINGER DRESSING

SERVES 4 TO 6

We are all in love with this quick and easy vegan salad. The dressing is extremely versatile, and you can use it on pretty much any combination of vegetables and noodles and rice to pull together an impromptu side. The nori is key. Sheets of dried seaweed that are roasted and seasoned for cooking and snacking, nori tastes like the sea. I love crumbling it on pretty much any salad to add a briny, salty kick. Tofu can be a tough sell, so when we asked our trusty recipe testers to give this one a go, we held our breath waiting for the feedback. We had nothing to be worried about. The combination of earthy noodles, crunchy cucumber, sweet-and-spicy dressing, and creamy tofu won everyone over, even the non–tofu lovers. Try tossing the tofu cubes in a little flour and frying them in a skillet with some vegetable oil for a crispy variation.

8 to 10 ounces dried buckwheat soba noodles (about 3 bundles)

2 tablespoons vegetable oil, such as canola

1 English cucumber, halved lengthwise and thinly sliced into half-moons

1 recipe Lemon-Ginger Dressing (page 308)

14 to 16 ounces firm tofu, cut into 1-inch cubes

1 cup fresh cilantro leaves (about ½ bunch)

1 bunch scallions (8 or 9), white and green parts thinly sliced (about 1 cup)

2 teaspoons kosher salt

1 teaspoon freshly ground black pepper

4 (8-inch-square) sheets unseasoned toasted nori (dried seaweed)

¼ cup white sesame seeds

In a large pot, bring about a gallon of water up to a rolling boil and add the soba noodles, making sure to stir, stir, stir and keep that water boiling. Cook the noodles until they are soft, 3 to 4 minutes, and drain in a colander. Pour ice water over the noodles to stop them from cooking and then toss them in a large bowl with the vegetable oil. This will keep the noodles from sticking together, which would make you (and us) sad.

Add the cucumbers to the noodles and toss with the Lemon-Ginger Dressing. Add the tofu, cilantro, and scallions and season with the salt and pepper. Gently toss again to combine. Distribute evenly among four to six bowls. Crumble the nori into small pieces and top each bowl evenly with nori and sesame seeds. Serve immediately.

GREEN PAPAYA SLAW

SERVES 4

Marvin, our longtime a.m. line cook, is in charge of making our green papaya slaw each morning. He shreds a dozen firm green papayas, all about the size of his head, and then pounds them with a rolling pin in the most gigantic mixing bowl we have. We always taste it together: Does it need more peanuts, more fish sauce, more heat? That moment when we find the perfect balance is one of the reasons I love to cook.

Every Southeast Asian country has some variation of a green papaya or mango salad. It offers great texture, bright and bold flavors, and stands out well on its own or as an awesome accompaniment to fish or grilled protein. This is an awesome summer barbecue go-to instead of the same macaroni salad you make every year.

Our version is dressed in *nuoc cham* and spiked with Thai bird chilies and peanuts. It is quick to assemble, pleasingly refreshing, and very spicy. The slightly tart flavor of the green papaya combines well with spice of the Thai bird chilies and the saltiness of the fish sauce. If we had our way, every table would order one to enjoy with their dinner. —*Chef Karen*

1 large unripe papaya (green, hard, and totally different from ripe papaya)

1 cup chopped roasted peanuts

½ cup Nuoc Cham (page 304)

4 fresh Thai bird chilies, thinly sliced, or 4 jalapeños, minced (use fewer chilies if you prefer less spice)

2 medium garlic cloves, minced

¼ cup fresh cilantro leaves (3 or 4 stems)

Using a vegetable peeler, peel the papaya. Slice it in half lengthwise and scrape out the seeds with a spoon. The inside of a green papaya is creamy white in color and very firm in texture. If you have a mandoline, use it to julienne the papaya into a large bowl in long, skinny strips. Otherwise, slice the papaya with a chef's knife into thin slices and then stack them and julienne them with your knife into long, super-skinny strips. The skinnier you can cut the papaya, the better. You should get 3 to 4 cups of shredded papaya. Add ¾ cup of the chopped peanuts to the bowl.

In a small bowl, mix together the Nuoc Cham, chilies, and garlic. Pour over the papaya and pound (using a pestle, the blunt end of a rolling pin, or the blunt end of the head of a wooden spoon) to infuse the flavors into the papaya. Go ahead and bang hard against the papaya to break it down. It's a great way to get your frustrations out! The texture of the papaya will go from very hard to soft and almost creamy. This is when you know it is almost ready; all the papaya is infused with the nuoc cham and the texture of the papaya has softened a bit. The Papaya Slaw can be made up to a day in advance and stored in an airtight container in the refrigerator. Be sure to toss again before serving. Divide the papaya and dressing among four small bowls and garnish evenly with the cilantro and the remaining ¼ cup peanuts.

CHRISTOPHER'S CHINESE CHICKEN SALAD

SERVES 4

This and every other Chinese chicken salad owes more than a little to California cuisine and therefore more than a lot to Wolfgang Puck and his lovely restaurant Chinois on Main in Santa Monica, California. If Christopher could plop our humble little eatery down right next to Chinois on Main, or maybe a beach in Venice, he would. This salad has everything: It is crunchy, tart, healthy, filling, spicy, and sweet, with a complex and savory charm. Supreming citrus is a way to add citrus to your dish without the tough membranes: Cut the skin and pith off the fruit and then use a small sharp knife to separate the flesh from the membranes. Alternatively, you can simply slice the fruit into thin slices. Try serving this warm as we sometimes do at Myers+Chang. We give it a good toss in the wok, which takes some of the snap out of the lettuce but amps up the spice and makes the chicken extra juicy.

1 medium garlic clove, smashed

1 pound boneless, skinless chicken breast

1 head romaine lettuce, shredded (6 to 8 cups)

2 medium celery stalks, thinly sliced (about 1 cup)

1 cup roasted, lightly salted cashews

4 or 5 scallions, white and green parts thinly sliced (about ½ cup)

½ cup chopped fresh cilantro (about ½ bunch)

½ teaspoon kosher salt

½ teaspoon freshly ground black pepper

¼ cup soy sauce

¼ cup extra-virgin olive oil

¼ cup light brown sugar

2 tablespoons sriracha

2 tablespoons unseasoned rice vinegar

2 teaspoons peeled and finely chopped fresh ginger (about ¾-inch knob)

2 seedless oranges, supremed (see headnote)

Fill a medium saucepan with water, add the garlic, and submerge the chicken in the water. Bring the water to a boil, turn off the heat, and cover the pan. Turn on a timer and let the chicken poach for 12 minutes. Test the chicken by slicing into the thickest part. If it is still pink, let the chicken continue to cook for another 4 to 5 minutes. When the chicken is cooked, remove it from the water and let cool. The chicken may be cooked up to 2 days in advance and

continued
↓

stored in an airtight container in the refrigerator.

Shred or cube the chicken into bite-size pieces and place in a large bowl along with the romaine, celery, cashews, scallions, and cilantro. Season with the salt and pepper. In a separate small bowl, whisk together the soy sauce, olive oil, brown sugar, sriracha, vinegar, and ginger. Pour over the salad and toss to combine well. Divide among four serving bowls. Top with the orange supremes and serve immediately.

THAI GINGER CHICKEN SALAD

SERVES 4

We try to give dishes their true name as often as we can, but sometimes that means a dish languishes on the menu like a wallflower at the prom. *Larb* or *laab* is a Laotian minced meat salad that is popular in Thai and Hmong cuisines. I first experienced it a few years before we opened Myers+Chang in a local hole-in-the-wall Cambodian restaurant. We ordered dish after dish of things I didn't know the name of; this spicy, salty, sharp salad was by far my favorite. I experimented with replicating it at home, adding more lemongrass, taking out some shallots, tweaking constantly until we opened the restaurant. I couldn't wait to put it on the menu, and I ate it pretty much every single day; it's that good. But not many of our guests were ordering it, and I couldn't figure out why. We changed the name from Chicken Laab Salad to Thai Ginger Chicken Salad, and now it's among our most popular lunch dishes. You can't judge a book by its cover, but your lunch order can certainly be swayed by a name. Make any number of variations with chopped beef, lamb, pork, even tofu. It's bright and fragrant with fresh herbs. You will make this again and again, and it will become a staple in your house like it has become in ours.

1 pound boneless, skinless chicken breast (or substitute ground chicken)

2 stalks lemongrass

4 tablespoons vegetable oil, such as canola

1 small shallot, thinly sliced (about 2 tablespoons)

1 tablespoon peeled and chopped fresh ginger (about 1-inch knob)

¾ teaspoon kosher salt

½ teaspoon freshly ground black pepper

8 ounces dried thin vermicelli rice noodles

1 cup fresh cilantro leaves (about ½ bunch)

1 cup fresh mint leaves (about 1 bunch)

1 cup fresh Thai basil leaves (about ½ bunch)

1 cup Nuoc Cham (page 304)

4 teaspoons Khao Koor (page 311)

8 Bibb lettuce leaves

Using a sharp chef's knife, slice the raw chicken breast into thin strips. Next, slice the other way and turn the strips into cubes. Then chop up the cubes so the chicken is almost a "ground" texture. (Alternatively, for an easy shortcut, you could just use 1 pound of ground chicken, but the *laab*

continued
↓

really benefits from bigger chunks of chicken, so this is only if you are super strapped for time.)

Peel and discard the dry, papery outer layers of the lemongrass; trim off the top two-thirds of the stalk, which is also dry and papery, along with the very base and discard. Finely chop the bottom third (5 to 6 inches) of the stalk, where the stem is pale and bendable. You should have about ¼ cup.

In a large, heavy, flat-bottomed skillet, heat 3 tablespoons of the vegetable oil over high heat. Add the lemongrass, shallots, and ginger and cook, stirring, until translucent, 1 to 2 minutes. Add the chicken and season with ½ teaspoon of the salt and ¼ teaspoon of the pepper. Continuously stir until the chicken is cooked through, 6 to 8 minutes. It will stay pale in color and will not turn brown. Transfer to a bowl and set aside.

Place the rice vermicelli noodles in a large metal, glass, or durable plastic bowl. Boil a kettle or saucepan full of water and pour the water over the noodles to cover. Help them soften by pushing them into the water with a wooden spoon or rubber spatula. Let sit for 5 to 6 minutes, until soft, and then drain. Toss with the vegetable oil to keep the noodles from sticking together and set aside.

Coarsely chop the cilantro, mint, and Thai basil leaves and add to the chicken. Add the Nuoc Cham and 2 teaspoons of the Khao Koor and mix thoroughly. Taste and adjust for seasoning, adding the remaining ¼ teaspoon of salt and ¼ teaspoon of pepper.

Place 2 lettuce leaves in the bottom of each of four serving bowls and divide the noodles evenly among the bowls. Divide the dressed chicken over the noodles, pour any remaining dressing evenly over the chicken, and sprinkle evenly with the remaining 2 teaspoons Khao Koor. Serve immediately.

TIGER'S TEARS

SERVES 3 TO 4

Cambodian legend has it that this salad is so spicy, it will make even a big strong tiger cry. We tell all our guests this tale when delivering their salad and then slyly keep an eye on them as they begin eating to see if they start to sweat . . . or shed tears. You can vary the heat by changing the amount of Thai bird chilies or jalapeños you use, but don't get too shy. The best part of eating this rare beef salad is fanning your face and feeling the heat wake up your insides. It's completely addictive and we have had guests visit us weekly since we've opened to get their fix.

1 pound flank, skirt, or hanger steak

½ cup Homemade Red Curry Paste (page 307) or jarred Thai red curry paste (we like Roland brand)

2 tablespoons vegetable oil, such as canola (for searing if you do not have a grill)

1 medium red bell pepper

1 medium yellow bell pepper

1 medium green bell pepper

½ cup Nuoc Cham (page 304)

¼ teaspoon kosher salt

¼ teaspoon freshly ground black pepper

½ cup fresh cilantro leaves (about ¼ bunch)

½ cup fresh mint leaves (about ½ bunch)

½ cup fresh Thai basil leaves (about ¼ bunch)

2 fresh Thai bird chilies, thinly sliced, or 2 jalapeños, minced

2 teaspoons Khao Koor (page 311)

Rub the steak all over with the curry paste and place it in a nonreactive container such as a plastic storage container or glass roasting pan. Marinate the meat overnight in the refrigerator. If you don't have time to marinate it overnight, let it sit for at least a few hours. The meat will be more tender and delicious the longer you marinate it.

If you have a grill, grill the steak to medium, about 8 minutes on each side, moving the steak in an X pattern so you get nice grill marks. Remove the steak from the grill and let rest for 20 minutes or so. If you don't have a grill, heat the vegetable oil in a large, heavy, flat-bottomed skillet on the stove over high heat. Sear the steak for 4 to 5 minutes on each side, then remove from the skillet and let it rest for 20 minutes. There is no point in grilling a beautiful piece of steak if you are not going to rest it properly. (Seriously, guys!) Resting the meat ensures that it stays juicy and pink. Once rested, chill the steak in the refrigerator until it is cool to the touch, about 30 minutes or up to 1 day if you want to grill the meat in advance. (Be sure to cover it well if you are storing it in the refrigerator overnight.) Slice the steak as thinly as possible against the grain for maximum tenderness (see Note). It should be beautifully rare with a hint of cooked meat all around.

Note: Slicing against the grain means to slice the steak against the natural meat fibers to break them up so the meat is easy to chew. Look to see how the meat would break apart if you tore it into pieces and slice it against this direction.

Using a chef's knife, remove the stem and thinly slice all the bell peppers (don't forget to use those tops and bottoms) and place in a large bowl. Add the steak and toss with the Nuoc Cham, salt, and pepper. Tear the cilantro, mint, and Thai basil leaves into small pieces with your fingers to release their aroma and add them to the salad. Add the chilies and toss well. Divide the salad evenly among three or four serving plates and sprinkle with the Khao Koor. Eat with reckless abandon!

AND THEN SOME

130 PAN-ROASTED SOY-GLAZED SALMON
WITH COOL CUCUMBER SALAD

133 RAINBOW TROUT WITH COCONUT RICE
AND CHILI-TOMATO JAM

136 TAMARIND-GLAZED COD WITH
VIETNAMESE MINT, JICAMA,
AND GRAPEFRUIT SLAW

139 INDONESIAN FRIED CHICKEN AND
GINGER-SESAME WAFFLES

145 PANKO-CRUSTED LEMON CHICKEN

148 BULGOGI BBQ SLOPPY "JO"

151 KOREAN BRAISED SHORT RIB TACOS
WITH KIMCHI-SESAME SALSA

153 TEA-SMOKED PORK SPARE RIBS

PAN-ROASTED SOY-GLAZED SALMON WITH COOL CUCUMBER SALAD

SERVES 4

You could say this is the recipe that started it all. When Christopher and I were dating, I would cook dinner for him and make him dishes that I grew up eating. There were a lot of stir-fries in our dating phase (there still are) and a few simple pan-roasted dishes. Christopher was used to Americanized Chinese food, which has a lot of sweet and fried and saucy. The meal I made that he loved most was salmon with soy, ginger, sriracha, sugar, and vinegar, served with a bowl of steaming white rice and some wokked vegetables. I made it at least once a week. This is the dish that made us both look at each other and say, "We should open a Chinese restaurant together." It's still my favorite dish we make, and we still eat it at least once a week.

¼ cup unseasoned rice vinegar

1 teaspoon sugar

1½ teaspoons kosher salt

1 teaspoon freshly ground black pepper

½ English cucumber, halved lengthwise and thinly sliced into half-moons

2 tablespoons vegetable oil, such as canola

Four 5-ounce skin-on salmon fillets

4 scallions, cut into thirds

1 recipe Salmon Sauce (recipe follows)

One 1-inch knob fresh ginger, peeled and thinly sliced

½ cup fresh cilantro leaves (about ¼ bunch)

Perfect White Rice (page 315) or Perfect Brown Rice (page 316)

1 recipe Crispy Shallots (page 312)

Preheat the oven to 325°F and place a rack in the center of the oven.

In a medium bowl, combine the vinegar, sugar, 1 teaspoon of the salt, and ½ teaspoon of the pepper and stir together. Add the cucumbers to the bowl to marinate in the dressing. Set aside.

Heat a large, heavy, flat-bottomed ovensafe skillet on the stove over high heat for 2 minutes. Add the vegetable oil, tilting the pan to cover the bottom evenly with the oil, and heat until it is almost smoking. Pat the salmon skin dry with a paper towel. Season both sides of the salmon fillets with the remaining ½ teaspoon salt and the

continued
↓

PAN-ROASTED
SOY-GLAZED
SALMON
WITH COOL
CUCUMBER
SALAD

continued

remaining ½ teaspoon black pepper and carefully add to the skillet skin-side down. Cook on high for 1 to 2 minutes, pushing down slightly on the salmon with a spatula to get exceptionally crispy skin (that's the good stuff!). Use a thin spatula to carefully flip the salmon fillets over. Add the Salmon Sauce to the skillet and sprinkle the scallions and sliced ginger over the fish and sauce. Transfer to the oven and bake for 4 to 5 minutes, until the salmon is cooked to medium.

Divide the rice among four shallow serving bowls and place 1 piece of salmon on top of each mound of rice, skin-side up. Spoon any remaining sauce, scallions, and ginger evenly onto the salmon and rice. Add the cilantro to the marinating cucumbers and garnish the salmon with the dressed cucumbers and the shallots. Serve immediately.

Salmon Sauce

MAKES ABOUT 1 CUP

½ cup soy sauce

¼ cup unseasoned rice vinegar

2 tablespoons sugar

One 2-inch knob fresh ginger, peeled and thinly sliced

1 tablespoon sriracha

IN A SMALL pot, combine the soy sauce, vinegar, sugar, ginger, sriracha, and ¼ cup water. Bring to a boil over high heat, stirring until the sugar has dissolved. Turn off the heat and set aside. The Salmon Sauce can be made up to 1 week in advance and stored in an airtight container in the refrigerator.

RAINBOW TROUT WITH COCONUT RICE AND CHILI-TOMATO JAM

SERVES 4

I am always working on "the perfect bite," i.e., a dish in which every bite tastes to the eater just the way I envision. I am totally obsessed with this idea. This trout dish is a perfect package of flavor and texture. Each bite gives you a bit of jam, crisp trout skin, flaky fish, and soft herby rice. We don't use tomatoes too often at the restaurant, but this jam, with tons of ginger, chili, and curry spices, makes sense. If you can't find trout, substitute cod or tilapia or other white fish. You want to find fish pieces that are thin enough that you can sandwich rice between them. Sometimes this is called "clear cut" at the fish counter; the bones are removed and each fish is split into two fillets, allowing you to fill each trout like a sandwich. —*Chef Karen*

4 butterflied rainbow trout, skin on and headless, deboned	1 recipe Coconut Rice (recipe follows)	1 cup Chili-Tomato Jam (page 310)
1 tablespoon kosher salt	¼ cup vegetable oil, such as canola	1 lime, quartered
2 teaspoons freshly ground black pepper		

Preheat the oven to 400°F and place a rack in the center of the oven.

Season the trout fillets with the salt and pepper on both sides. Measure about ¾ cup of the rice and fill the inside of one of the trout fillets, squishing and smushing it flat between the 2 halves until there is an even

amount throughout. Repeat with the rest of the rice and trout fillets.

In a large, heavy, flat-bottomed oven-safe skillet, heat the vegetable oil over high heat until it shimmers, about 1 minute. Gently place the trout packages in the oil and don't touch them for 2 minutes. Carefully flip the

continued
↓

trout fillets over using a thin metal spatula or a fish spatula. (If you don't have a fish "spat," get one; they are cheap and you will have it forever.) Transfer the pan to the oven and roast for 4 minutes. Remove the pan from the oven and carefully place each trout on a serving plate. Top with the Chili-Tomato Jam, distributing the jam evenly over the tops of the trout packages, and squeeze a wedge of lime over each one. Savor every perfect bite!

Coconut Rice

MAKES 3 CUPS

½ cup coconut milk

1 tablespoon sugar

2 teaspoons kosher salt

1 makrut lime leaf, or grated zest of 1 lime

2 cups Perfect White Rice (page 315) or leftover white rice from takeout

½ cup chopped fresh cilantro leaves (about ½ bunch)

4 or 5 scallions, white and green parts sliced (about ½ cup)

Grated zest and juice of 2 limes

IN A SMALL saucepan, combine the coconut milk, sugar, salt, and lime leaf and heat over medium heat. Put the rice in a bowl and pour the seasoned milk into the rice (not the other way around). Stir until the rice has absorbed the coconut milk and looks a little like risotto. Stir in the cilantro, scallions, lime zest, and lime juice. The

Coconut Rice can be made up to 2 days in advance and stored in an airtight container in the refrigerator. Remove the lime leaf before using.

TAMARIND-GLAZED COD WITH VIETNAMESE MINT, JICAMA, AND GRAPEFRUIT SLAW

SERVES 4

The game of "telephone" isn't great when you're trying to share information, but it can work wonders in the world of cooking. Each person takes what he or she "hears" or tastes in a recipe and then brings a different slant to the dish. This particular recipe started with Charles Phan at the Slanted Door. He makes a Vietnamese slaw that Mark Bittman wrote about in the popular *New York Times Diner's Journal* blog. I tried it, fell in love with it, and brought it to Myers+Chang. We originally offered it "as is" as a side salad and then experimented with it as a side to pan-roasted fish. Christopher loved the crisp, tart flavors of the salad with the fish and suggested something rich and caramel-y to balance out the brightness. Tamarind butter is sweet and tangy, and it brings the combination of flavors and textures together. Chef Phan, if you are ever in Boston, we would love to make this for you.

1 small jicama (if you can't find jicama, substitute an Asian pear, see Note, or peeled Granny Smith apple)

1½ cups thinly shredded green cabbage

3 medium carrots, coarsely shredded on the large holes of a box grater or using the grating blade of a food processor (about 1½ cups)

1 cup fresh mint leaves (about 1 bunch), torn into small pieces

2 small or 1 large grapefruit, supremed (see page 121)

Four 5-ounce skin-on cod fillets (or substitute hake or any other flaky white fish)

1½ teaspoons kosher salt

1 teaspoon freshly ground black pepper

2 tablespoons vegetable oil, such as canola

1 recipe Tamarind Butter (recipe follows)

1 recipe Vietnamese Dressing (recipe follows)

Using a sharp knife or vegetable peeler, carefully peel the rough papery outer skin of the jicama. Julienne enough of the jicama to make about 1½ cups. Reserve any remaining jicama for another use. Place the jicama in a medium bowl and toss with the cabbage, carrot, mint, and grapefruit. Set aside.

Season the fish on both sides with 1 teaspoon of the salt and ½ teaspoon of the pepper. In a large, heavy, flat-bottomed skillet, heat the vegetable oil on medium-high until it shimmers, about 1 minute. Carefully place the cod in the pan, skin-side down, and cook for 2 minutes without moving the fish. Using a thin metal spatula, flip the fish over and cook for about 4 minutes, until the flesh is opaque and flakes easily. Remove the pan from the heat and add the Tamarind Butter to the pan. Let the butter melt in the heat of the pan and spoon it evenly on top of the fish.

Season the slaw with the remaining ½ teaspoon salt and ½ teaspoon pepper and dress it with the Vietnamese Dressing, tossing lightly to coat. Divide the slaw and dressing among four plates and place 1 piece of cod on each. Spoon any remaining Tamarind Butter from the pan onto the fish. Serve immediately.

Note: Jicama is a crunchy root vegetable with a papery brown skin and a texture similar to water chestnut or Asian pear. You can find them in many Asian and Latin American grocery stores. To julienne jicama (or any round, firm vegetable) first slice it into thin slices, then stack the slices on top of one another and cut them into thin matchstick pieces.

Tamarind Butter

MAKES ABOUT ⅓ CUP

If you can't find the Indonesian sweet soy sauce, also called kecap manis, *substitute 1½ teaspoons soy sauce and 1½ teaspoons dark brown sugar.*

4 tablespoons (½ stick) unsalted butter, at room temperature

1 tablespoon tamarind concentrate

1 tablespoon Indonesian sweet soy sauce (kecap manis)

1 teaspoon kosher salt

IN A SMALL bowl, combine all the ingredients and beat vigorously with a wooden spoon until the mixture looks like cake frosting. The Tamarind Butter can be made up to 2 weeks in advance and stored in an airtight container in the refrigerator.

Vietnamese Dressing

MAKES ABOUT ⅓ CUP

3 tablespoons soy sauce

2 teaspoons fish sauce

2 teaspoons unseasoned rice vinegar

2 teaspoons light brown sugar

1 small garlic clove, finely minced

IN A SMALL bowl, whisk together all the ingredients. The Vietnamese Dressing can be made up to 1 month in advance and stored in an airtight container in the refrigerator.

INDONESIAN FRIED CHICKEN AND GINGER-SESAME WAFFLES

SERVES 2 AS A HEARTY MEAL OR 4 TO 6 AS A BIG SNACK

Christopher left home the day he graduated from high school to move to Los Angeles and become an actor. One of his favorite food haunts was Roscoe's, an LA institution that was (and still is) famous for their iconic soul food classic Fried Chicken and Waffles. When we opened Myers+Chang, he was eager for us to re-create this dish for our menu. Chef braises the chicken in plenty of turmeric, fish sauce, and coconut milk before frying it. She then blends together a tangy spicy sauce that we dub "surprising sauce" because of how many flavors hit your mouth when you eat it. The final touch is the waffle: Our version has lots of fresh ginger and sesame to give it plenty of flavor to stand up to the chicken and sauce. This was the dish that she challenged Bobby Flay with on his Food Network show *Beat Bobby Flay.* We can barely keep up with how many chickens we sell, it is so popular. Two of our favorite M+C guests, Andy and Ken, have dubbed it KFC: Karen's Fried Chicken!

1 fresh Thai bird chili or jalapeño

1 stalk lemongrass

1 tablespoon ground turmeric

One 3- to 4-pound whole chicken, split, with the backbone out and quartered (see Note)

1 tablespoon kosher salt, plus more for seasoning

1 teaspoon freshly ground black pepper

½ cup fish sauce

1 lime, halved

¾ cup coconut milk

2 to 3 quarts vegetable oil, such as canola, for frying (see Note, page 92)

1 recipe Ginger-Sesame Waffles (recipe follows)

1 recipe Honey-Sesame Butter (recipe follows)

1 recipe Surprising Sauce (recipe follows)

Thinly slice the Thai bird chili, making sure you are wearing gloves (and please don't touch your face). Set aside in a small bowl. Peel and discard the dry papery outer layers of the lemongrass; cut off the top two-thirds of the stalk, which is also dry and papery, along with the very base and discard. Thinly slice the bottom third of the stalk, where the stem is pale and bendable, and add to the bowl with the chili. Add the turmeric and stir to combine.

continued
↓

INDONESIAN
FRIED CHICKEN
AND GINGER-
SESAME
WAFFLES

continued

Lay the chicken pieces in a shallow baking dish. Season evenly with the salt and pepper and then sprinkle liberally with the fish sauce. Rub the chicken all over with the lemongrass mixture (get to know your bird!). Squeeze the lime all over the chicken. Throw the lime halves, skin and all, into the dish. Pour the coconut milk over the whole thing and turn to coat. Cover lightly with plastic wrap and marinate overnight (or as long as you have—the longer, the tastier) in the refrigerator.

Preheat the oven to 350°F and place a rack in the center of the oven.

Remove the chicken from the refrigerator, remove the plastic wrap, add about ½ cup water to the baking dish, and cover with aluminum foil. Roast for 35 minutes. Remove from the oven and let sit until

cool enough to handle. The chicken can be parbaked up to 2 days in advance; store it with the cooking liquid in an airtight container in the refrigerator.

In a large, deep, flat-bottomed saucepan, heat 3 to 4 inches of vegetable oil to 350°F or until a cube of bread fries to nice golden brown in 10 seconds. Shake the marinade off the chicken and fry a few pieces at a time, turning the pieces occasionally, until deep golden brown and an instant-read thermometer inserted into the thickest part of each piece registers 165°F, 10 to 12 minutes per side. Remove from the oil and drain on a paper towel–lined plate; salt each piece liberally when done. Serve with hot Ginger-Sesame Waffles smeared with Honey-Sesame Butter and with Surprising Sauce on the side, so you can make it wild or mild.

Note: You can often buy chickens this way, but if you can't, you can also use chicken pieces.

Ginger-Sesame Waffles

MAKES 3 LARGE BELGIAN-STYLE WAFFLES

Don't save these waffles just for this dish. They are so good, you'll make them for brunches and for snacking like we do. We serve them topped with vanilla ice cream on our weekend dim sum menu. Guests who order them invariably tell us they are one of the best things we make. Make sure your buttermilk and egg are at room temperature or they will cause the melted butter to solidify when you whisk them all together, and you'll end up with greasy waffles.

1 cup all-purpose flour

1 teaspoon baking powder

½ teaspoon baking soda

½ teaspoon kosher salt

1 cup buttermilk, at room temperature

1 large egg, at room temperature

5 tablespoons unsalted butter, melted and cooled

2 tablespoons sugar

2 tablespoons peeled and finely minced fresh ginger (about 2-inch knob)

2 tablespoons black sesame seeds

IN A LARGE bowl, stir together the flour, baking powder, baking soda, and salt. In a medium bowl, whisk together the buttermilk, egg, melted butter, sugar, ginger, and sesame seeds. Add the wet ingredients to the dry and fold together gently. Pour into a blazing-hot waffle iron and cook as directed according to the waffle iron instructions.

Note: A trick of the trade for even fluffier and lighter waffles: Separate the eggs and combine the yolks with the wet ingredients. In a clean medium bowl, whisk the whites into a frenzy until foamy and airy, about 1 minute, and fold them into the batter at the very end. This is what put Chef's waffles over the top on the Food Network!

Honey-Sesame Butter

MAKES ABOUT ¼ CUP

4 tablespoons (½ stick) unsalted butter, at room temperature

1 tablespoon honey

2 teaspoons toasted sesame oil

IN A SMALL bowl, mix together all the ingredients until well combined. The Honey-Sesame Butter can be made up to 2 weeks in advance and stored in an airtight container in the refrigerator. Bring to room temperature before using. **Pro tip:** If the honey is a little warm, it will be easier to incorporate.

Surprising Sauce

MAKES ABOUT ¾ CUP

We deemed this tart, spicy, sweet, funky sauce "surprising" because every time we ate it, we were wowed by the myriad flavors that kept hitting our mouths. Use it not just for this fried chicken but also as a sandwich condiment to wake up your lunch.

6 dried red Thai chilies

3 medium garlic cloves, chopped (about 1 tablespoon)

1 tablespoon peeled and chopped fresh ginger (about 1-inch knob)

1 tablespoon fish sauce

1 tablespoon sugar

¼ cup unseasoned rice vinegar

¼ cup fresh Thai basil leaves (2 or 3 stems)

1 tablespoon extra-virgin olive oil

1 tablespoon honey

1 teaspoon kosher salt

BREAK the chilies in half, break off the stems, and empty out and discard the inner seeds. (Either wear gloves while doing this or wash your hands thoroughly right after.) Place the chili pieces in a small pot with ¼ cup water, the garlic, and the ginger. Bring the water to a boil, then turn off the heat. Let sit until cool enough to handle. Transfer to a food processor and add the fish sauce and sugar. Process to a coarse paste. Add the vinegar and process again until blended. Add the Thai basil, olive oil, honey, and salt and pulse until chunky. The Surprising Sauce can be made up to a week in advance and stored in an airtight container in the refrigerator. Serve with the Indonesian fried chicken or other fried delights.

PANKO-CRUSTED LEMON CHICKEN

SERVES 4

One of Christopher's favorite Chinese takeout dishes is lemon chicken. He brought it home one day for me to try from one of the Chinese-American restaurants that dot the area around Myers+Chang, and I watched in awe as he gobbled it up. It was so neon! So candylike! So . . . unlike anything I had ever eaten! This is a bright, classy version of that heavy dish. The lemon is sweet, but high and bright at the same time, and the watercress is peppery and snaps through the sweetness. Make this recipe in two steps. If you have the time, marinate the chicken overnight or before you start your day in the morning so it gets a nice bath by dinnertime.

Four 5-ounce boneless, skinless chicken breast cutlets

Grated zest of 1 lemon

2 cups buttermilk

1 cup all-purpose flour

2½ teaspoons kosher salt, plus more for seasoning

1¼ teaspoons freshly ground black pepper

2 large eggs

2 tablespoons whole milk

2 cups panko bread crumbs

½ teaspoon garlic powder

½ teaspoon onion powder

½ teaspoon dry mustard powder

½ teaspoon paprika

2 cups vegetable oil, such as canola, plus more as needed

1 bunch watercress, trimmed (about 3 cups)

3 or 4 red radishes, thinly sliced

2 tablespoons extra-virgin olive oil

1 tablespoon freshly squeezed lemon juice

Perfect White Rice (page 315) or Perfect Brown Rice (page 316)

1 recipe Candied Lemon Sauce (recipe follows)

Pound the chicken breasts evenly until they are about ½ inch thick. (An easy trick is to place each breast between two pieces of plastic wrap so that you don't get raw chicken all over your cutting board. If you don't have a mallet, try a rolling pin!) Place the chicken breasts in a nonreactive dish such as a glass baking dish and rub with the lemon zest. Add the buttermilk

to cover the chicken, cover the container, and refrigerate overnight.

The next day, set up a breading station: On one plate, stir together the flour, 2 teaspoons of the salt, and 1 teaspoon of the pepper. In a medium bowl, crack the eggs and whisk in the milk. Make the seasoned panko crumbs next by stirring together the panko with the garlic powder, onion powder,

continued
↓

AND THEN
SOME

PANKO-
CRUSTED
LEMON
CHICKEN

147

continued

dry mustard, and paprika in a large bowl. One piece at a time, remove the chicken from the buttermilk and give it a shake, dip it into the flour, then the egg mixture, and then the panko. When all the chicken is well coated, heat 2 cups of the vegetable oil in a large, deep, flat-bottomed saucepan over medium-high heat. Fry each chicken cutlet separately, making sure it is deep golden brown on the outside and cooked all the way through, about 3 minutes on each side. Sprinkle a pinch of salt on each one as it comes out of the pan. Place on a paper towel–lined plate as you continue with the remaining cutlets. You may need to add 1 cup more oil after frying the first 2 pieces of chicken.

In a medium bowl, toss the watercress and radishes with the olive oil, lemon juice, remaining ½ teaspoon salt, and remaining ¼ teaspoon pepper.

Divide the rice among four serving plates, top with a chicken cutlet, spoon about ¼ cup of the Candied Lemon Sauce over the chicken, top with the watercress salad, and enjoy your M+C-style Lemon Chicken.

Candied Lemon Sauce

MAKES ABOUT 1 CUP

1 lemon

¾ cup sugar

2 tablespoons freshly squeezed lemon juice

2 tablespoons unseasoned rice vinegar

THINLY SLICE the lemon; you should get 10 to 12 slices. Remove any seeds and place the lemon slices in a small nonreactive pot with ½ cup of the sugar and ¼ cup water.

Bring the water to a boil, then reduce the heat to maintain a simmer. Stir continuously until the lemons are thick and syrupy, about 10 minutes. Take off the heat and set aside to cool. When cool, remove the lemon slices and chop them up. Discard any excess syrup.

IN A SMALL SAUCEPAN, combine the remaining ¼ cup sugar, the lemon juice, and the vinegar.

Bring to a boil just until the sugar has dissolved, then stir in the chopped candied lemon. The Candied Lemon Sauce can be made up to 1 month in advance and stored in an airtight container in the refrigerator. Bring up to room temperature before using. The sauce may be used warm or at room temperature.

BULGOGI BBQ SLOPPY "JO"

MAKES 4 BURGERS

Like many other things, the Chinese lay claim to the first "meat sandwich," too: It was called *roujiamou* and originated in the Shanxi province. Everyone's mom has a sloppy joe recipe, and I'm sure an argument can be made that their mom's is the best, if not the first. My mom's was straight from Hamburger Helper, and I loved it. Christopher's mother was famed for hers. Or as famous as one got from being on the front page of the *Newburyport Daily News's* food section . . . in 1964. She called it a "spoon burger." This is Chef Karen's homage to Mary Myers. She wanted to improve upon the texture of a traditional sloppy joe (soft verging on soggy), so she used thinly sliced flank steak with lots of kimchi cucumber pickles and potato chips to press into the sandwich. Karen and Mary would have gotten along famously—funny, feisty, and lippy as hell. Note that the cucumbers need about a day to pickle and the flank steak needs a long marinate. The dish comes together quickly the day of as long as you plan for these two items the night before or the morning of.

¼ cup sambal oelek

¼ cup toasted sesame oil

¼ cup sugar

¼ cup white sesame seeds

5 medium garlic cloves, smashed

1 cup low-sodium soy sauce

1 pound flank or skirt steak

4 soft rolls (we love the focaccia rolls from Flour Bakery or use Portuguese rolls or soft potato rolls)

2 tablespoons unsalted butter, at room temperature

1 recipe Korean BBQ Sauce (recipe follows)

1 recipe Kimchi Cucumbers (recipe follows; make a day in advance)

In a medium bowl, combine the sambal oelek, sesame oil, sugar, white sesame seeds, garlic, and soy sauce. Place the steak in a flat shallow pan and pour the soy mixture over it, turning to coat. Cover with plastic wrap and marinate overnight. Throw the marinade and steak together before you start your day and it will do its job by dinner.

Remove the steak from the pan and, using a sharp chef's knife, slice the steak as thinly as possible against the grain (see Note). Place the sliced meat and about ⅓ cup of the marinade in a large, heavy, flat-bottomed skillet and cook gently over low heat until the meat is cooked medium and just barely pink, 6 to 8 minutes.

Toast the rolls lightly and spread a little butter on them. Pile on the warm sliced beef and top with the Korean BBQ Sauce. Layer on the Kimchi Cucumbers so that you get one in every bite. **Pro tip:** Buy a mini bag of potato chips and add them to the sandwich—Christopher and Chef love it this way!

Note: Slicing against the grain means to slice the steak against the natural meat fibers to break them up so the meat is easy to chew. Look to see how the meat would break apart if you tore it into pieces and slice it against this direction.

Korean BBQ Sauce

MAKES ABOUT ⅔ CUP

1½ cups Basic Chicken Stock (page 313) or canned low-sodium chicken broth or water

1 bunch scallions (8 or 9), coarsely chopped

1 large carrot, coarsely chopped

1 medium yellow onion, coarsely chopped

3 medium garlic cloves

One 2-inch knob fresh ginger, peeled and chopped

2 tablespoons Korean red pepper paste (gochujang)

2 tablespoons low-sodium soy sauce

IN A LARGE flat-bottomed saucepan, combine the stock, scallions, carrot, onion, garlic, ginger, red pepper paste, and soy sauce and bring to a boil over medium-high heat. Reduce the heat to low and simmer gently for 30 minutes. Let cool briefly and then puree in a blender. Strain through a fine sieve. The Korean BBQ Sauce can be made up to 1 month in advance and stored in an airtight container in the refrigerator. Gently warm in a small saucepan over low heat before using.

Kimchi Cucumbers

MAKES 1 QUART (MORE THAN YOU NEED, BUT YOU ARE GOING TO WANT EXTRA TO SNACK ON)

2 English cucumbers

1 cup Korean chili powder, or ¼ cup hot red pepper flakes

1 bunch scallions (8 or 9), thinly sliced

4 medium garlic cloves, thinly sliced

¼ cup sugar

¼ cup fish sauce

¼ cup kosher salt

2 tablespoons shrimp paste in oil

SLICE the cucumbers crosswise about ¼ inch thick and place them in a large bowl. Add the chili powder, scallions, garlic, sugar, fish sauce, salt, and shrimp paste. Mix all together with your hands (be sure to wear gloves or you will stink for a week). Place in an airtight container and cover with plastic wrap, placing the plastic directly on top of the cucumbers. Place something heavy on top of the plastic to compress the cucumbers and seal the container well. The cucumbers will slowly release liquid and become submerged. Refrigerate for a minimum of 1 day before using. They will taste good tomorrow, and better in a week. Store in an airtight container in the refrigerator for up to 3 weeks.

KOREAN BRAISED SHORT RIB TACOS WITH KIMCHI-SESAME SALSA

MAKES 8 TACOS

Gourmet food trucks have become so popular they are like smartphones and social media—we can hardly remember a time before them. But I do. I remember when I first heard about the Kogi Taco Truck in LA. It took the city by storm in late 2008 with its active Twitter presence and $2 short rib tacos. The truck championed cheap street food that was inventive, well-made, fresh, and flavorful. I almost flew to LA just to try them, but we were getting crushed that holiday season, so instead I read everything I could about what they were making: homemade tortillas, Korean short rib barbecue, fresh cilantro salsa with kimchi and sesame. My mouth watered more with each article I found. Christopher challenged me to come up with something similar, so I looked up pictures of the tacos, blew them up so I could scrutinize each bite, and created this recipe. The salsa is terrific on meats and fish and chicken, so don't just limit it to the tacos. The short rib recipe is a keeper as well. We make big batches and freeze it all so we always have some on hand. Make the components in advance, and you'll have lunch or dinner as quickly as if you placed an order at the Kogi truck.

½ Asian pear, cored

1 large napa cabbage leaf, thinly sliced (about ½ cup)

8 soft corn tortillas

Braised Short Ribs (page 314)

16 large sprigs fresh cilantro

About 3 tablespoons sriracha

1 recipe Kimchi-Sesame Salsa (recipe follows)

1 lime, cut into 8 pieces

Preheat the oven to 350°F and place a rack in the center of the oven.

Cut the Asian pear into matchstick-size pieces and toss in a small bowl with the napa cabbage. Set aside. Wrap the corn tortillas in aluminum foil and place in the oven until warmed through, 8 to 10 minutes. While the tortillas are warming up, heat the short ribs in a medium saucepan over medium heat until hot. Remove the tortillas from the oven and place them on a flat work surface. Evenly arrange the pear-cabbage mixture in a line in the middle of each tortilla. Drain

continued

KOREAN
BRAISED
SHORT RIB
TACOS WITH
KIMCHI-
SESAME
SALSA

———————
continued

the short rib with a fork and divide it evenly on top of the pear-cabbage. Drizzle with a little sriracha, adding more if you like spice. Add 2 sprigs of cilantro and finish with about 2 tablespoons of the Kimchi-Sesame Salsa for each taco. Fold the tacos over and garnish each with a lime wedge. Squeeze the lime into the taco before eating.

Kimchi-Sesame Salsa

MAKES ABOUT 1 CUP

½ cup chopped fresh cilantro (about ½ bunch)

3 scallions, white and green parts sliced (about ⅓ cup)

3 tablespoons chopped kimchi

1 tablespoon plus 1 teaspoon white sesame seeds

1 tablespoon plus 1 teaspoon sesame oil

2 teaspoons peeled and finely chopped fresh ginger (about ½-inch knob)

1 medium shallot, minced

1 small garlic clove, minced

2 teaspoons soy sauce

2 teaspoons sugar

2 teaspoons unseasoned rice vinegar

2 teaspoons chili oil

Juice of 1 lime

½ teaspoon kosher salt

½ teaspoon freshly ground black pepper

IN A MEDIUM bowl, mix together all the ingredients until well combined. The Kimchi-Sesame Salsa can be made up to 2 days in advance and stored in an airtight container in the refrigerator.

TEA-SMOKED PORK SPARE RIBS

SERVES 4

If Yankee Candle Company ever puts out an "umami"-scented candle (and they already have "Man Town" and "Leather Couch," so why not?), these ribs will be exactly what they're looking for. They are cooked in a traditional Chinese red braise, which is a slow-braising technique that imparts a deep red color to the meat. Then they are smoked with black tea. Finally, they are topped with a sugar-pepper mixture that caramelizes at the end, turning these ribs into meat candy. You'll be engrossed by the whole cooking process: All the colors and shapes in the braise! The smoke billowing out of the pot! The bonfire smell that lingers all night! The end result is the epitome of savory. Many of our guests call these meat candy, and they are so tasty that someone once begged me to make an ice cream out of them. (I declined.)

1 bunch scallions (8 or 9), halved

1 large carrot, sliced into ½-inch-thick rounds

1 large yellow onion, quartered

½ cup dried shiitake mushrooms

¼ cup dried red Thai chilies

6 medium garlic cloves, smashed

One 1-inch knob fresh ginger, sliced

4 whole star anise

2 dried bay leaves

1 whole cinnamon stick

1 tablespoon fennel seeds

1 tablespoon coriander seeds

1 teaspoon whole cloves

4 pounds Louisiana-style pork ribs or St. Louis–style pork spare ribs

2 cups Basic Chicken Stock (page 313) or canned low-sodium chicken broth

1 cup low-sodium soy sauce

½ cup Shaoxing cooking wine (or substitute dry sherry or dry white wine)

½ cup black Chinkiang vinegar

½ cup black tea leaves (any basic black tea leaf will work)

½ cup sugar

½ cup uncooked white rice

¼ cup Sichuan peppercorns

¼ cup light brown sugar

Preheat the oven to 350°F and place a rack in the center of the oven.

In a large braising dish or Dutch oven, combine the scallions, carrots, onion, dried mushrooms, dried chilies, garlic, ginger, star anise, bay leaves, cinnamon stick, fennel, coriander, and cloves and mix together to distribute evenly on the bottom of the dish. Place the ribs directly on top of the vegetables and pour the stock, soy sauce, Shaoxing, and vinegar over the whole thing. Cover the dish tightly

continued
↓

with aluminum foil (or the lid, if using a Dutch oven). Place on the stove over high heat for 10 minutes. Turn off the heat and move the braising dish to the oven. Cook for 2½ hours. Remove from the oven and let cool. The ribs should be almost falling off the bone.

To smoke the ribs, you need a large braising dish or Dutch oven as well as a wire rack that fits inside. If you have two large braising dishes, use the second one; otherwise, remove the cooked ribs from the braising dish and clean it so you can use it to smoke the ribs. Line the bottom and sides of the braising dish or Dutch oven with a large sheet of aluminum foil. Add the black tea leaves, sugar, and white rice and give it a stir. Place a wire rack on top, making sure it is tall enough so that it is not touching the tea or the rice. Place the ribs on the rack, cover the whole dish tightly with aluminum foil (or the lid, if using a Dutch oven), place the dish over high heat, and immediately start a timer for 12 minutes. After about 5 minutes, you should start to see the ribs smoke. (Please open the windows!) After the first whiff of smoke, turn off

the heat and remove the dish from the stove. When the timer goes off, carefully remove the foil or the lid. The ribs can be made up to 2 days in advance and stored in an airtight container in the refrigerator.

Turn the oven temperature up to 400°F. In a small skillet, toast the Sichuan peppercorns over medium-low heat until they start to become fragrant and floral and pop a bit, 4 to 6 minutes. Use a spice grinder, coffee grinder, or mortar and pestle to grind them to a powder. Cut the ribs into 5-bone sections and place them on a baking sheet. Mix together the Sichuan peppercorns and brown sugar in a small bowl and spread evenly on top of the ribs. Pour a few tablespoons of water on top of each 5-bone section directly onto the sugar-pepper mix to moisten. Place in the oven and cook for 6 to 8 minutes, until the sugar-pepper mix has melted and the ribs are piping hot. Remove from the oven and place on a large platter. Pour any juices over all the ribs. Serve family-style and definitely eat with your hands!

DUMPLINGS

158 SHIITAKE MUSHROOM AND SPINACH DUMPLINGS WITH CLASSIC DUMPLING SAUCE

161 EDAMAME, WASABI, AND MUSTARD GREEN DUMPLINGS WITH BLACK VINEGAR–WASABI DIPPING SAUCE

164 LEMONY SHRIMP DUMPLINGS WITH KIMCHI-YOGURT DIPPING SAUCE

167 JUICY DUCK AND GINGER DUMPLINGS

171 MAMA CHANG'S PORK AND CHIVE DUMPLINGS WITH BLACK PEPPER–SCALLION SAUCE

176 BRAISED SHORT RIB DUMPLINGS WITH SICHUAN CHILI OIL

SHIITAKE MUSHROOM AND SPINACH DUMPLINGS WITH CLASSIC DUMPLING SAUCE

MAKES 40 TO 50 DUMPLINGS

Being a dumpling on the menu at Myers+Chang sitting next to Mama Chang's Pork and Chive Dumplings is like sitting next to Charlize Theron on your fat day. In other words, when we created this dish, it had to have some *jingling! Jingling* is something like a Chinese word for "chutzpah." At least my mom says it is after Christopher described what "chutzpah" meant. Hmmm. Someone might want to Google Translate this. These dumplings are stuffed full of garlicky sautéed spinach and earthy shiitakes with some tofu to bind it all together. They are healthy and full of flavor and they embody *jingling.*

2 cups dried shiitake mushrooms

4 large napa cabbage leaves, thinly sliced (about 2 cups)

1½ teaspoons kosher salt

4 tablespoons vegetable oil, such as canola, plus more as needed

2 medium garlic cloves, sliced

1 pound fresh baby spinach

½ teaspoon freshly ground black pepper

¼ teaspoon red pepper flakes

1 cup crumbled firm tofu (about 8 ounces)

1 tablespoon soy sauce

1 tablespoon peeled and finely chopped fresh ginger (about 1-inch knob)

2 teaspoons toasted sesame oil

1 teaspoon black Chinkiang vinegar

One 16-ounce package round dumpling wrappers (we like Twin Marquis brand)

1 recipe Classic Dumpling Sauce (recipe follows)

In a medium saucepan, bring about 4 cups water to a boil. Place the shiitake mushrooms in a medium bowl and pour the boiling water over them to cover. Let sit for 10 to 15 minutes to allow the mushrooms to rehydrate.

Place the cabbage in a large bowl with 1 teaspoon of the salt. Toss well and set aside for at least 10 minutes.

Drain the mushrooms and let cool. When they are cool enough to handle, slice off any woody stems and mince the mushrooms very fine. You can do this by hand or pulse them in a food processor if you have one. Set aside.

In a wok or a large, heavy, flat-bottomed skillet, heat 2 tablespoons of the vegetable oil over high heat until it shimmers, about 1 minute. Add the garlic, give it a quick stir, and then add the spinach. Stir immediately and season with ¼ teaspoon of the salt, ¼ teaspoon of the black pepper, and the red pepper flakes. Cook, stirring, until the leaves are wilted, about 1 minute, and remove them from the pan. Place in a colander, let cool slightly, and squeeze any excess liquid out with your hands. Coarsely chop the spinach and set aside.

Take the cabbage out of the bowl and squeeze hard with your hands. You will be amazed with the amount of water that comes out. Very finely chop the cabbage.

In a large bowl, combine the cabbage, mushrooms, spinach, and tofu. Add the soy sauce, ginger, sesame oil, vinegar, remaining ¼ teaspoon salt, and remaining ¼ teaspoon black pepper. Mix very well using your hands; it is really important that all the ingredients are distributed evenly.

Fill a small bowl with warm water. Lay a dumpling wrapper on a clean work surface and scoop about 1 tablespoon of the filling into the center of the wrapper. Dip your finger in the water and paint all around the edge of the wrapper to moisten. Fold the wrapper over in half to look like a half-moon. (This always reminds me of making a taco shell.) Pinch just the top of the wrapper together, leaving the sides exposed and open. Start pleating the left side of the dumpling: Hold the dumpling on the top, fold a pleat on one side of the wrapper about halfway down the arc toward the center of the dumpling, and press it into the facing side of the wrapper. Repeat the pleating almost to the bottom of the arc so that you have two pleats on the left side of the dumpling. Repeat the pleating process on the right side of the dumpling, again pleating toward the center. When the dumpling is completely pleated, you should be able to sit the dumpling on its bottom and it will look like a little love seat. The smooth side of the dumpling will be the seat, and the pleated side will be the back of the couch. Continue with the rest of the dumpling wrappers and filling until the filling has been used up. The dumplings can be made in advance and stored uncooked for up to 3 weeks in an airtight container in the freezer. The easiest way to freeze them is to place them on a flat plate or tray and

continued
↓

SHIITAKE
MUSHROOM
AND SPINACH
DUMPLINGS
WITH CLASSIC
DUMPLING
SAUCE

continued

freeze until dumplings are completely frozen, and then transfer to a resealable freezer bag or an airtight container and return them to the freezer. Thaw in the refrigerator on a flat plate overnight or for at least 6 hours before cooking.

In a large, heavy, flat-bottomed skillet with a lid or a nonstick skillet with a lid, heat the remaining 2 tablespoons of oil over medium-high heat. When the oil starts to shimmer, carefully lay as many dumplings as will comfortably fit on their bottoms in the skillet and turn the heat down to medium. Cook without moving the pan until the bottoms of the dumplings are golden brown, about 3 minutes. Check by lifting them up with your fingers and peeking underneath. Add about 2 tablespoons water to the pan and immediately cover with the lid. The pan will sizzle and steam up immediately, so don't be startled. Shake the pan from time to time to keep the dumplings from sticking. Let the dumplings steam for 2 minutes, at which point most of the water will have evaporated. Add another 2 tablespoons water to the pan, cover, and steam again. Turn off the heat, keep covered, and let rest for 1 minute. Uncover and turn the heat back to medium-high to crisp up the dumplings. Remove from the pan. Continue in the same manner to cook the remaining dumplings, adding 1 tablespoon of vegetable oil to the pan at a time as needed. Serve crispy-side up with the Classic Dumpling Sauce.

Classic Dumpling Sauce

MAKES ABOUT ¾ CUP

This classic dumpling sauce can be paired with any of the dumplings in this book. You can also add more or less sriracha or substitute wasabi for a different kind of kick.

½ cup soy sauce

2 tablespoons peeled and finely chopped fresh ginger (about 2-inch knob)

1 tablespoon Chinkiang black vinegar

2 teaspoons sriracha

2 teaspoons toasted sesame oil

IN A SMALL bowl, stir together all the ingredients. Store in an airtight container in the refrigerator for up to 1 month.

EDAMAME, WASABI, AND MUSTARD GREEN DUMPLINGS WITH BLACK VINEGAR–WASABI DIPPING SAUCE

MAKES ABOUT 50 DUMPLINGS

Joanne and I were in one of our weekly meetings, and we got to talking about the opening menu at M+C. She told me that when developing the restaurant, she had always thought there would be an edamame dumpling on the menu. The next week, I surprised her with this variation. I talk to my team a lot about different kinds of spices: how the tingle of Sichuan peppercorn is different than fresh chili and hot pepper heat, which is different from the "nose spice" that is associated with Chinese hot mustard and wasabi. I love the burn of wasabi, and I decided to marry creamy edamame beans with sharp mustard greens and enhance the peppery taste of the greens with wasabi. This vegetarian dumpling packs tremendous flavor in each little bite. Different wasabis have different heat, so start with less and add more upon tasting if you want to amp up the spice. —*Chef Karen*

6 napa cabbage leaves, thinly sliced (about 3 cups)

1 tablespoon plus 2 teaspoons kosher salt

½ cup vegetable oil, such as canola, plus more as needed

1 pound mustard greens, chopped into ½-inch pieces

1 teaspoon freshly ground black pepper

1 teaspoon red pepper flakes

2 cups shelled edamame beans (if using frozen beans, defrost before using)

1 cup crumbled firm tofu (about 8 ounces)

⅓ cup soy sauce

1 to 2 tablespoons wasabi powder or paste

1 tablespoon toasted sesame oil

1 tablespoon black Chianking vinegar

One 16-ounce package round wheat dumpling wrappers (we like Twin Marquis brand)

1 recipe Black Vinegar–Wasabi Dipping Sauce (recipe follows)

Place the napa cabbage in a large bowl with 1 tablespoon of the salt. Toss well and set aside for at least 10 minutes.

While the cabbage is resting, in a wok or large, heavy, flat-bottomed skillet, heat ¼ cup of the vegetable oil over high heat until it shimmers, about

continued ↓

EDAMAME,
WASABI, AND
MUSTARD
GREEN
DUMPLINGS
WITH BLACK
VINEGAR–
WASABI
DIPPING SAUCE

continued

1 minute. Add the mustard greens and season with 1 teaspoon of the salt, the black pepper, and the red pepper flakes. Add ¼ cup water to the pan and cover. Cook the greens, stirring from time to time, for 3 minutes. Remove the cover and taste the greens; they should be soft but still have a bit of bite. Remove from the pan and transfer to a plate to cool. When the greens are cool, squeeze them out over the sink to remove any residual water. Place on a cutting board and chop well.

Take the cabbage out of the bowl and squeeze hard with your hands. You will be amazed with the amount of water that comes out. Very finely chop the cabbage.

In a large bowl, combine the mustard greens, cabbage, edamame, tofu, soy sauce, wasabi powder, sesame oil, vinegar, and remaining 1 teaspoon salt. Mix very well with your hands. Get in there! The tofu will mix almost completely into the filling, and you want to make sure the wasabi is incorporated well so you don't get any sneaky hot pockets.

Fill a small bowl with warm water. Lay a dumpling wrapper on a clean work surface and scoop about 1 tablespoon of the filling into the center of the wrapper. Dip your finger in the water and paint all around the edge of the wrapper to moisten. Fold the wrapper over in half to look like a half-moon and seal tight. Continue with the rest of the dumpling wrappers and filling until the filling has been used up. The dumplings can be made in advance and stored uncooked for up to 3 weeks in an airtight container in the freezer. The easiest way to freeze them is to place them on a flat plate or tray and freeze until the dumplings are completely frozen, then transfer them to a resealable freezer bag or an airtight container and return them to the freezer. Thaw in the refrigerator on a flat plate overnight or at least 6 hours before cooking.

You need a large, heavy, flat-bottomed skillet with a lid or a nonstick skillet with a lid. Heat the skillet over medium-high heat and add 2 tablespoons of the vegetable oil. When the oil starts to shimmer, carefully lay as many dumplings as will comfortably fit on their side in the skillet and turn the heat down to medium. Cook without moving the pan until the dumplings are golden brown on the bottom, about 3 minutes. Check by lifting them up with your fingers and peeking underneath. When the dumplings are golden brown, add about 2 tablespoons water to the bottom of the pan and immediately cover with the lid. The pan will sizzle and steam up immediately, so don't be startled. Shake the pan from time to time to keep the dumplings from sticking. Let the dumplings steam for 2 minutes, at which point most of the water will have evaporated. Add another 2 tablespoons water to the pan, cover, and steam again. Turn off the heat, keep covered, and let rest for 1 minute. Uncover and turn the heat back up to medium-high to crisp up the dumplings. Remove from the pan. Continue in the same manner to cook the remaining dumplings, adding 1 tablespoon of vegetable oil to the pan at a time as needed. Serve seared-side up with the Black Vinegar–Wasabi Dipping Sauce.

Black Vinegar-Wasabi Dipping Sauce

MAKES ½ CUP

¼ cup low-sodium soy sauce

2 tablespoons black Chinkiang vinegar

2 tablespoons peeled and grated fresh ginger (about 2-inch knob)

2 teaspoons toasted sesame oil

1 teaspoon wasabi powder or paste

IN A SMALL bowl, whisk together all the ingredients until the wasabi powder has dissolved. Store in an airtight container in the refrigerator for up to 1 month.

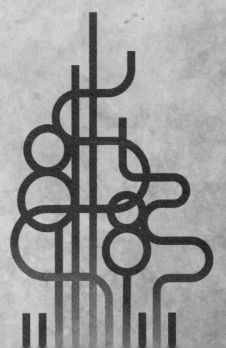

LEMONY SHRIMP DUMPLINGS WITH KIMCHI-YOGURT DIPPING SAUCE

MAKES 30 TO 35 DUMPLINGS

A few years prior to opening Myers+Chang (when it was barely a thought in our heads), I was flipping through *Food & Wine* and read an article about über-talented chef Anita Lo in NYC and some lemony shrimp dumplings she was crushing on. I filed it away for "someday." That someday came when we were planning the menu for our new restaurant and I wanted to offer a slew of dumplings in addition to the classic pork and chive. I had imagined exactly how these would taste, and we worked on the filling until our recipe matched the taste vision in my head. I knew the shrimp had to be snappy and crisp, not pasty, and that the lemon had to be super bright. Ginger pairs well with lemon (and with shrimp), so that went into the mix as well. Water chestnuts add nice crunch, and the egg white holds it all together. The Kimchi-Yogurt Dipping Sauce came about a year after M+C's opening, when Christopher declared that these needed an upgrade. He was right; this dipping sauce turns a really good dumpling into a really, really fabulous dumpling.

1 pound medium or large raw shrimp, peeled, deveined, and chopped into ½-inch pieces (about 3 cups)

¼ cup coarsely chopped water chestnuts

2 tablespoons grated lemon zest (from 1 or 2 lemons)

1 scallion, white and green parts finely chopped (about 2 tablespoons)

1 tablespoon peeled and finely chopped fresh ginger (about 1-inch knob)

1 tablespoon cornstarch

1 tablespoon soy sauce

About ½ egg white (do your best to split an egg white in half)

30 to 35 square wonton wrappers

3 tablespoons vegetable oil, such as canola, plus more as needed

1 recipe Kimchi-Yogurt Dipping Sauce (recipe follows)

Place the shrimp on a few paper towels and blot any excess liquid. In a medium bowl, mix the shrimp, water chestnuts, lemon zest, scallions, ginger, cornstarch, soy sauce, and egg white.

Fill a small bowl with warm water. Lay a wonton wrapper on a clean work surface and spoon about 1 tablespoon of the filling into the center of the wrapper. Dip your finger in the water and moisten the edges of the wrapper.

continued
↓

LEMONY
SHRIMP
DUMPLINGS
WITH KIMCHI-
YOGURT
DIPPING SAUCE

continued

Fold up the bottom half of the wrapper over the shrimp, press down slightly so the filling spreads to the right and left sides of the wrapper, and then continue to fold up so you have a cigar-shaped tube with the seam of the dumpling on the bottom. Seal the sides of the tube by pressing down the edges of the wrapper. Continue with all the wrappers. The dumplings can be assembled up to 1 day in advance and stored in the refrigerator in an airtight container.

In a large, heavy, flat-bottomed skillet, heat 2 tablespoons of the vegetable oil over medium-high heat. When the oil starts to shimmer, place as many dumplings as will comfortably fit in the skillet, seam-side down and a few inches apart. Turn down the heat to medium and cook, shaking the pan gently, for about 5 minutes until the bottoms of the dumplings turn golden brown. When the dumplings are golden brown, add about 2 tablespoons water to the bottom of the pan and immediately cover with the lid. The pan will sizzle and steam up immediately, so don't be startled. Shake the pan from time to time to keep the dumplings from sticking. Let the dumplings cook for another minute or so, until the water has evaporated, then lift up the lid, add another 2 tablespoons water, cover, and continue to cook for another minute or so. Repeat one more time; the total cooking time is 8 to 9 minutes. Remove from the pan. Continue in the same manner to cook the remaining dumplings, adding 1 tablespoon of vegetable oil to the pan at a time as needed. Arrange on a serving platter crisped-side up and serve with the Kimchi-Yogurt Dipping Sauce.

Kimchi-Yogurt Dipping Sauce

MAKES ABOUT 1 CUP

½ cup Greek yogurt

2 scallions, white and green parts finely chopped (about ¼ cup)

2 tablespoons minced kimchi

1 tablespoon soy sauce

1 tablespoon freshly squeezed lemon juice

½ medium garlic clove, minced

¼ teaspoon kosher salt

Large pinch of freshly ground black pepper

STIR together all the ingredients in a small bowl. The Kimchi-Yogurt Dipping Sauce can be made up to 3 days in advance and stored in an airtight container in the refrigerator.

JUICY DUCK AND GINGER DUMPLINGS

MAKES 35 TO 45 DUMPLINGS

These are my favorite dumplings to make. I love how the duck fat melts in the dumplings reminiscent of *xiao long bao* or traditional soup dumplings. I fold them bellybutton-style (see page 67) and they look like tortellini, which reminds me of my year living and cooking in Italy and making tons of teeny tiny tortellini with the *nonnas* in Modena. I serve them in the rich, gingered braising liquid from the duck legs. I get so happy every time I make them that I do a little "happy dumpling dance." (Ask me when you are at the restaurant, and I will do it for you.) If you can't find duck legs, substitute bone-in, skin-on chicken legs with thighs attached. —*Chef Karen*

5 Long Island duck legs, or 3 Moulard duck legs (or substitute 3 or 4 bone-in, skin-on chicken legs with thigh attached; about 2 pounds)

2 tablespoons plus 1 teaspoon kosher salt

1 teaspoon freshly ground black pepper

2 medium yellow onions, diced

3 medium carrots, diced

One 2-inch knob fresh ginger, unpeeled, thinly sliced into coins

5 whole star anise

2 dried bay leaves

Two 12-ounce cans dark beer (porters and stout work well)

1 tablespoon peeled and grated fresh ginger (about 1-inch knob)

One 16-ounce package square dumpling wrappers (we like Twin Marquis brand)

3 tablespoons vegetable oil, such as canola, plus more as needed

Preheat the oven to 400°F and place a rack in the center of the oven.

Season the duck legs with 2 tablespoons of the salt and the pepper, rubbing the seasoning in well with your hands. In a large braising dish or Dutch oven, combine the onions, carrots, ginger, star anise, and bay leaves. Place the duck legs on top of the vegetables and pour 2 cups water and the beer over the duck legs. The braising liquid should only come halfway up the duck legs so that the skin gets crispy. Make sure the pan is large enough so that the duck legs do not crowd the pan too much and the fat can render out evenly. Place in the oven, uncovered, and braise for 2 hours. When the legs are done, the

continued
↓

meat will pull apart easily from the bones. Remove the pan from the oven. When cool enough to handle, remove the duck legs from the pan and let them cool a bit until they are just warm and you can separate the meat, skin, and any remaining fat from the bone.

Strain the braising liquid through a cheesecloth or a fine sieve into a small pot and place on the stove over low heat to keep warm.

Remove the star anise and bay leaves from the vegetables that are strained out and discard. Chop all the vegetables into small pieces. Finely chop all the duck meat and skin and add to the chopped vegetables. Season with the remaining 1 teaspoon salt and the ginger. Mix the filling well with your hands and set aside.

Fill a small bowl with warm water. Lay a dumpling wrapper on a clean work surface and scoop 1 tablespoon of the filling into the center of the wrapper. Dip your finger in the water and paint the edges of the wrapper. Fold the square into a triangle with the top of the wrapper pointing up like a little hat. Press the top edges together and then seal the dumpling, working your way down the sides. Draw the bottom two corners of the triangle together

to form a kerchief shape. Dab a bit of water on the edges of the corners and press tightly to seal. Repeat with the remaining filling and wrappers. The dumplings can be made up to 1 week in advance and stored uncooked in an airtight container in the freezer. The easiest way to freeze them is to place them on a flat plate or tray and freeze until the dumplings are completely frozen, then transfer them to a resealable freezer bag or an airtight container and return them to the freezer. Thaw in the refrigerator on a flat plate before cooking.

You need a large, heavy, flat-bottomed skillet with a lid or a nonstick skillet with a lid. Heat the skillet over medium-high heat and add 2 tablespoons of the vegetable oil. When the oil starts to shimmer, carefully lay as many dumplings as will comfortably fit on their flat side in the skillet and turn the heat down to medium. Cook without moving the pan until the dumplings are golden brown on the bottom, about 3 minutes. Check by lifting them up with your fingers and peeking underneath. When the dumplings are a golden brown, add about 2 tablespoons water to the bottom of the pan and immediately cover with the lid. The pan will sizzle and steam up immediately, so don't be startled. Shake the pan from time

continued
↓

to time to keep the dumplings from sticking. Let the dumplings steam for 2 minutes, at which point most of the water will have evaporated. Add another 2 tablespoons water to the pan, cover again, and steam again. Turn off the heat, keep covered, and rest for 1 minute. Uncover and turn the heat back up to medium-high to crisp up the dumplings. Remove from the pan. Continue in the same manner to cook the remaining dumplings, adding 1 tablespoon of oil to the pan at a time as needed. Divide the dumplings among serving bowls and pour a bit of the duck braise over them. Serve immediately.

MAMA CHANG'S PORK AND CHIVE DUMPLINGS WITH BLACK PEPPER–SCALLION SAUCE

MAKES 40 TO 50 DUMPLINGS

Making dumplings with my mom is one of the earliest childhood food memories I have. I remember Mom setting up the kitchen table with a huge bowl of filling, dumpling wrappers covering the whole table, and the two of us going to town folding as fast as we could before the wrappers dried out. Well, she folded as fast as she could; the folded dumplings looked like little couches to me and I would play house with them and my dozens of LEGO people. My brother was a notoriously picky eater and he ate about four things, dumplings being one of them. So Mom would make and freeze them on the weekends and pull them out during the week for his dinner. The first thing she and my dad do when they visit us in Boston is make a trip to Myers+Chang, sit at the food bar, and order these to make sure we are still making them properly. She's never shy about sharing her feedback. We all watch her out of the corner of our eyes and breathe a sigh of relief when she gives a thumbs-up.

8 large napa cabbage leaves, thinly sliced (about 4 cups)

1 tablespoon kosher salt

1 pound ground pork (don't choose super lean ground pork or your dumplings will be dry)

1 cup minced fresh garlic chives or regular fresh chives

3 tablespoons soy sauce

1 tablespoon peeled and finely chopped fresh ginger (about 1-inch knob)

2 teaspoons toasted sesame oil

One 16-ounce package round wheat dumpling wrappers (we like Twin Marquis brand)

4 tablespoons vegetable oil, such as canola, plus more as needed

1 recipe Black Pepper–Scallion Sauce (recipe follows)

Place the cabbage in a large bowl with the salt. Toss well and set aside for at least 10 minutes.

In a large bowl, combine the ground pork, garlic chives, soy sauce, ginger, and sesame oil and use your hands to mix all the ingredients thoroughly together. Set aside.

continued
↓

MAMA
CHANG'S
PORK AND
CHIVE
DUMPLINGS
WITH BLACK
PEPPER–
SCALLION
SAUCE

continued

Take the cabbage in your hands and squeeze as hard as you can. You will be amazed by the amount of water that comes out. Squeeze out as much water as you can and add the cabbage to the pork mixture. Mix well with your hands until the filling is well combined.

Fill a small bowl with warm water. Lay a dumpling wrapper on a clean work surface and scoop about 1 tablespoon of the filling into the center of the wrapper. Dip your finger in the water and paint all around the edge of the wrapper to moisten. Fold the wrapper over in half to look like a half-moon. (This always reminds me of making a taco shell.) Pinch just the top of the wrapper together, leaving the sides exposed and open. Start pleating the left side of the dumpling: hold the dumpling on the top, fold a pleat on one side of the wrapper about halfway down the arc toward the center of the dumpling and press it into the facing side of the wrapper. Repeat the pleating almost to the bottom of the arc so that you have two pleats on the left side of the dumpling. Repeat the pleating process on the right side of the dumpling, again pleating toward the center. When the dumpling is completely pleated, you should be able to sit the dumpling on its bottom and it will look like a little love seat. The

smooth side of the dumpling will be the seat and the pleated side will be the back of the couch. Continue with the rest of the dumpling wrappers and filling until the filling has been used up. The dumplings can be made up to 1 week in advance and stored uncooked in an airtight container in the freezer. The easiest way to freeze them is to place them on a flat plate or tray and freeze until the dumplings are completely frozen, then transfer them to a resealable freezer bag or an airtight container and return them to the freezer. Thaw in the refrigerator on a flat plate before cooking.

You need a large, heavy, flat-bottomed skillet with a lid or a nonstick skillet with a lid. Heat the skillet over medium-high heat and add 2 tablespoons of the vegetable oil. When the oil starts to shimmer, carefully add as many dumplings as will comfortably fit in the skillet and turn the heat down to medium. Cook without moving the pan until the dumpling bottoms are golden brown, about 3 minutes. Check by lifting them up with your fingers and peeking underneath. Add about 2 tablespoons water to the bottom of the pan and immediately cover with the lid. The pan will sizzle and steam up immediately, so don't be startled. Shake the pan from time to time to keep the dumplings

from sticking. Let the dumplings steam for 2 minutes, at which point most of the water will have evaporated. Add another 2 tablespoons water to the pan, cover, and steam again. Wait till the water has mostly evaporated again and repeat one last time with a final 2 tablespoons water. Turn off the heat, keep covered, and let rest for 1 minute.

Uncover and turn the heat back to medium-high to crisp up the bottoms. Remove from the pan. Continue in the same manner to cook the remaining dumplings, adding 1 tablespoon of oil to the pan at a time as needed. Serve immediately with the Black Pepper–Scallion Sauce.

Black Pepper–Scallion Sauce

MAKES JUST OVER ¾ CUP

Christopher loves Mama Chang's dumplings (and Mama Chang), but he wasn't nuts about the original traditional dipping sauce we served them with. Because these dumplings are so classic, he wanted a jazzy peppery sauce to dip them in. We tested three or four different variations, each with a little more of this or a little less of that. Two versions stood out, and in a moment of culinary genius, Christopher mixed them together and created this sauce.

2 scallions, white and green parts finely chopped (about ¼ cup)

1 medium garlic clove, minced

2 tablespoons sugar

2 tablespoons black Chinkiang vinegar

1½ tablespoons soy sauce

1 tablespoon sriracha

1 tablespoon vegetable oil, such as canola

1 tablespoon toasted sesame oil

1 tablespoon chili oil

1 tablespoon freshly ground black pepper

PLACE all the ingredients in a blender and blend quickly until combined but not totally smooth. Store in an airtight container in the refrigerator for up to 1 month. Stir well before using.

BRAISED SHORT RIB DUMPLINGS WITH SICHUAN CHILI OIL

MAKES 35 TO 45 DUMPLINGS

I made these special dumplings for Lunar New Year during the Year of the Goat. I used braised goat for that batch, and we passed small plates of food around the dining room for a wild dim sum celebration. I adapted this recipe to use our Asian braised short rib that we make every week for our banh mi at lunch. The rich braised short rib stands up to the fierce chili oil and is crazy addictive. These dumplings are steamed instead of cooked like pot stickers. We fold them "big hug"–style (see page 67) so they kind of resemble an Italian cappelletti. —*Chef Karen*

1 recipe Braised Short Ribs (page 314)

One 16-ounce package round dumpling wrappers (we like Twin Marquis brand)

1 recipe Sichuan Chili Oil (recipe follows)

Drain the short ribs of any juices, reserving about ¼ cup of the juices, and shred the meat finely. Return the reserved juices to the meat to keep it moist. We are going to use what we call the "big hug" fold on these dumplings. Fill a small bowl with warm water. Lay out a dumpling wrapper on a clean work surface and scoop 1 tablespoon of the braised short rib in the center of the wrapper. Dip your finger in the water and use it to paint the edges of the wrapper. Fold the dumpling round in half, pushing out any excess air, and seal the edges of the wrapper all around. Join and seal the two pointed ends together below the base of the dumpling. Dab a bit of water on the ends for a better pinched seal. Repeat until you have used all the braised short rib. The dumplings can be made in advance and stored uncooked for up to 3 weeks in an airtight container in the freezer. The easiest way to freeze them is to place them on a flat plate or tray and freeze until dumplings are completely frozen, then transfer them to a resealable freezer bag or an airtight container and return them to the freezer. Thaw in the refrigerator on a flat plate before cooking.

continued
↓

**BRAISED
SHORT RIB
DUMPLINGS
WITH SICHUAN
CHILI OIL**

___

continued

Fill a large skillet with about 1 inch of water and place on the stove over high heat until the water boils. Line a bamboo steamer with a lettuce leaf or parchment paper and put as many dumplings as will comfortably fit without touching into the steamer. Cover with the lid and place the steamer directly in the water in the skillet. If you don't have a bamboo steamer, use a double boiler lined with a lettuce leaf or piece of parchment paper instead. Cook on high for 6 to 8 minutes, until the wrappers are cooked through. Transfer the dumplings to a small bowl and dress with a generous spoonful of the Sichuan Chili Oil. Serve immediately.

Sichuan Chili Oil

MAKES ABOUT ¾ CUP

1 tablespoon Sichuan peppercorns

¼ cup chili oil

¼ cup black Chinkiang vinegar

2 tablespoons soy sauce

2 teaspoons peeled and grated fresh ginger (about 1-inch knob)

1 teaspoon Dijon mustard

IN A SMALL skillet, toast the Sichuan peppercorns over medium-low heat until they start to become fragrant and floral and pop a bit, 4 to 6 minutes. Use a spice grinder, coffee grinder, or mortar and pestle to grind them to a powder. In a blender or in a medium bowl using a whisk, combine the ground Sichuan peppercorns, chili oil, vinegar, soy sauce, ginger, and mustard. The Sichuan Chili Oil can be made up to 2 weeks in advance and stored in an airtight container in the refrigerator. Whisk together to recombine before serving.

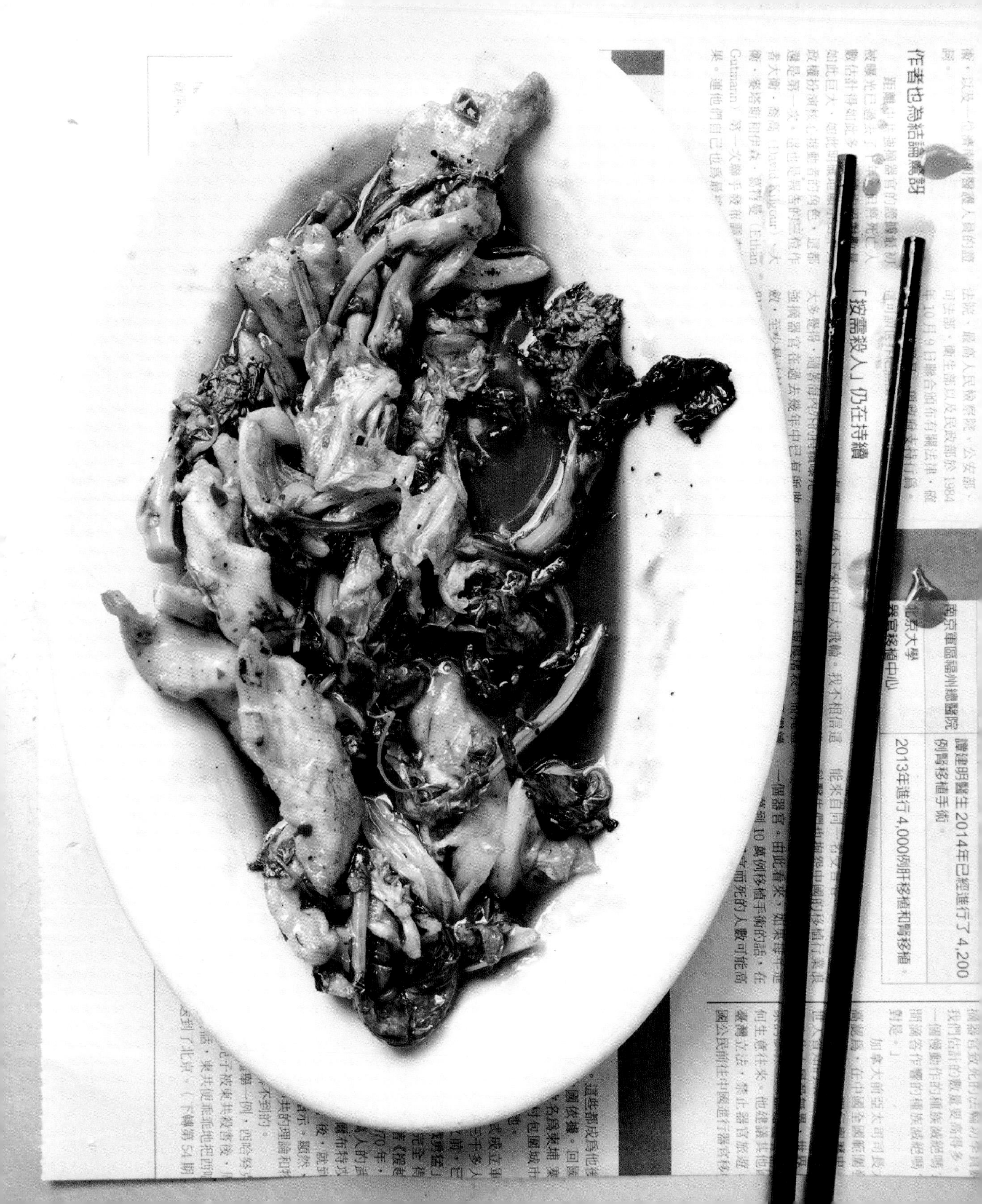

WOK

182 RED CURRY CAULIFLOWER WITH TOFU

185 CHICKEN AND RAPINI STIR-FRY

187 CLAMS IN CHINESE BLACK BEAN SAUCE

189 WOK-ROASTED LEMONGRASS MUSSELS
WITH GARLIC TOAST

193 SPICY SILKY TOFU

194 TRIPLE PORK MUSHU STIR-FRY

196 RAINBOW BEEF

RED CURRY CAULIFLOWER WITH TOFU

SERVES 4

When Chef Karen first started at Myers+Chang, she immediately became obsessed with all the new ingredients and flavors she was surrounded by. Her background to that point had been mostly with Italian and Middle Eastern cooking, and she immersed herself in this new vocabulary of chili, lemongrass, ginger, garlic, and galangal. Learning how to make an outstanding homemade curry paste was one of the first projects she tackled. You can easily buy red curry paste at the grocery store in the same way you buy spaghetti sauce or salad dressing. But no cook worth her salt was going to just unscrew a jar and start cooking. (That doesn't mean you can't. Sometimes life gets in the way and you need a shortcut.) Making curry from scratch is a lot less daunting than you think, and it lasts for weeks in the freezer. Tofu and cauliflower soak up the spicy intense curry to make a deliciously saucy stir-fry that begs to be eaten over a bowl of fragrant rice.

1 medium cauliflower (about 2 pounds)

¼ cup vegetable oil, such as canola

14 to 16 ounces firm tofu, cut into ½-inch cubes and blotted dry with a paper towel

1 teaspoon kosher salt

1 recipe Vegetarian Curry Sauce (recipe follows)

Perfect White Rice (page 315) or Perfect Brown Rice (page 316)

1 cup fresh cilantro leaves (about ½ bunch)

Fill a large pot with water and bring it up to a rolling boil. Using a sharp chef's knife, trim and divide the head of cauliflower into 1- to 2-inch florets. Bite-size pieces are very chopstick friendly. You should have about 4 cups of florets. When the water is boiling, add the cauliflower and cook for 2 minutes. Drain immediately and set aside.

Heat a wok or large, heavy, flat-bottomed skillet over high heat and add the vegetable oil. When the oil starts to shimmer, carefully add the tofu (be careful not to splash oil on yourself!) and brown on all sides. Turn the heat off, and using a slotted spoon, transfer the tofu to a paper towel–lined plate. Keep the oil in the wok and turn the heat back to high. Add the cauliflower and season with the salt. Toss for 6 to 8 minutes to get some nice char on the cauliflower. Add the Vegetarian Curry Sauce, turn the heat down to medium, and simmer the cauliflower in the sauce for 5 minutes. Return the tofu to the wok and gently stir for 2 minutes. You want the tofu to absorb the curry and flavor but not break up totally and get mushy. Divide the rice among four bowls and evenly divide the cauliflower and tofu on top of the rice. Garnish with the cilantro.

Vegetarian Curry Sauce

MAKES ABOUT 1 CUP

¼ cup Homemade Red Curry Paste (page 307) or jarred Thai red curry paste (we like Roland brand)

2 tablespoons vegetable oil, such as canola

½ cup coconut milk

2 tablespoons light brown sugar

1 tablespoon Madras curry powder

1 tablespoon kosher salt

1 lime, quartered

IN A LARGE saucepan, combine the curry paste and vegetable oil. Cook over medium heat, stirring with a rubber spatula, for 2 minutes to toast the curry paste and release the flavors. Add the coconut milk, brown sugar, curry powder, and salt and continue to stir. Squeeze the juice of the lime wedges into the curry and throw the spent wedges in as well. Simmer over low heat for 10 minutes, whisking frequently to keep the curry smooth. Remove the lime wedges and turn off the heat. The Vegetarian Curry Sauce can be made up to 3 days in advance and stored in an airtight container in the refrigerator. As it cools, the sauce will thicken.

CHICKEN AND RAPINI STIR-FRY

SERVES 4

We put this stir-fry on our opening menu as a nod to guests looking for the traditional chicken and broccoli they were used to ordering at their local Chinese takeout joint. We wanted something familiar enough to entice these guests but different enough to showcase what we were doing. Our opening chef, Alison, Christopher, and I had gone to dim sum brunch in Chinatown a few weeks before opening the restaurant; we grabbed one of every dish off the rolling carts, including steamed Chinese broccoli dressed with just a squeeze of oyster sauce. It was simple, salty, sweet, and by far our favorite pick of the brunch. Back in the kitchen, we tried making this with rapini (which is also commonly referred to as broccoli rabe). The sharpness of the rapini cut through the sweetness of the oyster sauce, and once we added chicken and some napa cabbage, we had our dish.

1 tablespoon cornstarch

1 tablespoon Shaoxing cooking wine (or substitute dry sherry or dry white wine)

1 large egg white

1 pound boneless, skinless chicken breast, cut thinly into 2 x ¼-inch strips

2 cups vegetable oil, such as canola (See Note, page 92)

1 pound rapini, trimmed and cut into 2-inch pieces

4 large napa cabbage leaves, thinly sliced (about 2 cups)

½ teaspoon kosher salt

1 teaspoon freshly ground black pepper

1 teaspoon red pepper flakes

1 teaspoon chili oil

1 recipe Chicken Stir-Fry Sauce (recipe follows)

1 cup fresh cilantro leaves (about ½ bunch)

Perfect White Rice (page 315) or Perfect Brown Rice (page 316)

In a medium bowl, stir together the cornstarch, Shaoxing wine, and egg white. Add the chicken strips to the bowl and use your hands to coat the chicken thoroughly in the mixture. Marinate the chicken in an airtight container in the refrigerator for at least 30 minutes or up to 1 day.

Now we are going to velvet the chicken (for more on velveting, see page 65). Place a few paper towels on a large plate and set aside. Heat the vegetable oil in a wok or deep skillet until the oil reaches 250°F. (Test the heat by placing a piece of chicken in the oil; it should float immediately.) Working in batches,

continued
↓

carefully add the chicken to the hot oil and cook until the strips just turn white, about 30 seconds, using a wooden spoon or chopsticks to gently separate them. (We are going to cook the chicken again, so don't worry if it does not seem cooked all the way through.) Quickly remove the chicken strips from the wok as soon as they turn white and drain on the paper towel–lined plate. Carefully pour out the oil into a heat-safe container and set aside.

<u>Wipe out the hot wok</u> with a paper towel and heat over high heat for 30 seconds. Measure out ¼ cup of the velveting oil and return it to the wok.

Add the rapini and stir for 1 minute to coat with the oil. Add ½ cup water to the wok and cover. Cook for about 5 minutes, until the rapini is wilted and no longer raw and bitter tasting. Add the napa cabbage and season with the salt, black pepper, red pepper flakes, and chili oil. Stir a few times and return the chicken to the wok. Stir for 2 minutes. Add the Chicken Stir-Fry Sauce and toss until the chicken and rapini are nicely covered in sauce and the chicken is cooked through, 3 to 4 minutes more. Add the cilantro and toss one last time. Divide the stir-fry among four bowls and serve with rice.

Chicken Stir-Fry Sauce

MAKES ABOUT 1 CUP

1 tablespoon cornstarch

¼ cup oyster sauce

¼ cup low-sodium soy sauce

¼ cup Basic Chicken Stock (page 313) or canned low-sodium chicken broth

IN A SMALL bowl, whisk together the cornstarch and 4 tablespoons cold water with a fork until smooth. Set aside.

IN A MEDIUM saucepan, bring the oyster sauce, soy sauce, and stock to a boil over medium-high heat. Whisk in the cornstarch slurry until the sauce thickens and becomes shiny, 3 to 4 minutes. The Chicken Stir-Fry Sauce can be made up to 1 week in advance and stored in an airtight container in the refrigerator. It gets quite gelatinous once refrigerated but will liquify as soon as you cook it.

CLAMS IN CHINESE BLACK BEAN SAUCE

SERVES 3

Chinese fermented black beans are salted and fermented soybeans and nothing like what gets stuffed in your burrito. They are deeply funky and pair really well with shellfish. This simple dish can be made in a flash, except for the soaking-the-beans part. Don't skimp on soaking them overnight or your dish will be waaaay salty. You'll find fermented black beans packaged in bags in Asian grocery stores near the vacuum-sealed dried mushrooms. We love this sauce in any stir-fry, so don't just limit it to saucing clams.

24 littleneck clams

½ cup sake

1 recipe Black Bean Sauce (recipe follows)

1 tablespoon unsalted butter

1 bunch English watercress, trimmed

Place the clams in a large bowl and fill with cold water. Wait a few minutes and drain. Refill, wait, and drain three more times to make sure the clams are clean, outside and in.

In a large stockpot, combine the clams, sake, and ¼ cup water and bring to a boil over high heat. Reduce the heat to medium, cover tightly, and steam for 6 to 8 minutes. Start checking at

6 minutes and steam until all the clams open (discard any that do not open). Add the Black Bean Sauce and ¼ cup water. Bring up to a simmer and swirl in the butter.

Divide the clams among three bowls, eight clams each, and spoon the sauce over the top. Garnish with the watercress and serve.

Black Bean Sauce

MAKES ABOUT 1 CUP

½ cup dried fermented black beans, soaked overnight in 6 cups water

2 tablespoons vegetable oil, such as canola

2 medium garlic cloves, minced

1 tablespoon peeled and finely chopped fresh ginger (about 1-inch knob)

½ cup Shaoxing cooking wine (or substitute dry sherry or dry white wine)

1 tablespoon sugar

DRAIN the water from the black beans and rinse three times. This will remove all the residual salt. Set aside.

IN A MEDIUM flat-bottomed skillet, heat the vegetable oil over medium heat. Add the garlic and ginger and sauté until soft and translucent, about 1 minute. Add the black beans, Shaoxing wine, and sugar. Reduce the heat to low, mash the beans a little with the back of a spoon, and cook for about 5 minutes, until they are soft. Set aside. The Black Bean Sauce can be made up to 1 week in advance and stored in an airtight container in the refrigerator.

WOK-ROASTED LEMONGRASS MUSSELS WITH GARLIC TOAST

SERVES 2

These mussels started out as an experiment for our opening chef, Alison. She wanted to try a dry-fried mussel dish because of something she had read about: throwing mussels in a really hot, dry pan so they pop open and pick up a smoky, roasted-in-the-fire-at-the-beach kind of flavor. Cooking mussels this way also means their liquid reduces instantly as soon as they open, which concentrates their flavor. Mussel broth is always the best part of mussels, anyway. Cooking shellfish is much easier than people think. Whether as an appetizer or a meal, once you make these mussels, they will become a new dinner go-to.

1 stalk lemongrass

6 medium garlic cloves

2 tablespoons chopped fresh cilantro stems

1 tablespoon fish sauce

1½ teaspoons freshly ground black pepper

½ teaspoon kosher salt

½ cup extra-virgin olive oil

2 pounds PEI mussels, cleaned, scrubbed, and debearded (see Note)

1½ cups white wine

4 slices crusty white bread, or 1 small French baguette, split in half

3 tablespoons unsalted butter

1 tablespoon freshly squeezed lime juice

2 teaspoons sugar

1 fresh Thai bird chili or jalapeño, sliced

1 cup fresh cilantro leaves (about ½ bunch)

Peel and discard the dry, papery outer layers of the lemongrass; trim off the top two-thirds of the stalk, which is also dry and papery, along with the very base and discard. Coarsely chop the pale, bendable inner core. You should have about 2 tablespoons chopped lemongrass. Mince 3 of the garlic cloves and add to the lemongrass. Add the cilantro stems and finely mince all three ingredients together.

Place in a small bowl and stir in the fish sauce, ½ teaspoon of the black pepper, and the salt. It will look like a rough pesto. Set aside. The lemongrass mixture can be made up to a day in advance and stored in an airtight container in the refrigerator.

In a wok or large flat-bottomed saucepan, heat the olive oil over medium heat for about 30 seconds.

continued
↓

Thinly slice 2 of the garlic cloves into and add to the oil. Add the lemongrass mixture and cook, stirring, until the garlic starts to brown, 1 to 2 minutes. Add the mussels and wine. Turn the heat up to high, cover the pot, and cook for 5 minutes.

While the mussels are cooking, toast the bread until golden brown and spread with 1 tablespoon of the butter. Split the remaining garlic clove in half and run the cut side over the buttered sides of the bread. Set aside.

Take a peek inside the pot. When the liquid is boiling and the mussels have opened, add the remaining 1 teaspoon black pepper, the lime juice, sugar, and chili. Stir in the remaining 2 tablespoons butter with a wooden spoon. Cook over high heat for 2 minutes to incorporate the butter. Fold in the cilantro leaves and discard any unopened mussels. Divide the mussels between two bowls and pour the broth over the mussels. Serve with the garlic toast.

Note: A trick on cleaning mussels is to cover them in cold water for about 20 minutes or so, and they will spit out any sand that might be inside of them.

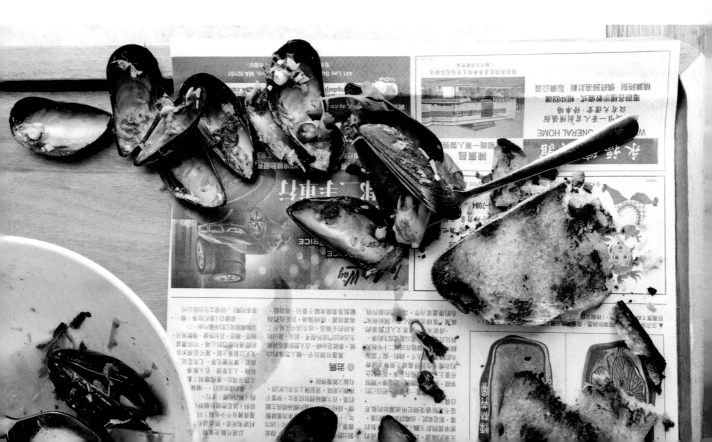

SPICY SILKY TOFU

SERVES 3 TO 4

I grew up eating tofu at almost every meal, and it's my personal mission to convert tofu haters into tofu lovers. I'm certain that no one really hates tofu. They are simply misinformed. One of our cookbook bibles, *Hot Sour Salty Sweet*, has a gorgeous recipe for Luscious Tofu with Chili Oil that inspired us to use tofu as a foil for spicy pork in chili oil. The hot, spicy, intense sauce works brilliantly against the creamy, mild tofu. Kimchi snuck its way in here as we were developing the recipe after we got takeout at a local Korean-Japanese restaurant; they had a pork, tofu, and kimchi stew that made us sweat and beg for more. No one who starts out saying they don't eat tofu ends up turning down this recipe. We love it and you will too.

3 tablespoons vegetable oil, such as canola

14 to 16 ounces firm tofu, cut into 1-inch cubes and patted dry with a paper towel

¾ pound ground pork

½ bunch scallions (4 or 5), cut into thirds

½ pound baby bok choy, trimmed and halved (if small) or quartered (if large)

½ cup coarsely chopped kimchi

3 tablespoons low-sodium soy sauce

1 tablespoon plus 1 teaspoon chili oil

½ teaspoon kosher salt

½ teaspoon freshly ground black pepper

¼ teaspoon red pepper flakes

½ cup fresh cilantro leaves (about ¼ bunch)

Perfect White Rice (page 315) or Perfect Brown Rice (page 316)

In a wok or large, heavy, flat-bottomed skillet, heat the vegetable oil over high heat until it is almost smoking, about 90 seconds. Add the tofu and lightly sear on all sides, 2 to 3 minutes. Remove from the wok with a slotted spoon and let drain on a paper towel–lined plate.

Add the pork and scallions to the wok, still over high heat. Cook, stirring with a wooden spoon, until the pork browns and the scallions soften, 2 to 3 minutes. Add the bok choy and toss for 2 minutes more. Add the kimchi and toss for 30 seconds more. Return the tofu to the wok and season with the soy sauce, chili oil, salt, black pepper, and red pepper flakes. Cook, stirring to evenly distribute the seasonings, for about 30 seconds. Add the cilantro leaves and give one final toss. Place in a large serving bowl and serve family-style with rice.

TRIPLE PORK MUSHU STIR-FRY

SERVES 4 TO 6

Chinese food is pretty much always eaten family-style. Plates come to the table when they're ready, and you dig in and make a meal out of a little bit of this and that and a lot of rice. Sharing, laughing, slurping, and really getting into your food is what it's all about. We love any dish we can put on our menu that encourages you to play with your food, such as mushu pork. Grab a tortilla, paint it with sauce, add scallions, fill with stir-fried pork and cabbage, and eat like an Asian burrito. In addition to pork loin, we add applewood-smoked bacon and Chinese sausage to our mushu to make it extra special and porky. Our specialty produce supplier, Jim, who has been selling to the top restaurants in Boston for more than two decades and is as food obsessed as we are, calls this one of his all-time favorite dishes in the city. Jim, now you can make it at home!

12 mushu pancakes

8 tablespoons vegetable oil, such as canola

1 pound pork loin, thinly sliced into 2 x ¼-inch strips

¾ cup coarsely diced Chinese sausage

2 large eggs, lightly whisked

10 large napa cabbage leaves, thinly sliced (about 5 cups)

6 slices thick-cut applewood-smoked bacon, cooked until crispy and chopped into small squares

1 recipe Mushu Sauce (recipe follows)

2 bunches scallions (16 to 18): 1 bunch thinly sliced into rounds, 1 bunch sliced on an angle into thin strips

1 cup fresh cilantro leaves (about ½ bunch)

If you have a steamer, set it up with water; if you have a bamboo steamer (see Note), set it up with about ½ inch of water in a large pot over the stove. Steam the pancakes until they are warm and set aside while you cook the pork. (If you don't have a steamer, you can microwave the pancakes for about 30 seconds for a similar and easy result.)

While the pancakes are steaming, in a wok or large, heavy, flat-bottomed skillet, heat 6 tablespoons of the vegetable oil over high heat until the oil starts to smoke, about 90 seconds. Add the pork strips and cook, stirring, until the strips turn white, 4 to 5 minutes. Remove the pork with a slotted spoon and transfer to a paper towel–lined plate. In the same oil, cook the Chinese sausage, stirring, for 20 seconds. Add the eggs and turn the heat down to medium, stirring continuously until they are lightly scrambled, about 1 minute. Remove the eggs and sausage from the wok and place in the bowl on top of the pork.

Wipe out the wok with a paper towel. Add the remaining 2 tablespoons vegetable oil and turn the heat back up to high. When the oil starts to shimmer, toss in the napa cabbage

and cook, stirring, to soften and slightly char the cabbage, 3 to 4 minutes. Add the bacon and toss. Return the pork, egg, and sausage back to the wok and toss to combine. Add the Mushu Sauce and toss to evenly mix in and reduce the sauce, 2 to 3 minutes. Add the scallion rounds and the cilantro and give one final stir. Divide among four to six serving plates and serve with the scallion strips and the warmed mushu pancakes.

Note: You can get bamboo steamers for a few dollars in many Asian markets; invest in a few and you'll start steaming everything you can get your hands on.

Mushu Sauce

MAKES ABOUT 1 CUP

2 teaspoons cornstarch

⅓ cup hoisin sauce

⅓ cup low-sodium soy sauce

¼ cup sugar

2 tablespoons unseasoned rice vinegar

1 teaspoon hot Sichuan bean paste

1 teaspoon toasted sesame oil

IN A SMALL bowl, whisk together the cornstarch and 1 tablespoon cold water until smooth to make a slurry (see Note). In a small saucepan, whisk together the hoisin sauce, soy sauce, sugar, vinegar, bean paste, and sesame oil and bring up to a boil. Whisk in the cornstarch slurry. Set aside. The Mushu Sauce can be made up to

1 week in advance and stored in an airtight container in the refrigerator.

Note: Don't use warm or hot water because it will cause the cornstarch to seize up into small lumps that won't dissolve no matter how hard you whisk, which is why you can't mix it directly into the sauce.

RAINBOW BEEF

SERVES 4

I wish we could say that this dish came from my mom or my grandmother in Taiwan, but the truth is that our opening chef, Alison, learned to make Rainbow Beef in culinary school in New York. We were tossing around ideas for our opening menu, and she recalled this dish being the one to introduce her to the joys of using hot Sichuan bean paste. I almost always have a jar of this pungent sauce in the fridge at home. It's salty, funky, and spicy and great in pretty much any stir-fry. Here we toss it with thin strips of beef and colorful peppers; served with a big mound of fluffy rice, it makes a quick and comforting dinner.

1 pound top round sirloin or London broil	¼ cup vegetable oil, such as canola	1 recipe Rainbow Sauce (recipe follows)
1 large red bell pepper	1 medium yellow onion, thinly sliced	1 cup fresh cilantro leaves (about ½ bunch)
1 large green bell pepper	1 bunch scallions (8 or 9), cut into thirds	Perfect White Rice (page 315) or Perfect Brown Rice (page 316)
1 large yellow bell pepper		

Trim the steak into ½-inch slices, making sure to slice against the grain (see Note). If the steak is thick, you can slice it through the middle, lengthwise first, so you are left with two thinner pieces. Then you can slice each thinner piece into thin slices, turning them into chopstick-friendly pieces. Set aside.

Trim the bell peppers by cutting off the tops and bottoms and slicing down one side so you can open up the pepper and lay it out flat. Trim off the ribs (the soft white parts that poke out of the pepper) and slice the pepper into

2 x ¼-inch matchstick-size pieces. Set aside.

In a wok or large, heavy, flat-bottomed skillet, heat the vegetable oil over high heat until it starts to smoke, about 90 seconds. Add the beef and stir quickly until the beef starts to lose some of its red color, about 1 minute. Remove the beef and transfer to a paper towel–lined plate.

Add the onions to the wok and cook, stirring continuously, for 1 minute. Add the scallions and bell peppers and toss a few times to combine the vegetables. Stir for 1 minute more. Add the beef, give the whole mixture a quick stir, and then add the Rainbow Sauce. Cook, stirring continuously, for 2 to 3 minutes to reduce the sauce. Add the cilantro at the last minute and divide the beef among four plates, or serve family-style on a platter, along with rice.

Note: Slicing steak against the grain means to slice against the natural meat fibers to break them up so the meat is easy to chew. Look to see how the meat would break apart if you tore it into pieces and slice it against this direction.

Rainbow Sauce

MAKES ABOUT 1 CUP

½ cup low-sodium soy sauce

¼ cup oyster sauce (we like Maekrua brand)

¼ cup hot Sichuan bean paste

2 tablespoons toasted sesame oil

1 tablespoon freshly ground black pepper

IN A MEDIUM saucepan, combine all the ingredients and bring to a boil over high heat, whisking continuously. The Rainbow Sauce can be made up to 2 weeks in advance and stored in an airtight container in the refrigerator.

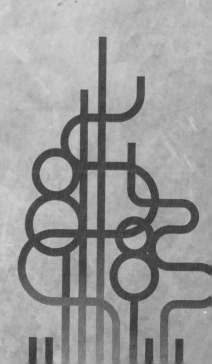

NOODLES

200 WILD MUSHROOM LO MEIN

202 GINGER-SCALLION CRAB AND
CRISPY VERMICELLI STIR-FRY

207 WOK-CHARRED UDON NOODLES WITH
CHICKEN AND BOK CHOY

210 SURF AND TURF BLACK PEPPER
SHANGHAI NOODLES

214 BACON AND CALAMARI PAD THAI

217 SICHUAN DAN DAN NOODLES

220 TWICE-COOKED LAMB BELLY STIR-FRY
WITH SLIPPERY CELLOPHANE NOODLES

223 BEEF AND CHINESE BROCCOLI
CHOW FUN

WILD MUSHROOM LO MEIN

SERVES 4 TO 6

This dish reminds me of Italy in the fall, with the earthy mushrooms, bright mint, and bitter chicory. Early on in my cooking career, I spent a year as the chef of a tiny *enoteca* in Modena in the Emilia-Romagna region where I learned to make pasta by hand. I practiced each day and created chalkboard specials with linguine, orecchiette, and fusilli featuring the best of the farmers' market that morning. Here I combine the rich flavors I fell in love with then with soft lo mein noodles, funky miso paste, and a splash of soy to create an umami bomb that is very Asian and decidedly Myers+Chang. It is rich and flavorful and works as a full meal or a side dish. When my sister and I were kids, we used to fight over the water chestnuts in our takeout lo mein, so I made sure to add a good amount to this dish so there are enough to go around. —*Chef Karen*

1 pound mixed wild mushrooms (cremini, shiitake, trumpet, yellowfoot, and hen of the woods are all great)

1 cup chopped fresh mint leaves (about 1 bunch)

¼ cup extra-virgin olive oil

1 tablespoon kosher salt

1 teaspoon freshly ground black pepper

1 pound thin dried lo mein wheat noodles

¼ cup vegetable oil, such as canola

2 small leeks, cleaned and thinly sliced into rounds

1 cup canned sliced water chestnuts, drained

¾ cup Fun Sauce (page 306)

2 tablespoons unsalted butter, at room temperature

1 teaspoon red miso paste

2 cups chopped radicchio (about ½ medium head)

2 cups hand-torn, bite-size pieces frisée (about ½ medium bunch)

<u>Trim any woody stems</u> off the mushrooms and slice them in half or quarters depending on their size so that they are roughly the size of a half dollar. In a large bowl, toss the mushrooms with the mint, olive oil, salt, and pepper.

<u>Heat a wok</u> or a large, heavy, flat-bottomed skillet over high heat. When the wok is hot, add the mushrooms and cook, stirring frequently, for 5 minutes. Turn off the heat and scrape the mushrooms out onto a plate to cool. The mushrooms can be made up to 3 days in advance and stored in an airtight container in the refrigerator.

In a large pot, bring about a gallon of water to a boil. Drop in the lo mein noodles and cook for 6 minutes. Drain into a colander. Rinse the noodles immediately with cold water to stop the cooking and keep them from sticking together.

In the same wok or skillet, heat the vegetable oil over high heat and swirl it around until it shimmers, about 1 minute. Add the leeks and toss until they become translucent and soft, about 1 minute. Add the water chestnuts and the mushrooms and stir, stir, stir. Add the noodles and Fun Sauce and toss to reduce the sauce and mix everything together, 2 minutes. In a small bowl, stir together the butter and the miso paste and add to the noodles along with 2 tablespoons water. Toss well to mix in thoroughly. Add the radicchio and frisée and toss a few more times. The lettuces should stay firm to give a contrasting bite to the stir-fry. Divide among four to six bowls and eat with chopsticks and an open heart.

GINGER-SCALLION CRAB AND CRISPY VERMICELLI STIR-FRY

SERVES 4

Given our proximity to Chinatown, we are always careful to let people know we are not a traditional Chinese restaurant. Rather, we define ourselves as being influenced and inspired by all Asian cuisines; if it tastes great and uses items from our ingredient larder, then we want to make it for you. This dish was inspired by the traditional Thai dish *mee krob*, crisp noodles tossed with a sweet-and-sour sauce with lots of lime or lemon. We were coming out of a particularly long and cold winter in Boston (compared to those short mild winters we see . . . not!), and we were starting to feel spring creep up ever so slowly. This light, bright stir-fry filled with pea tendrils and the first English peas of the season hinted at the warm sun and longer days that were just around the corner.

Picking crab is time- and labor-intensive, but if you have many hands, the task goes quickly. Sit around the table with your family or friends, pick crabs, and catch up on quality time. If you can't find pea tendrils, feel free to substitute spinach or any other mild green leafy vegetable.

3 cups vegetable oil, such as canola, for frying (see Note, page 92)	1 pound fresh or frozen shucked crab meat	½ teaspoon red pepper flakes
6 ounces thin dried uncooked rice vermicelli noodles	1 cup shelled English peas, or frozen green peas	¾ pound pea tendrils, trimmed, or baby spinach
1 medium garlic clove, sliced	1 recipe Scallion Sauce (recipe follows)	12 fresh Thai basil leaves
1 leek, cleaned and sliced into ¼-inch rings	2 tablespoons unsalted butter	12 fresh mint leaves
		1 lemon, cut into 4 wedges

Set out a platter lined with paper towels to catch the noodles after they fry. In a large deep saucepan, heat the vegetable oil to 350°F. Break up the noodles into four smaller bunches and drop them one at a time into the hot oil. Fry until they puff up and are airy and crispy; they fry up in a matter of seconds, so be prepared. Use tongs to break up and loosen the noodles as they fry. They will double in size and taste crunchy, not hard or raw. Transfer to the paper towel–lined platter to drain and then divide among four serving bowls. Carefully pour out the oil into a heat-safe container and set aside.

In a wok or large, heavy, flat-bottomed skillet, measure out 2 tablespoons of the noodle-frying oil and heat over high heat. Add the garlic and when the garlic dances, add the leeks and toss until they start to soften and char, 1 to 2 minutes. Add the crabmeat and English peas and give a quick stir. Add the Scallion Sauce and toss. Add the butter and red pepper flakes and swirl to emulsify. Finish with the pea greens, basil, and mint. Toss until the pea greens wilt, 1 to 2 minutes. Spoon the crab mixture evenly over the crispy vermicelli noodle nests. Squeeze a lemon wedge over each serving and enjoy the sunshine.

Scallion Sauce

MAKES ABOUT 1 CUP

¼ cup vegetable oil, such as canola

1 bunch scallions (8 or 9), white and green parts finely chopped (about 1 cup)

½ cup peeled and finely chopped fresh ginger (about 8-inch piece)

1 tablespoon kosher salt

½ cup Basic Chicken Stock (page 313) or canned low-sodium chicken broth

1 tablespoon soy sauce

1 tablespoon unseasoned rice vinegar

IN A MEDIUM saucepan, heat the vegetable oil over medium heat until it shimmers. Add the scallions and ginger and season with the salt. Cook for 1 minute, then add the stock, soy sauce, and vinegar. Turn the heat up to high and cook for 2 minutes. Turn off the heat and set aside. The Scallion Sauce can be made up to 3 days in advance and stored in an airtight container in the refrigerator.

WOK-CHARRED UDON NOODLES WITH CHICKEN AND BOK CHOY

SERVES 4

When Karen became our chef, one of our first meetings was to go through the menu item by item so she could learn the story behind each dish. This dish, I told her, was one of our top sellers and had been on our menu since opening day, and we would never ever take it off the menu. About four years into her tenure with us, she surprised us at one of our weekly tastings with a fabulous chicken-udon-vegetable dish called Hong Kong noodles that we inhaled. We all looked at one another and whispered, "Maybe we could take the udon off and put this one on . . . ?" Open the floodgates! The new dish was on our menu for all of about three weeks before we yanked it and reinstated this original udon dish. As scrumptious as the new udon was, our guests clamored for the standby. And for good reason. It's a classic dish that hits all the right notes: juicy tender chicken, crisp greens, bouncy udon noodles, and a spicy rich sauce to bind it all together. Pro tip: Keep your wok very hot while making the stir-fry or everything will steam instead of char. If you don't have a wok, use a large, heavy skillet. Cast iron is the closest way to get a high-heat char on this dish.

One 16-ounce package fresh udon noodles

2 cups plus 1 tablespoon vegetable oil, such as canola (See Note, page 92)

1 tablespoon cornstarch

1 tablespoon Shaoxing cooking wine (or substitute dry sherry or dry white wine)

1 large egg white

1 pound boneless, skinless chicken breasts, thinly sliced into 2 x ¼-inch strips

8 heads baby bok choy, root ends trimmed and leaves separated (about 1 pound)

½ medium yellow onion, thinly sliced

1 recipe Udon Sauce (recipe follows)

½ teaspoon red pepper flakes

In a large pot, bring about a gallon of water to a rolling boil. Add the udon noodles and cook for 6 minutes. Drain into a large bowl, rinse with cold water, and toss with 1 tablespoon of the vegetable oil to keep the noodles from sticking together. Set aside.

continued ↓

In a medium bowl, stir together the cornstarch, Shaoxing wine, and egg white. Add the chicken strips to the bowl and use your hands to coat the chicken thoroughly in the mixture. Marinate the chicken in an airtight container in the refrigerator for at least 30 minutes or up to 1 day.

Now we are going to velvet the chicken (see page 65). Place a few paper towels on a large plate and set aside. Heat the remaining 2 cups vegetable oil in a wok or deep skillet until the oil reaches 250°F. (Test the heat by placing a piece of chicken in the wok; it should float immediately.) Working in two or three batches, carefully add the chicken to the hot oil and cook until the strips just turn white, about 30 seconds, using a wooden spoon or chopsticks to gently separate them. (We are going to cook the chicken again, so do not worry if it does not seem cooked all the way through.) Quickly remove the chicken strips from the wok as soon as they turn white and drain on the paper towel–lined plate. Carefully pour out the oil into a heat-safe container and set aside.

Wipe out the hot wok with a paper towel and heat over high heat for 30 seconds. Measure out 2 tablespoons of the velveting oil and add it to the wok. Add the bok choy leaves and onions and stir continuously with a spatula or wooden spoon for about 3 minutes. Remove the vegetables from the wok and place on the same plate as the chicken.

Wipe out the wok again and heat over high heat for 30 seconds. Measure out another 2 tablespoons of the velveting oil and add to the wok. When the wok starts to smoke, add the reserved udon noodles. Don't stir them immediately; let them cook in the hot oil for at least 2 to 3 minutes to give them a nice char. When the noodles start to pick up some color, stir with a wooden spoon and then add the chicken and vegetables. Stir to combine everything and finish cooking the chicken, 2 to 3 minutes. Add the Udon Sauce and the red pepper flakes and stir to distribute the sauce and coat the noodles thoroughly and evenly. Divide among four plates and serve immediately.

Udon Sauce

MAKES ABOUT 1 CUP

1 tablespoon cornstarch

⅓ cup oyster sauce

¼ cup hoisin sauce

2 tablespoons Shaoxing cooking wine (or substitute dry sherry or dry white wine)

1½ tablespoons unseasoned rice vinegar

1½ tablespoons sambal oelek

2 teaspoons low-sodium soy sauce

1 teaspoon sugar

1 teaspoon toasted sesame oil

½ teaspoon fish sauce

IN A SMALL bowl, whisk together the cornstarch and 2 tablespoons cold water until smooth to make a slurry (see Note, page 195). In a medium saucepan, combine the oyster sauce, hoisin sauce, Shaoxing wine, vinegar, sambal oelek, soy sauce, sugar, sesame oil, and fish sauce. Whisk together and bring to a boil over medium-high heat. Add the cornstarch slurry and whisk continuously for 20 seconds, or until the sauce thickens. Remove from the heat. The Udon Sauce can be made up to a week in advance and stored in an airtight container in the refrigerator. Bring to room temperature before using. (It will be thick and gelatinous.)

SURF AND TURF BLACK PEPPER SHANGHAI NOODLES

SERVES 4 TO 6

Our dry cleaning bill at the restaurant is pretty minimal: the occasional chef's coat when we have an event to attend to or the stack of pashminas we offer to our patio guests on chilly early autumn evenings. But one fall, it spiked. We had added Black Pepper Peel-and-Eat Shrimp to the menu, and it was off-the-charts popular. It was also extraordinarily messy. The shrimp were coated with a sticky, buttery, peppery sauce that people couldn't get enough of. And invariably it ended up on pants, coats—everywhere. We had to pull it, but not before we figured out how to take the dish and refashion it into an easier-to-eat stir-fry. Our sous chef at the time, Kevin, worked tirelessly on this until he had captured the addictive spiciness of the shrimp and added it to Shanghai wheat noodles and steak to make a surf and turf hit. The bonus? No more sauce-stained blouses.

One important thing to remember when "wokking it out" is that all your ingredients need to be tight! Everything cut into strips and ready to go. Be a pro and get all the prep done ahead of time, and you will impress yourself at how well this comes together.

One 16-ounce bag fresh thick Shanghai-style noodles (we use Twin Marquis brand), or 12 ounces dried linguine noodles

1 medium red bell pepper

1 medium green bell pepper

1 medium yellow bell pepper

¼ cup vegetable oil, such as canola

1 pound top round sirloin or strip steak, thinly sliced into 2 x ¼-inch strips

1 medium yellow onion, thinly sliced

1 cup sliced garlic chives or regular fresh chives, cut into 2-inch pieces

1 cup bean sprouts

1 tablespoon peeled and finely chopped fresh ginger (about 1-inch knob)

1 medium garlic clove, thinly sliced

18 to 20 raw medium (36/40) shrimp, peeled and deveined

1 recipe Black Pepper Sauce (recipe follows)

2 tablespoons unsalted butter

1 cup fresh cilantro leaves (about ½ bunch)

1 cup chopped roasted unsalted peanuts

2 tablespoons freshly squeezed lime juice

In a large pot, bring about a gallon of water to a rolling boil. Add the noodles. If using fresh noodles, boil for 3 to 4 minutes; if using dried noodles, boil until the noodles are just past al dente and soft when you bite into them, about 10 minutes. Drain the noodles in a colander and immediately rinse with cold water to stop them from cooking further. Set aside.

Trim the bell peppers by cutting off the tops and bottoms and slicing down one side so you can open up the pepper and lay it out flat. Trim off the ribs (the soft white parts that poke out of the pepper) and thinly slice the peppers into 2 x ¼-inch matchstick-size pieces. Set aside.

Have a large plate ready near the stove. In a wok or large, heavy, flat-bottomed skillet, heat 2 tablespoons of the vegetable oil over high heat and swirl it around until it shimmers and starts to smoke, about 90 seconds. Add about half the beef and stir quickly until it starts to brown. Add about half the bell peppers, half the onions, half

the garlic chives, half the bean sprouts, half the ginger, and half the garlic. Toss until the vegetables start to yield and soften, about 4 minutes. Add half the shrimp and stir for 1 minute more.

Remove the beef, vegetables, and shrimp from the wok with a slotted spoon and place on the large plate. With the heat still on high, give the Black Pepper Sauce a vigorous stir to recombine all the ingredients, add half the sauce to the juices in the wok, and bring to a boil. Whisk in 1 tablespoon of the butter and swirl to emulsify the sauce. Add about half the cooked noodles and coat with the sauce. Return the beef, vegetables, and shrimp to the wok and toss for 2 minutes until the stir-fry is shiny and everything is well coated with sauce.

Divide among two or three bowls. Repeat the whole process with the remaining ingredients and divide among another two or three bowls. Sprinkle the bowls evenly with the cilantro leaves, peanuts, and lime juice. Serve immediately.

Black Pepper Sauce

MAKES ABOUT 1¼ CUPS

If you can't find the kecap manis, substitute 1½ teaspoons soy sauce and 1½ teaspoons dark brown sugar.

½ cup oyster sauce

1 tablespoon low-sodium soy sauce sauce

1 tablespoon Indonesian sweet soy sauce (kecap manis)

1 tablespoon freshly ground black pepper

2 tablespoons freshly squeezed lime juice

1 tablespoon sugar

1 tablespoon fish sauce

IN A MEDIUM saucepan, combine the oyster sauce, soy sauce, sweet soy sauce, black pepper, and ½ cup water and bring to a boil over medium-high heat. Turn down the heat to medium-low and whisk until the mixture thickens, 1 to 2 minutes. Turn off the heat; the sauce should be shiny and coat the back of a spoon. Whisk in the lime juice, sugar, and fish sauce. The Black Pepper Sauce can be made up to 2 weeks in advance and stored in an airtight container in the refrigerator.

BACON AND CALAMARI PAD THAI

SERVES 4 TO 6

I am always going to order pad thai. It doesn't matter if I am at the hottest new Southeast Asian spot where the chef is serving her modern interpretation of the dish, or the joint around the corner where I get takeout on Monday nights. Salty, sweet, funky—it is what I crave all the time. My sous chef, Ashley, knows how much I love it and created this fun, fresh version for a special at Myers+Chang. She replaces the standard chicken and shrimp with bacon and calamari, and it has fresh shredded cabbage and lots of lime on top. I love it. Every now and then, I ask her to bring it back so we can share it for lunch when we are working together. —*Chef Karen*

1 pound dried wide rice noodles or rice sticks (we like Twin Marquis brand)

¼ cup plus 1 tablespoon vegetable oil, such as canola

1 medium garlic clove, thinly sliced

One 1-inch knob fresh ginger, peeled and cut into matchstick-size pieces

1 small yellow onion, thinly sliced

2 large eggs, beaten

½ pound calamari rings and tentacles (about 1 cup)

1 recipe Pad Thai Sauce (recipe follows)

2 cups bean sprouts (about ½ pound)

1 cup fresh cilantro leaves (about ½ bunch)

1 bunch scallions (8 or 9), white and green parts thinly sliced (about 1 cup)

8 slices thick-cut bacon, cooked and chopped into ½-inch pieces

2 cups thinly sliced red cabbage (about ½ small head)

1 cup fresh Thai basil leaves (about ½ bunch)

1 cup roasted unsalted peanuts

1 lime, quartered or cut into 6 wedges

In a large pot, bring about a gallon of water to a boil. Drop in the noodles and cook for 2 minutes. Drain the noodles in a colander and toss with 1 tablespoon of the vegetable oil to keep them from sticking together. Set aside.

Heat a wok or large, heavy, flat-bottomed skillet over high heat and

add the remaining ¼ cup vegetable oil. Add the garlic and ginger and stir for 10 seconds. Add the onion and stir until soft and translucent, 2 to 3 minutes. Turn the heat down to medium and add the beaten eggs. Stir constantly to make "scrambled eggs." Once the egg is cooked, add the calamari and stir for about 10 seconds. As the calamari cooks,

continued
↓

the rings will firm up and the tentacles will curl. Add the Pad Thai Sauce and the noodles and stir and toss to evenly coat the noodles with the sauce. Let the sauce reduce a bit until glossy and the noodles start to absorb the sauce, about 1 minute. Throw in the bean sprouts, cilantro, scallions, and bacon and toss for 3 minutes. Divide among four to six bowls and garnish each with a neat pile of shredded cabbage, Thai basil, roasted peanuts, and a lime wedge. Instruct your guests to squeeze the lime over the top and mix all the toppings together before eating.

Pad Thai Sauce

MAKES ABOUT 1½ CUPS

½ cup tamarind concentrate

½ cup fish sauce

¼ cup honey

¼ cup unseasoned rice vinegar

3 medium garlic cloves, minced (about 1 tablespoon)

1 teaspoon red pepper flakes

2 tablespoons cornstarch

IN A SMALL saucepan, combine the tamarind concentrate, fish sauce, honey, vinegar, garlic, and red pepper flakes and bring up to a boil. In a small bowl, whisk together the cornstarch and 2 tablespoons cold water unti smooth to make a slurry (see Note, page 195). Whisk the slurry into the tamarind sauce and reduce the heat to low. Simmer, whisking continuously, for 2 minutes. As the cornstarch cooks, it will thicken up the sauce. Remove from the heat and let cool. The Pad Thai Sauce can be made up to 3 days in advance and stored in an airtight container in the refrigerator.

SICHUAN DAN DAN NOODLES

SERVES 6

This whole recipe calls for twenty-six ingredients—but don't let that scare you off. It will be worth the shopping time, we promise. You may find that you start using some of these ingredients in your everyday cooking. We hope so. We opened the restaurant with cold Taiwanese Dan Dan Noodle Salad (page 109), and our guests asked us why we didn't offer the more common hot Sichuan-style version. Sichuan Dan Dan Noodles are made with pork and lots of spices, and the best versions make your nose and tongue tingle with the buzz of Sichuan peppercorns. When Chef Karen joined us, she brought her Italian cooking expertise and essentially riffed off an Italian Bolognese sauce to make the best Sichuan-inspired pork ragu you'll ever eat. The pickled mustard greens are essential to the dish; they add a sharp, sour funk that makes the noodles sing.

One 16-ounce bag fresh thick Shanghai-style noodles (we use Twin Marquis brand), or 12 ounces dried linguine

1 recipe Pork Ragu (recipe follows)

1 tablespoon unsalted butter

2 cups bean sprouts (about ½ pound)

1 cup chopped pickled mustard greens (see Note)

1 cup fresh cilantro leaves (about ½ bunch)

4 or 5 scallions, white and green parts thinly sliced (about ½ cup)

In a large pot, bring about a gallon of water to a boil. Add the noodles. If using fresh noodles, boil for 3 to 4 minutes; if using dried noodles, boil for about 10 minutes, until they are just past al dente and soft when you bite into them. Drain the noodles in a colander and rinse with cold water to stop the cooking. Set aside.

In a wok or a large, heavy, flat-bottomed skillet, combine the Pork Ragu,

butter, and 3 tablespoons water and cook over medium-high heat, stirring frequently. Add the noodles and toss and cook until the noodles are hot and completely coated with sauce, about 1 minute. Add the bean sprouts, mustard greens, and cilantro and toss until they are incorporated. Divide among six bowls and garnish each with a heaping tablespoon of the scallions. Serve immediately.

Note: You can find pickled mustard greens in a jar or bag in the jarred food aisle of an Asian grocery store.

Pork Ragu

¾ teaspoon whole Sichuan peppercorns

2 tablespoons vegetable oil, such as canola

1 medium carrot, diced (about ½ cup)

1 teaspoon kosher salt

1 teaspoon freshly ground black pepper

1 small yellow onion, diced (about 1 cup)

1 medium celery stalk, diced (about ½ cup)

1 medium garlic clove, sliced

1 scallion, green part finely chopped (about 1 tablespoon)

1 teaspoon peeled and finely chopped fresh ginger (about ½-inch knob)

¼ cup soy sauce

1 tablespoon hot Sichuan bean paste

2 teaspoons black Chinkiang vinegar

½ teaspoon Chinese five-spice powder

¼ teaspoon ground ginger

1 cup Basic Chicken Stock (page 313) or canned low-sodium chicken broth

¼ cup tomato paste

2 teaspoons chili oil

½ pound ground pork

½ cup thinly sliced fresh shiitake or white button mushrooms (about 5)

IN A SMALL skillet, toast the Sichuan peppercorns over medium-low heat until they start to become fragrant and floral and pop a bit, 4 to 6 minutes. Use a spice grinder, coffee grinder, or mortar and pestle to grind them to a powder. Set aside.

IN A LARGE saucepan or Dutch oven, heat the vegetable oil over high heat until it shimmers, about 1 minute. Add the carrots and season with ½ teaspoon of the salt and ½ teaspoon of the black pepper. Cook the carrots, stirring frequently, until caramelized and golden, about 2 minutes. Add the onion and celery and cook, stirring occasionally, until they are all golden brown, about 8 minutes. Add the garlic, scallion, and ground ginger. Stir until all the vegetables are softened, another 2 minutes. Add the soy sauce, hot bean paste, vinegar, five-spice, and ginger. Stir frequently until the liquid has reduced slightly and the ragu base thickens, 2 to 3 minutes; this helps build all the flavors in the ragu. Add the stock, tomato paste, chili oil, ground Sichuan peppercorns, and ¼ cup water. Season with the remaining ½ teaspoon salt and ½ teaspoon black pepper and bring up to a simmer. Add the ground pork and use a wooden spoon to break up the pork into the liquid. Turn the heat down to maintain a very low simmer and cook, stirring frequently, for about 30 minutes. Add the sliced mushrooms and simmer over very low heat, stirring frequently, for another 15 to 20 minutes. The Pork Ragu can be made up to 3 days in advance and stored in an airtight container in the refrigerator.

TWICE-COOKED LAMB BELLY STIR-FRY WITH SLIPPERY CELLOPHANE NOODLES

SERVES 4

This is the first dish I put on the menu at Myers+Chang. I remember looking at the menu and being surprised that there was no lamb on it. I love the unctuous, intense flavor of lamb, and knowing that a lot of mutton is eaten in Mongolia and Northern China, I made sure to perfume this dish with the cumin and coriander that are so common in that region. People can be put off by the gaminess of lamb, so I turned it into "bacon" and crisped it in the wok. The first time I tasted it, I knew this would change many opinions about lamb. By pairing the lamb with the classic green beans and mustard, this dish turns a traditional pairing into a modern Myers+Chang star. I'm proud that it has become one of Christopher's all-time favorite dishes. —*Chef Karen*

1 pound long beans, cut into 2-inch pieces, or 1 pound green beans

16 ounces sweet potato starch or mung bean starch cellophane noodles

4 tablespoons vegetable oil, such as canola

1 recipe Lamb Belly Bacon (recipe follows)

2 medium leeks, cleaned and thinly sliced (about 2 cups)

8 large napa cabbage leaves, thinly sliced (about 4 cups)

¾ cup Fun Sauce (page 306)

4 tablespoons Chinese Hot Mustard Sauce (page 304)

1 cup fresh cilantro leaves (about ½ bunch), for garnish

2 tablespoons sesame seeds, for garnish

Fill a large bowl with ice water and set aside. Fill a large pot with water and bring to a rolling boil. Add the beans and cook them ever so slightly just until the color changes, about 2 minutes for long beans and about 1 minute for green beans. Quickly remove the beans from the water with a slotted spoon or dump the beans and water into a strainer. Plunge them into the ice water to stop the cooking. Remove the beans from the water and pat them dry with a paper towel. Set aside.

Fill the pot again with water and bring to a rolling boil. Drop in the cellophane noodles and turn off the heat. Let the noodles soak for 8 minutes, then drain. Toss them with 1 tablespoon of the vegetable oil to keep them from sticking together and set aside.

Heat a wok or large, heavy, flat-bottomed skillet over high heat and add the remaining 3 tablespoons vegetable oil. Add the cellophane noodles and cook for 1 minute, so they are warm and have a bit of char. Divide among four bowls.

In the same wok or skillet, lay half the sliced Lamb Belly Bacon as flat as possible and heat over medium heat until crispy, 2 to 3 minutes. Remove with a slotted spoon and place on a paper towel–lined plate.

Leaving the fat from the lamb in the wok, start the stir-fry. Add about half the leeks and toss until they are soft, about 1 minute. Add about half the long beans and cook for another 1 minute. Add about half the napa cabbage and cook, stirring frequently, for another 1 minute. Return the Lamb Belly Bacon to the wok, add about half the Fun Sauce, and toss for 1 minute. Add 2 tablespoons of the Chinese Hot Mustard Sauce to finish the dish, give it a final stir, and divide between two bowls.

Repeat with the remaining stir-fry ingredients to make two more bowls. Garnish all the bowls evenly with cilantro and sesame seeds and serve immediately.

Lamb Belly Bacon

1 whole cinnamon stick, broken

1 teaspoon cumin seeds

1 teaspoon coriander seeds

¼ teaspoon whole Sichuan peppercorns

¼ teaspoon red pepper flakes

2 pounds lamb belly (also known as boneless lamb breast)

¼ cup packed light brown sugar

½ cup plus 3 tablespoons black Chinkiang vinegar

2 celery stalks, cut into "smiles" about an inch wide

2 scallions, halved

1 small yellow onion, coarsely chopped

1 small carrot, cut into rounds

1 medium garlic clove, sliced

One 1-inch knob fresh ginger, peeled and cut into coins

1 cup Basic Chicken Stock (page 313) or canned low-sodium chicken broth

½ cup low-sodium soy sauce

IN A SMALL saucepan, toast the cinnamon stick, cumin, coriander, Sichuan peppercorns, and red pepper flakes over very low heat for 3 to 4 minutes, until you are able to smell the spices warming. Rub the toasted spices over the lamb belly. Sprinkle the brown sugar and 3 tablespoons of the vinegar over the lamb belly and rub that in as well. Refrigerate, covered, in a nonreactive container or a shallow glass baking dish for at least 24 hours or up to 3 days.

PREHEAT the oven to 350°F and place a rack in the center of the oven.

IN A LARGE braising dish or Dutch oven, scatter the celery, scallions, onions, carrots, garlic, and ginger evenly on the bottom. Lay the lamb belly directly on the vegetables and evenly pour the Chicken Stock, the remaining ½ cup of black vinegar, and soy sauce over the top. Cover the dish tightly with aluminum foil (or cover with the lid if using a Dutch oven). Place directly on the stove over high heat and heat for 5 minutes. Remove from the stove, place in the oven, and braise for 1½ hours. Remove from the oven and when cool enough to handle, remove the lamb belly from the dish and place on a rack on a baking sheet to cool. It will have shrunk to about half the original size and it will be very fragrant. Discard the vegetables and excess juice. Once cool, wrap the belly tightly in plastic wrap and place in the freezer until completely cool and firm, about 15 minutes or up to an hour. Use a sharp knife and slice the belly lengthwise into ¼-inch strips. (These should resemble bacon!) Slice the strips into thirds so that they will be easier to eat. The Lamb Belly Bacon can be made up to 4 days in advance and stored in an airtight container in the refrigerator.

BEEF AND CHINESE BROCCOLI CHOW FUN

SERVES 4

We were literally days away from opening Myers+Chang when our opening chef, Alison, and I took a look at the almost-finalized menu and realized we needed more noodle dishes. We had to come up with something fast and killer that would be easy to execute and train our cooks on. We started flipping through a bunch of takeout Chinese menus and both of us said at the same time: "Beef and broccoli!" But of course we wanted to do it our way. American broccoli was out; Chinese broccoli (*gai lan*) was in. Alison loaded up the sauce with lots of pepper because she loves steak au poivre, and she wanted our beef to be really peppery. She made it really gingery, too. Ginger is awesome with beef because it cuts through the richness and intensity of the meat. When you put them together, the beef gets a lift and tastes lighter and cleaner; the ginger doesn't end up tasting like ginger so much as it melts into the background. I love chewy, floppy flat rice noodles so we added those. You can find fresh rice noodles in the refrigerated section of Asian grocery stores near the produce. This has become one of our all-time most popular dishes.

10 ounces London broil or flank steak, thinly sliced in 2 x ¼-inch strips

1 recipe Fun Sauce (page 306), chilled

¼ teaspoon freshly ground black pepper

6 tablespoons vegetable oil, such as canola

1 pound gai lan (Chinese broccoli), regular broccoli, or rapini, trimmed and cut into 2-inch pieces

½ medium yellow onion, thinly sliced

1 pound fresh wide flat rice noodles, cut into 1-inch strips

2 scallions, white and green parts finely chopped (about ¼ cup)

1 tablespoon peeled and chopped fresh ginger (about 1-inch knob)

3 medium garlic cloves, minced (about 1 tablespoon)

Place the beef in a medium bowl. Measure out about half the Fun Sauce (don't use it warm or it will start to cook the beef) and add it to the beef along with the pepper, mixing to coat. (Keep the remaining Fun Sauce in an airtight container in the refrigerator.) Cover the bowl with plastic wrap and marinate in

continued
↓

the refrigerator for at least a few hours or up to overnight. If you do this before you start your day, you'll be ready to go by dinnertime.

In a wok or a large, heavy, flat-bottomed skillet, heat 2 tablespoons of the vegetable oil over high heat until it shimmers, about 1 minute. Add the gai lan and onions and use a wooden spoon or spatula to stir continuously for 3 minutes. Add about 3 tablespoons water to the hot wok and stirr for another 2 to 3 minutes. The water will turn to steam as it hits the hot wok and continue to cook the vegetables. Turn off the heat and transfer the vegetables to a plate or large bowl. Set aside.

Wipe out the wok with a paper towel. Heat the wok over high heat for 30 seconds. Add 2 tablespoons of the vegetable oil and coat the wok again. Remove the beef from the refrigerator, drain any sauce into a bowl, and set the sauce aside. Add the beef to the wok, stirring immediately and continuously, and stir-fry for 2 minutes. Turn off the

heat and transfer the meat to the same plate/bowl as the vegetables.

Wipe out the wok again with another paper towel and heat over high heat for 30 seconds. Add the remaining 2 tablespoons vegetable oil and coat the bottom of the wok. Add the rice noodles and stir to coat with oil. Add the scallions, ginger, garlic, and 2 tablespoons water and cook for 1 minute. Add the beef and vegetables and toss for 1 minute. Add the remaining Fun Sauce from the refrigerator along with the drained sauce from the beef and stir for 2 minutes. Shut off the heat, stir one final time, and divide among four bowls. Serve immediately.

VARIATION: To make vegetarian Tofu and Chinese Broccoli Chow Fun, omit the beef and substitute 14 to 16 ounces firm tofu, cut into 1-inch cubes. Do not marinate the tofu. Proceed with the stir-fry directions substituting the tofu cubes for the beef and add all the Fun Sauce at the end of the stir-fry as instructed.

RICE AND
GRAINS

228 GENMAI FRIED RICE

231 THE GREEN MONSTER

233 CURRIED DUCK AND WHEAT BERRIES

236 NASI GORENG (Indonesian Fried Rice)

240 KIMCHI QUINOA BOKKEUMBOP

GENMAI FRIED RICE

SERVES 4 TO 6

I learned how to properly fry rice from my mom, who learned from her mom. Our opening chef, Alison, says the first time she saw me make fried rice, it was a wow moment for her. Prior to our cooking together, she had only ever had sad greasy fried rice with dried-up bits of char sui pork and peas from a takeout joint. It was a few weeks before our opening, and Christopher, Alison, and I were menu planning at our house and starving. We had a fridge full of random ingredients for recipe testing. I toasted up a bit of leftover rice with some scallions until it was partly crispy, threw in some vegetables, and added a little egg, soy, and cilantro. It was fragrant, healthy, and delicious. We decided a version of that quick snack deserved a place on the menu. The Genmai uses brown rice, and we add the egg on top to better coat the rice with creamy yolk and make it richer. We throw in a handful of garlic to amp up the flavor. Toasted garlic + greens + rice = happiness.

Make the genmai in two batches to ensure there is enough room in your wok for everything to get nice and charred. (If you try to make this in one batch, everything will be a bit mushy. Trust me—we have tried.) Be sure to have all of your ingredients measured and ready to go so the cooking goes smoothly and you avoid chaos in the kitchen.

Two 8-inch-square sheets toasted nori (dried seaweed)

2 tablespoons white sesame seeds

1 cup vegetable oil, such as canola

4 to 5 scallions, white and green parts cut into 1-inch pieces

3 medium garlic cloves, thinly sliced

6 large napa cabbage leaves, thinly sliced (about 3 cups)

½ head broccoli, separated into florets (about 2 cups)

1 cup shelled edamame

5 cups cooked day-old brown rice

3 teaspoons kosher salt

2 teaspoons red pepper flakes

2 teaspoons freshly ground black pepper

2 teaspoons unsalted butter

4 to 6 large eggs

Preheat the oven to 350°F and place a rack in the center of the oven.

Toast the nori sheets and the sesame seeds on a baking sheet in the oven until they are lightly toasted, for 5 minutes. Remove from the oven, let cool, and crumble and tear the nori into small pieces. Place all into a small bowl. This is the garnish. The garnish can be made up to 1 month in advance and stored in an airtight container at room temperature.

In a wok or a large, heavy, flat-bottomed skillet, heat ¼ cup of the vegetable oil over high heat until it shimmers, about 1 minute. Add about half the chopped scallions and half the sliced garlic and stir for 20 seconds until they start to turn golden. Add about half the napa cabbage and half the broccoli florets and toss until the vegetables start to soften, 1 to 2 minutes. Add half the edamame and stir for another 2 minutes. Add 2½ cups of the rice,

1½ teaspoons of the salt, 1 teaspoon of the red pepper flakes, 1 teaspoon of the black pepper, and ¼ cup of the vegetable oil. Stir over high heat, breaking up any rice clumps, until the rice is charred, about 4 minutes, and turn off the heat. Divide the rice among two or three bowls and set aside. Clean out the wok and repeat with the other half of the ingredients. Divide the rice among two or three more bowls.

In a large skillet, melt the butter over medium-high heat. Carefully crack the eggs into the pan. Cook until the tops of the whites are set but the yolks are still runny, 2 to 3 minutes. If the butter starts to spit, it is a sign that the heat is too high. In this case, turn the heat down to low. When the sunny-side-up eggs are ready, remove the pan from the heat. Using a metal spatula, remove the eggs and garnish each bowl with a sunny-side-up egg. Evenly sprinkle with the nori garnish. Serve, instructing your guests to break up the egg and stir it well into the rice.

THE GREEN MONSTER

SERVES 6

When winter starts in Boston, we all tend to hunker down under the covers and eat meat loaf for five months (not that there is anything wrong with that). We wanted to create a stir-fry dish that satisfied our cravings for something rich and delicious but that is good for us as well in those dark months. The Green Monster is "everything green"—Brussels sprouts, kale, peas, edamame, spinach, leeks, avocado, cucumber, or whatever is awesome and in season—wok charred with chewy, nutty farro, and rich pistachio-lemongrass pesto. Garnished with avocado and pickled cucumbers, this dish is bright and rich with lots of texture and flavor. When we described the dish to our staff, Rich, our bar-back, said, "Can we call it the Green Monster??!!" and we did. Named after the iconic wall at Fenway park, the Green Monster is a home run. —*Chef Karen*

2 teaspoons kosher salt

2 cups uncooked farro

¼ cup extra-virgin olive oil

1 medium leek, cleaned and thinly sliced (about 1 cup)

6 to 8 Brussels sprouts, thinly sliced (about ¾ cup)

1 cup baby spinach

½ cup shelled edamame beans

½ cup fresh or frozen green peas

½ cup Lemongrass Pesto (recipe follows)

½ teaspoon freshly ground black pepper

1 medium avocado, diced

1 English cucumber, diced

Bring a large pot of water to a rolling boil and add 1 teaspoon of the salt. Add the farro and cook, stirring occasionally, until the farro is cooked through and pleasantly chewy when you bite into it, 10 to 12 minutes. Drain in a colander and set aside.

In a wok or a large, heavy, flat-bottomed skillet, heat the olive oil over high heat until it shimmers, about 1 minute. Add

the leeks and Brussels sprouts and stir with a wooden spoon until they are soft, about 1 minute. Add the cooked farro and toast in the pan, stirring continuously until it all starts to smell nutty and delicious, 3 to 5 minutes. Add the spinach, edamame, and peas and toss until the spinach wilts and the edamame and peas are warmed through, 2 to 3 minutes. Reduce the heat to medium and add the pesto. Stir

continued
↓

to blend the pesto into the farro and vegetables. Season with the remaining 1 teaspoon salt and the pepper. Divide among six serving bowls and top each bowl evenly with diced avocado and cucumber. Serve immediately.

Pro tip: You can eat this cold like a pasta salad the next day!

Lemongrass Pesto

MAKES 1 CUP

You can easily halve this recipe to make exactly what you need for the Green Monster, but it is so flavorful and bright you will want to have some extra to stir into soups and salads. Plus, it keeps well in the freezer.

2 stalks lemongrass

2 medium garlic cloves, peeled

2 teaspoons kosher salt

¼ cup extra-virgin olive oil

½ cup shelled raw pistachios

1 makrut lime leaf, thinly sliced, or grated zest of 1 lime

1 cup fresh Thai basil leaves (10 to 12 stems)

PEEL and discard the dry, papery outer layers of the lemongrass; trim off the top two-thirds of the stalk, which is also dry and papery, along with the very base and discard. Coarsely chop the bottom third (5 to 6 inches) of the stalk, where the stem is pale and bendable. You should have about ¼ cup chopped lemongrass. Set aside.

PLACE the garlic and salt in a food processor. With the processor running, drizzle in about half the olive oil and process into a paste. Add the pistachios and pulse until they become crumbly. Add the chopped lemongrass and lime leaf and pulse to combine. Add the remaining olive oil and 2 tablespoons water and process until the pesto is nice and creamy. Add another 1 tablespoon water if needed to loosen the pesto. Finally, add the basil, pulsing to incorporate all the ingredients together fully. Be careful not to overprocess or the pesto will be brown and yucky. The Lemongrass Pesto can be made up to 3 days in advance and stored in an airtight container in the refrigerator or in the freezer for up to 2 months. Use in soups and mix into pasta salads for a hit of fresh lemony nutty flavor.

CURRIED DUCK AND WHEAT BERRIES

SERVES 4

Chef Karen makes an amazing red curry paste. One of the most popular ways in which she serves it is simply with wokked cauliflower. I wanted to find another way to show it off, she wanted to pizzazz up our menu with some underutilized ingredients, and the happy result is this marvelous stir-fry. Duck is really rich and fatty, so we braise it until the fat renders out and makes the meat tender and juicy. Wheat berries are addictively chewy and marry perfectly with the curry. Each component is easily prepared in advance, so when you want to make dinner, all this comes together really quickly.

1 cup uncooked wheat berries, farro, or barley

¼ cup vegetable oil, such as canola

2 medium carrots, coarsely shredded on the large holes of a box grater or using the grating blade of a food processor (about 1 cup)

½ cup coarsely diced Chinese sausage

1 recipe Braised Duck (recipe follows)

1 recipe Curry Sauce (recipe follows)

1 cup fresh Thai basil leaves

In a large pot, bring about a gallon of water up to a boil. When the water is at a rolling boil, add the wheat berries and stir. Turn the heat down to medium so the water stays at a simmer and cook the wheat berries for about 1 hour and 10 minutes. When they are done, they will be soft but still have a bit of bite to them. Drain the wheat berries and set aside. The wheat berries can be made up to 3 days in advance and stored in an airtight container in the refrigerator.

In a wok or large, heavy, flat-bottomed skillet, heat the vegetable oil over high heat until it shimmers, about 1 minute. Add the shredded carrots and Chinese sausage and stir-fry for 1 minute. Add the Braised Duck and wheat berries and stir until everything is hot and nicely charred, for 4 minutes. Add the Curry Sauce and stir until the sauce is well mixed into the berries and duck, about 1 minute. Toss in the basil, give a quick stir, divide among four bowls, and serve immediately.

Braised Duck

MAKES ABOUT 2 CUPS SHREDDED MEAT

5 Long Island duck legs, or
3 Moulard duck legs, or 3 to
4 bone-in, skin-on chicken legs
with thigh attached (about
2 pounds)

2 tablespoons kosher salt

1 teaspoon freshly ground
black pepper

2 medium yellow onions, diced

3 medium carrots, diced

One 2-inch knob fresh ginger,
unpeeled, thinly sliced into coins

5 whole star anise

2 dried bay leaves

Two 12-ounce cans dark beer
(porters and stout work well)

PREHEAT the oven to 400°F and place a rack in the center of the oven.

SEASON the duck legs with the salt and pepper, rubbing in the seasoning well with your hands. In a large braising dish or Dutch oven, combine the onions, carrots, ginger, star anise, and bay leaf. Place the duck legs on top of the vegetables and pour 2 cups water and the beer over the duck legs. The braising liquid should only come halfway up the duck legs so that the skin gets crispy. Make sure the pan is large enough that the duck legs do not crowd the pan too much so the fat will render out evenly. Place in the oven, uncovered, and braise for 2 hours. When the legs are done, the meat will easily pull away from the bones. Remove the pan from the oven. When cool enough to handle, remove the duck legs from the pan and let them cool a bit until they are just warm. Separate the meat, skin, and any remaining fat from the bone. Shred the meat and discard the skin, bones, and braising vegetables. The Braised Duck can be made up to 3 days in advance and stored in an airtight container in the refrigerator.

Curry Sauce

MAKES ABOUT 1 CUP

½ cup coconut milk

¼ cup Homemade Red Curry Paste (page 307) or jarred Thai red curry paste (we like Roland brand)

1 lime, quartered

3 tablespoons sugar

1 tablespoon Madras curry powder

1 tablespoon freshly squeezed lime juice

1 tablespoon kosher salt

2 teaspoons fish sauce

1 medium garlic clove, sliced

IN A MEDIUM saucepan, whisk together the coconut milk and the curry paste over medium heat until combined. Add the lime wedges, sugar, curry powder, lime juice, salt, fish sauce, and garlic. Cook, stirring continuously with a wooden spoon or rubber spatula, for about 10 minutes. The curry will be nice and thick and a beautiful yellow color.

Set aside to cool. Pluck out the lime wedges. The Curry Sauce can be made up to 3 days in advance and stored in an airtight container in the refrigerator.

NASI GORENG (INDONESIAN FRIED RICE)

SERVES 4

Nasi goreng is a very pretty and exotic Indonesian name . . . for fried rice! It's hard to say if this is the best or most popular or most craveable dish at Myers+Chang, but it is in the top three for sure. This dish has breadth and funk and umami in spades. It's seductively spicy and with pineapple acting as a foil to the spice, the flavor opens up and you just can't get enough of it. It is a real labor of love to make because you start with making a flavor base called *terasi* that stinks to high heaven and will smell up your kitchen for at least a day. We were worried that not having an 800°F wok would compromise this dish in a home kitchen. But all the testers for this dish—Valerie, Anne, Sandy, Tracey, and Lisa—were unanimous in calling it a knockout.

Make the *nasi* in two batches to ensure there is enough room in your wok for everything to get nice and charred. (If you try to make this in one batch, everything will be a bit mushy. Trust me—we have tried.) Be sure you have all of your ingredients measured and ready to go so the cooking goes smoothly and you avoid chaos in the kitchen.

½ cup vegetable oil, such as canola

12 ounces ground pork

24 medium (36/40 count) raw shrimp, peeled and deveined

1½ cups small-diced pineapple

1 bunch scallions (8 or 9), white and green parts chopped (about 1 cup)

4 teaspoons Terasi (recipe follows)

3 teaspoons kosher salt

5 cups day-old cooked white rice

1 cup fresh Thai basil leaves

2 teaspoons unsalted butter

4 large eggs

4 tablespoons sambal oelek

4 tablespoons thinly sliced scallions, white and green parts, for garnish

1 recipe Crispy Shallots (page 312)

In a wok or a large, heavy, flat-bottomed skillet, heat ¼ cup of the vegetable oil over high heat until it shimmers, about 1 minute. Add half the pork and cook, stirring continuously with a spatula or wooden spoon, until the pork starts to brown. Be careful not to splash the oil! Add half the shrimp to the wok and stir until they start to turn pink, 1 to 2 minutes. Add half

continued
↓

the pineapple and half the chopped scallions and cook over high heat, stirring, for 2 minutes. Add 2 teaspoons of the terasi and 1½ teaspoons of the salt. Stir vigorously to make sure everything in the wok is seasoned well. Add half the rice and break up any clumps with the spatula. Add about half the basil and toss for 2 minutes. Divide the rice between two bowls. Clean out the wok and repeat with the second half of the ingredients. Divide the rice between two additional bowls.

In a large skillet, melt the butter over medium-high heat. Carefully crack the eggs into the pan. Cook until the tops

of the whites are set but the yolks are still runny, 2 to 3 minutes. If the butter starts to spit, it is a sign the heat level is too high. In this case, turn the heat down to low. Remove the pan from the heat and use a spatula to remove each egg from the pan.

Garnish each bowl with a sunny-side-up egg, 1 tablespoon of the sambal, 1 tablespoon of the sliced scallions, and 1 tablespoon of the shallots. When you eat this, break the egg up and mix it into the rice with the sambal, shallots, and scallions. There is nothing quite like it!

Terasi

MAKES 3 TO 4 TABLESPOONS

Terasi is the smoky condiment that gives nasi goreng all its character and charm. It smells very, very, very strong while it cooks. It will be smoky and spicy! Do not be alarmed—this is supposed to happen. Open your windows and turn your fan on high. We only make this before we open for service and only after we have opened up all the doors of the restaurant and loading dock area to get as much fresh air as possible into the kitchen.

2 teaspoons vegetable oil, such as canola

1 medium shallot, thinly sliced into rings

3 scallions, white and green parts thinly sliced

3 medium garlic cloves, sliced

4 fresh Thai bird chilies, sliced, including seeds

1½ teaspoons shrimp paste

PREHEAT the oven to 200°F and place a rack in the center of the oven. Go open all your windows—even if it's the dead of winter.

IN A SMALL skillet, heat the vegetable oil over medium heat. When the oil starts to shimmer, add the shallot, scallions, garlic, and chilies. Fry, stirring continuously, until everything is very, very dark, almost black and burnt looking, 15 to 20 minutes. Add the shrimp paste and fry for 1 minute until it caramelizes. Spread out onto a small baking sheet and toast in the oven for 20 to 25 minutes. Remove from the oven and let cool. It should be crunchy and not wet. You should be able to crumble it between your fingers. Place it in a coffee or spice grinder and pulse until it is like a coarse powder or chop it up with a knife. The Terasi can be made up to a week in advance and stored in an airtight container at room temperature.

KIMCHI QUINOA BOKKEUMBAP

SERVES 4 TO 6

I love to replace the rice in regular fried rice dishes with different whole grains and cereals. Here we take a traditional *bokkeumbap*, a Korean kimchi fried rice, and replace the rice with quinoa. Quinoa is considered a "superfood," which means it's full of fiber and protein and easy to digest. The quinoa is stir-fried with hearty bulgogi (Korean barbecue beef) and kimchi, another food with superpowers. This dish is satisfying and healthy at the same time. Throw a fried egg on it, and it's perfect for breakfast. —*Chef Karen*

½ cup low-sodium soy sauce

¼ cup sambal oelek

¼ cup toasted sesame oil

¼ cup sugar

¼ cup white sesame seeds

5 medium garlic cloves, smashed

1 pound shaved steak (see Note)

1 cup shelled raw unsalted pistachios

1 tablespoon extra-virgin olive oil

1 teaspoon Korean chili powder

½ teaspoon kosher salt

1½ cups uncooked red or white quinoa (we like the red for color, but they are the same)

½ cup vegetable oil, such as canola

½ head broccoli, cut into florets (about 2 cups)

2 medium carrots, coarsely shredded on the large holes of a box grater or using the grating blade of a food processor (about 1 cup)

1 cup shelled edamame beans

1½ cups finely chopped kimchi

2 tablespoons soy sauce

In a medium bowl, combine the low-sodium soy sauce, sambal oelek, sesame oil, sugar, sesame seeds, and garlic. Place the steak in a flat shallow pan and pour the soy mixture over it, turning to coat. Cover with plastic wrap and marinate in the refrigerator overnight. (Or throw the marinade and steak together before you start your day, and it will do its job pretty well by dinner.)

Preheat the oven to 325°F and place a rack in the center of the oven.

In a small bowl, toss together the pistachios, olive oil, Korean chili powder, and salt. Place on a baking sheet and toast in the oven until the pistachios are lightly toasted, 8 to 10 minutes. Remove the nuts from the oven and pour them into a small bowl. (Don't leave them on the baking sheet or they may continue to cook and then burn.) The pistachios can be made up to 1 week in advance and stored in an airtight container at room temperature.

240

In a large pot, bring about a gallon of water up to a boil. Add the quinoa and stir until it starts to float and the water comes to a boil. Cook for 10 minutes, then drain through a fine strainer. Let cool. The quinoa can be made up to 3 days in advance and stored in an airtight container in the refrigerator.

In a wok or large, heavy, flat-bottomed skillet, heat ¼ cup of the vegetable oil over high heat until it shimmers, about 1 minute. Drain and discard any excess marinade from the steak (it's okay if the sesame seeds remain) and add the steak to the wok. Stir quickly for 3 minutes. Remove the steak and set aside. Wipe out the wok. Add the remaining ¼ cup vegetable oil and heat until it shimmers. Add the broccoli and stir over high heat for 1 minute. Add the cooked quinoa and stir for another 2 minutes. Add the carrots and edamame and toss for another 2 minutes. Add the steak, kimchi, and soy sauce, and stir all together for another 5 minutes. Divide among four to six bowls and top evenly with the roasted pistachios.

Note: Ask your butcher for this, or slice 1 pound flank or skirt steak very thinly with a sharp knife.

SIDES

244 HAKKA EGGPLANT

247 SWEET-AND-SOUR BRUSSELS SPROUTS

249 CHINESE WATER SPINACH WITH
FERMENTED TOFU

250 RED MISO–GLAZED CARROTS

252 GINGER-SCALLION BOK CHOY

254 KUNG PAO CHICKPEAS

256 SICHUAN ZUCCHINI AND
SUMMER SQUASH

259 SMASHED FINGERLING POTATOES WITH
THAI CHILI JAM (Nam Prik Pao)

262 LONG BEANS AMANDINE WITH
HOMEMADE XO BROWN BUTTER

HAKKA EGGPLANT

SERVES 6 AS A SIDE

Papa Chang eats everything. I mean *everything*. It's a running joke at the end of any meal that if there is additional food at the table, we put it in front of him and little by little he somehow manages to demolish it. He's got a healthy metabolism and a complete appreciation of all food. He calls himself an equal opportunity eater. Before we opened Myers+Chang, Christopher and I often had dinner at a local Taiwanese restaurant called Taiwan Cafe around the corner from our house. We took my parents there, and my dad went nuts over this traditional dish. He typically leaves ordering up to us because he's happy with pretty much anything, but at Taiwan Cafe he always makes sure we order this. So I knew we had to create a version for our restaurant. The important ingredients are the thick dark soy sauce which adds a licorice-y taste and tons of Thai basil, which lends a different dose of the anise kick that is already present in the dish. The technique of cooking it first with a decent amount of oil before tossing it in the wok and cooking it again is pretty indulgent and what makes it special.

3 pounds medium Japanese eggplant (9 or 10 eggplants)

½ cup extra-virgin olive oil

1½ teaspoons kosher salt

1 teaspoon freshly ground black pepper

1 recipe Hakka Sauce (recipe follows)

1½ teaspoons red pepper flakes (use less if you are not a big spice fan)

1 cup fresh Thai basil leaves (about ½ bunch)

Preheat the oven to 350°F and place a rack in the center of the oven.

With a sharp knife, remove the stem from each eggplant and split the eggplant top to tail into two long pieces. Lay the flat sides down on a cutting board and cut each piece into 1-inch chunks. Do the same to the rest of the eggplant. Place all the eggplant in a large bowl. In a small bowl, whisk together the olive oil, salt, black pepper, and ½ cup water. Pour the mixture over the eggplant and toss very well with your hands. Transfer the eggplant to a large baking dish or a rimmed baking sheet (pouring any remaining liquid over the eggplant) and bake for 15 to

continued
↓

20 minutes. When it is done, the eggplant will be soft and you should be able to prick it easily with a fork. Remove from the oven and set aside.

Place a wok or large, heavy, flat-bottomed skillet on the stove and heat over high heat. Add the eggplant (no need to add oil) directly to the wok and stir for 1 minute. Add the Hakka Sauce and red pepper flakes. Toss and cook until the eggplant is well coated with sauce, 3 to 4 minutes. Add the basil and give the whole thing a good toss. Place in a large bowl and serve family-style.

Hakka Sauce

MAKES ABOUT 1¼ CUPS

½ cup hoisin sauce

½ cup low-sodium soy sauce

3 tablespoons Shaoxing cooking wine (or substitute dry sherry or dry white wine)

2 tablespoons unseasoned rice vinegar

1 teaspoon black Chinkiang vinegar

1 teaspoon thick soy sauce

1 teaspoon sugar

1 tablespoon cornstarch

IN A MEDIUM saucepan, whisk together the hoisin sauce, low-sodium soy sauce, Shaoxing wine, rice vinegar, black vinegar, thick soy sauce, and sugar and bring to a boil over medium-high heat.

IN A SMALL bowl, whisk together the cornstarch and 2 tablespoons cold water until smooth to make a slurry (see Note, page 195). Whisk the slurry into the pot. Simmer, while whisking, until it is shiny and coats the back of a spoon, 1 to 2 minutes. Remove from the heat. The Hakka Sauce can be made up to 1 week in advance and stored in an airtight container in the refrigerator.

SWEET-AND-SOUR BRUSSELS SPROUTS

SERVES 4 AS A SIDE

These Brussels sprouts have a crazy cult following at M+C.
It might be the most popular dish I have ever created. I got the idea while wedding-dress shopping in New York City with my mom and sister. We were all getting hangry and stopped into the closest bar to grab a snack. When the Brussels sprouts arrived fried, I knew they were onto something. Even my mom, who hates Brussels sprouts, ate them. When Brussels sprouts go out of season, we make this dish with broccoli or romanesco; however, nothing but those sweet little sprouts draws as much commotion. Every spring when we pull them off the menu to make way for more seasonal dishes, we inevitably field dozens of frantic queries about why they are no longer available. Be sure to plan ahead when making these. The pickled shallots need to be started at least four hours in advance. —*Chef Karen*

¼ cup sugar

¼ cup unseasoned rice vinegar

2 teaspoons red pepper flakes

6 tablespoons vegetable oil, such as canola

1 pound Brussels sprouts, trimmed and halved

2 teaspoons kosher salt

1 teaspoon freshly ground black pepper

1 recipe Pickled Shallots (page 312), drained

½ cup coarsely chopped fresh mint (about ¼ bunch)

In a small saucepan, combine the sugar, vinegar, and red pepper flakes and bring to a boil. Reduce the heat and simmer the sauce until it is the consistency of thin maple syrup, 3 to 4 minutes. Set aside. This is the hot and sweet sauce, and it provides the sweet component to the dish. It can be made up to 3 weeks in advance and stored in an airtight container in the refrigerator.

In a wok or a large, heavy, flat-bottomed skillet, heat the vegetable oil over high heat until it shimmers, about 1 minute. Throw the Brussels sprouts in the pan and sprinkle with the salt and pepper. The oil will splatter, so be careful! Don't stir for 2 to 3 minutes, allowing the Brussels sprouts to fry and char on the bottom. (You may even want to walk away so you are not

continued
↓

tempted to fuss with them.) Once they are charred on the bottom, start stirring them every minute or so until they soak up all the oil, about 3 minutes more. Add about ¼ cup water to the wok and turn down the heat to medium. Let the water evaporate, shaking the wok and moving around the Brussels sprouts so they can finish cooking. Taste one to see if it is cooked; you want it to be cooked through but still have some bite. Transfer the Brussels sprouts to a large bowl and toss with the hot and sweet sauce, shallots, and fresh mint. Serve immediately.

CHINESE WATER SPINACH WITH FERMENTED TOFU

SERVES 3 TO 4

This is one of those simple home-style sides that almost seemed too basic to offer at the restaurant or print in a cookbook. But unless you grew up eating Taiwanese food, you may not have ever tasted *furu*-style cooked vegetables. To explain the flavor and make it more familiar, we liken it to the salty, funky taste of miso paste. Fermented tofu is also called tofu cheese or preserved tofu "*furu*," and the tofu cubes come packed in brine in jars. Look for it in the jarred condiment section of Asian grocery stores. It's most often used as a condiment for rice and porridge, or stir-fried into greens as we do here. Water spinach is called *kong xin cai*, "hollow heart vegetable" in Chinese, because its stems are hollow. Substitute any leafy green if you can't find water spinach, although the crunch of the stems goes especially well with the bold sauce. Be sure to serve this dish with rice. Like most Chinese food, it's not meant to be eaten alone, but instead as part of a bigger meal and always, always with rice.

1 pound Chinese water spinach, regular spinach, Swiss chard, or other leafy green

1 tablespoon plus 2 teaspoons fermented bean curd

3 tablespoons vegetable oil, such as canola

3 medium garlic cloves, thinly sliced

Perfect White Rice (page 315) or Perfect Brown Rice (page 316)

Trim off the tough stems of the water spinach and cut into 2-inch pieces. Wash very thoroughly and drain well in a colander. Place the fermented tofu in a small bowl and whisk in about 1 tablespoon water to loosen the tofu into a saucelike consistency. Add more water if needed to loosen the sauce. Set aside.

In a wok or a large, heavy, flat-bottomed skillet, heat the vegetable oil over high heat until it shimmers, about 1 minute. Add the garlic and stir for 30 seconds. When the garlic turns golden brown, add the water spinach and keep tossing and stirring until the water spinach is wilted and softened, 3 to 4 minutes. Stir in the fermented tofu sauce and toss until all the water spinach is well covered in sauce. Transfer to a serving platter and serve family-style with rice.

RED MISO-GLAZED CARROTS

SERVES 3 TO 4

These carrots are like grown-up candy. We whip rich red miso into soft butter and throw heaping spoonfuls of it into carrots that are charred in the wok. It's our version of the classic French side dish of butter-glazed carrots. You can find miso in the refrigerated section in Asian grocery stores. It is made from fermented soybeans and is salty and unctuous and the epitome of umami.

1½ pounds carrots, sliced on an angle about ¼ inch thick

3 tablespoons unsalted butter, at room temperature

1 tablespoon red miso paste

1½ teaspoons light brown sugar

1 teaspoon freshly squeezed lemon juice

2 tablespoons vegetable oil, such as canola

1 bunch scallions (8 or 9), green parts only, thinly sliced (about ½ cup)

Bring a large pot of water to a boil and blanch the carrots until they are no longer raw but still a bit crisp, 2 to 3 minutes. Drain the carrots and set aside.

In a medium bowl, combine the butter, miso paste, brown sugar, and lemon juice and beat vigorously with a wooden spoon until it is fluffy like cake frosting.

In a wok or a large, heavy, flat-bottomed skillet, heat the vegetable oil over high heat until it shimmers, about 1 minute. Add the carrots to the wok and shake to even them out. Let them char a bit without moving them, 2 to 3 minutes. Shake the pan and add the miso butter and about two-thirds of the scallions. Toss the carrots in the butter until the butter has melted and starts to brown and the carrots are cooked through, 3 to 4 minutes. Remove from the heat, place on a large serving plate, and garnish with the remaining scallions.

GINGER-SCALLION BOK CHOY

SERVES 4

When I am not eating at Myers+Chang, I often stop at the neighborhood Chinese BBQ shop on my way home from work to pick up takeout. The glistening chickens, ducks, roasted pork, and ribs hanging in the window are hard to pass by, and they make for a quick, easy meal. I always request an extra side of what I call "green sauce" to mix into the rice and meat. It's a salty, gingery scallion mixture that goes great with pretty much everything. I asked Chef if she could replicate this for us.

She picked up the method of pouring hot oil over the ginger and the scallions, which releases their flavor and fragrance, from David Chang's *Momofuku* cookbook. Bok choy is a workhorse in our kitchen, and cooking it with this sauce spikes it with terrific flavor while still letting the crunchy vegetable shine. To turn this vegetable side into a meal, add some cooked chicken or stir-fried tofu.

1 recipe Ginger-Scallion Sauce
(recipe follows)

2 pounds baby bok choy,
trimmed and halved (if small) or
quartered (if large)

In a wok or a large, heavy, flat-bottomed skillet, heat 2 tablespoons of the Ginger-Scallion Sauce over high heat for 30 seconds. Add the bok choy and 2 tablespoons water. Toss the bok choy until it just begins to wilt, about 1 minute. Add the remainder of the Ginger-Scallion Sauce and cook, stirring continuously, until the bok choy leaves are cooked and the white parts are still crunchy, 3 to 5 minutes. Divide among four plates or serve on a large platter family-style.

252

Ginger-Scallion Sauce

MAKES ABOUT 1½ CUPS

2 bunches scallions (16 to 18), green and white parts thinly sliced (about 2 cups)

¼ cup peeled and finely chopped fresh ginger (about 4-inch knob)

1 tablespoon kosher salt

⅓ cup vegetable oil, such as canola

¼ cup tamari

¼ cup unseasoned rice vinegar

IN A MEDIUM glass or stainless steel bowl, stir together the scallions, ginger, and salt. Let sit for 20 minutes to bring out the flavor and moisture. In a small saucepan, heat the vegetable oil over medium-high heat until it shimmers. Pour the oil over the ginger-scallion mixture. Let sit for 10 minutes to cool. Whisk in the tamari and vinegar. The Ginger-Scallion Sauce can be made up to 3 days in advance and stored in an airtight container in the refrigerator.

KUNG PAO CHICKPEAS

SERVES 3 TO 4

You can find kung pao chicken on pretty much every Chinese takeout menu. It's a staple for anyone who orders late-night Chinese food, and it is one of those Americanized Chinese dishes that everyone I know grew up with—except me. Chef and Christopher were trading stories about their favorite takeout dishes and raving about the addictiveness of a super-spicy, garlicky, well-made kung pao dish. I was skeptical that it could really be that tasty, but then Chef came up with a brilliant idea to make me a vegan version with chickpeas. I was sold. It's crunchy and earthy, and I love it over a bowl of hot fluffy rice.

One 15-ounce can chickpeas, drained, rinsed, and shaken dry

2 teaspoons cornstarch

4 tablespoons vegetable oil, such as canola

8 dried red Thai chili peppers

3 scallions, white and green parts cut into 1-inch pieces

1 small red onion, cut into 1-inch cubes

1 red pepper, cut into 1-inch squares

1 green pepper, cut into 1-inch squares

1 large celery stalk, cut into 1-inch pieces

½ cup unsalted roasted peanuts or cashews

One 5-ounce can whole water chestnuts, drained and quartered

1 recipe Kung Pao Sauce (recipe follows)

In a small bowl, toss the chickpeas with the cornstarch. In a wok or a large, heavy, flat-bottomed skillet, heat 2 tablespoons of the vegetable oil over high heat until it shimmers, about 1 minute. Add the cornstarch-coated chickpeas and stir until the chickpeas start to color, 4 to 6 minutes. Some of the cornstarch may stick to the pan, but it will melt off when the rest of the ingredients are added. Remove the chickpeas from the wok.

Add the remaining 2 tablespoons oil to the wok and heat over high heat until it shimmers, about 1 minute. Add the chilies and stir until they start to blacken, about 1 minute. Add the scallions, onion, bell peppers, celery, peanuts, and water chestnuts and cook, stirring frequently, until the vegetables start to soften but are still somewhat crisp, 2 to 3 minutes. Return the chickpeas to the wok, add the Kung Pao Sauce, stir to combine, and bring to a boil, 2 to 3 minutes. Place in a large serving bowl.

Kung Pao Sauce

MAKES ABOUT ¾ CUP

⅓ cup low-sodium soy sauce

3 tablespoons unseasoned rice vinegar

2 tablespoons sambal oelek

1 tablespoon minced garlic (about 3 medium cloves)

1 tablespoon peeled and finely chopped fresh ginger (about 1-inch knob)

1 tablespoon sugar

2 teaspoons cornstarch

IN A SMALL BOWL, whisk together all the ingredients with 2 tablespoons water. The Kung Pao Sauce can be made up to 1 week in advance and stored in an airtight container in the refrigerator.

SICHUAN ZUCCHINI AND SUMMER SQUASH

SERVES 4 TO 6

When Chef Karen was introduced to the basic Sichuan ingredient hot bean paste, it opened up her culinary world to a whole new flavor profile. The bean paste plus Sichuan peppercorns create a sauce that is spicy and irresistible. I loved seeing how she took an ingredient traditionally used to flavor meat and tofu and noodles and added it to vegetables and salads. This simple preparation with summer squash and zucchini is salty, hot, sweet, and crunchy. The trick is to get your wok rip-roaring hot so the zucchini and squash char and don't get soggy. The whole process takes under five minutes and will have you practicing your lightning-speed wok moves.

1 tablespoon unsalted butter

½ cup pepitas (pumpkin seeds) or sunflower seeds

1 tablespoon sugar

1 teaspoon kosher salt

½ teaspoon freshly ground black pepper

3 medium yellow summer squash (1 to 1½ pounds)

3 medium zucchini (1 to 1½ pounds)

¼ cup vegetable oil, such as canola

1 recipe Sichuan Dressing (recipe follows)

12 fresh Thai basil leaves, torn by hand into small pieces

In a small skillet, melt the butter over medium heat. Add the pepitas and toss frequently until they start to heat and you hear popping sound (like popped corn). Sprinkle the sugar, salt, and pepper evenly over the pepitas and toss over medium-high heat until they are golden in color and well coated with the salt-sugar mixture, about 8 minutes. Spread them out on a plate to cool. The pepitas can be made up to 2 weeks

in advance and stored in an airtight container at room temperature.

Using a sharp chef's knife, slice the yellow squash and zucchini into ¼-inch-thick rounds. Set aside.

In a wok or a large, heavy, flat-bottomed skillet, heat the vegetable oil over high heat until it shimmers, about 1 minute. Carefully add the squash and

256

zucchini and toss until they start to char, 6 to 8 minutes. Keep tossing and after another minute, add the Sichuan Dressing. Toss to coat well and add the Thai basil leaves. Toss once more to wilt the basil leaves. Divide among four to six bowls and garnish evenly with the pepitas.

Sichuan Dressing

MAKES ABOUT 1¼ CUPS

2 tablespoons whole Sichuan peppercorns

2 medium garlic cloves

1 large shallot, coarsely chopped

¼ cup hot Sichuan bean paste

1 tablespoon red pepper flakes

¼ cup vegetable oil, such as canola

¼ cup chili oil

¼ cup unseasoned rice vinegar

IN A SMALL skillet over medium-low heat, toast the Sichuan peppercorns until they start to become fragrant and floral and pop a bit, 4 to 6 minutes. Transfer to a blender and add the garlic, shallot, hot bean paste, and red pepper flakes and blend for 2 to 3 minutes, scraping down the sides of the blender jar occasionally, until the mixture is broken down pretty well. With the blender running on low speed, add the vegetable oil, chili oil, and vinegar and blend until it all comes together. The Sichuan Dressing can be made up to 2 weeks in advance and stored in an airtight container in the refrigerator.

人生隨遇

SMASHED FINGERLING POTATOES WITH THAI CHILI JAM (NAM PRIK PAO)

SERVES 4

Sometimes when I create new dishes, it's really just about what I'm craving at the time. In this case, one of our servers, Kimya, kept asking me for mashed potatoes for staff meal, and it made me realize we had never had potatoes on our menu. This is a Thai version of the Spanish tapas dish *patatas bravas*, rich with *nam prik pao* and lots of smoke from the wok. If you don't have a wok, sear these in a hot skillet and they will be just as delicious. The starchy fingerling potatoes are the ideal vehicle for the heat of the jam. If you want to eat them cold, add a spoonful of Greek yogurt and serve as potato salad. *Nam prik pao* is an essential Thai condiment. It is roasted chili peppers cooked to a jammy consistency, intensely flavored but not in your face, a little oceany and a little smoky. If you want to buy it, it often comes in a jar labeled "chili paste in oil." But trust me, the work is worth it on this one! —*Chef Karen*

2 pounds fingerling potatoes

2 tablespoons extra-virgin olive oil

1 tablespoon plus 1 teaspoon kosher salt

2 sprigs fresh rosemary

2 sprigs fresh thyme

5 medium garlic cloves

¼ cup vegetable oil, such as canola

1 recipe Nam Prik Pao (recipe follows)

½ cup fresh cilantro leaves (about ¼ bunch)

Place the potatoes in a large stockpot and fill with cold water. Add the olive oil, 1 tablespoon of the salt, the rosemary, thyme, and garlic. Bring to a boil over high heat. When the water is boiling, turn the heat down to medium and simmer for about 15 minutes, or until the potatoes are just cooked through. Drain the potatoes, discard the herb sprigs and garlic cloves, and gently "smash" or flatten the potatoes with the heel of your palm, which is easy to do when they are nice and warm. Smashing them ensures that you are

continued ↓

SMASHED
FINGERLING
POTATOES
WITH THAI
CHILI JAM
(NAM PRIK
PAO)

———

continued

getting lots of surface area to crisp up when you fry them. The potatoes can be cooked and smashed up to 3 days in advance and stored in an airtight container in the refrigerator.

In a wok or a large, heavy, flat-bottomed skillet, heat about half the vegetable oil over high heat until it shimmers, about 1 minute. Carefully add about half the smashed potatoes and sprinkle with ½ teaspoon of the salt. Cook, without stirring, until the potatoes get crispy, 3 to 4 minutes, and then give them a toss. Repeat three or four times until the potatoes are crispy and charred throughout. Remove the potatoes from the wok and repeat with the remaining vegetable oil, potatoes, and salt. Return the first batch of cooked potatoes to the wok and add the nam prik pao, tossing until the potatoes are well coated. Serve on a large platter, family-style, garnished with the cilantro.

Nam Prik Pao

MAKES 3 TO 4 TABLESPOONS

¼ cup dried red Thai chili peppers (about 12)

2 tablespoons vegetable oil, such as canola

2 medium shallots, thinly sliced

One 1-inch knob fresh ginger, peeled and thinly sliced

2 medium garlic cloves, thinly sliced

2 teaspoons tamarind concentrate

1 teaspoon shrimp paste

1 teaspoon fish sauce

1 teaspoon light brown sugar

1 teaspoon unseasoned rice vinegar

PLACE the dried chilies in a small bowl and pour boiling water over them to cover. Cover tightly with a piece of plastic wrap and steam for 10 minutes. Remove the chilies from the water; they should be nice and soft. Coarsely chop them, seeds and all, and set aside. In a small skillet, heat the vegetable oil over medium-high heat. When the oil starts to shimmer, add the chopped chilies and fry for 2 minutes, stirring frequently. Add the shallots, ginger, and garlic and turn the heat down to low. Gently cook for 3 minutes, until the shallots and garlic are translucent. Add the tamarind concentrate, shrimp paste, fish sauce, brown sugar, and vinegar. Cook gently for 6 to 8 minutes, stirring, until the mixture becomes thick and jammy. Turn off the heat and let cool for 10 minutes. Turn the mixture out onto a cutting board and finely chop the whole mess with a sharp chef's knife until it is sticky and pasty, or run it through a food processor. The Nam Prik Pao can be made up to 1 week in advance and stored in an airtight container in the refrigerator.

LONG BEANS AMANDINE WITH HOMEMADE XO BROWN BUTTER

SERVES 4 TO 6

I love to update an American holiday classic. My mom used to open a frozen box of Birds Eye green beans and toasted almonds for special occasions, and my sister, Jenny, and I would go crazy for it. Here I dress up Chinese long beans with XO sauce that I mellow with a bit of nutty, fragrant brown butter. XO might be the funkiest, most flavorful condiment there is. It is a spicy seafood sauce from Hong Kong made with handfuls of dried seafood cooked down with sweet cured ham, garlic, ginger, and chilies. It keeps indefinitely in the freezer, so make a lot of it, store it in small containers, and use it all through the year to amp up vegetables, soups, and sauces. Try to find Chinese long beans, which are chewy and hearty and come in long bundles 1 to 2 feet long. They look like green beans on steroids. Look for beans that are flexible but not limp and have no dark spots. If you can't find long beans, substitute fresh green beans (not frozen or canned), and cook them a little less than you would normally to retain some crunch and chew.

—*Chef Karen*

2 tablespoons unsalted butter

2 tablespoons sugar

2 teaspoons kosher salt

1 cup sliced natural almonds

1 pound long beans, cut into thirds, or 1 pound green beans

¼ cup XO Brown Butter (recipe follows)

½ teaspoon freshly ground black pepper

In a large, heavy, flat-bottomed skillet, heat the butter over medium-high heat until it starts to foam. Add the sugar and 1½ teaspoons of the salt and swirl around. Add the almonds and toss, toss, toss until they are well coated, the butter from the pan starts to disappear, and the almonds become a brittle, 2 to 3 minutes.

Don't walk away from the pan or the nuts might burn. Transfer to a plate, spread in an even layer, and let cool. Wipe the pan clean with a paper towel.

Fill a large bowl with ice water and set aside. Fill a large pot with water and bring to a rolling boil. Add the beans and cook them ever so slightly just until the color changes, about 2 minutes for long beans and about 1 minute for green beans. Quickly remove the beans from the water with a slotted spoon or dump the beans and water into a strainer. Plunge them into the ice water to stop the cooking. Remove the beans from the water and pat them dry with a paper towel. Set aside.

Heat the skillet over medium-high heat and add the XO Brown Butter. Throw in the long beans and stir with a wooden spoon until the beans are soft and well covered with the brown butter, about 3 minutes. Season with the remaining ½ teaspoon salt and the pepper. Transfer the beans to a large platter, top with the sliced almonds, and serve family-style.

XO Brown Butter

MAKES ABOUT ⅔ CUP

½ cup (1 stick) unsalted butter

2 tablespoons dried shrimp

2 tablespoons dried scallops
(substitute more dried shrimp
if you can't find dried scallops)

½ cup vegetable oil, such
as canola

2 tablespoons chopped
Chinese sausage

One ¼-inch knob ginger,
coarsely chopped

1 dried red Thai chili pepper

1 medium garlic clove, sliced

2 tablespoons unseasoned
rice vinegar

¾ teaspoon kosher salt

MELT the butter in a small saucepan over medium heat until the solids fall to the bottom and the remaining butter turns a beautiful golden-brown hazelnut color, 8 to 10 minutes. Strain the butter from the solids into a heat-resistant bowl using a fine sieve and let sit until cool to the touch. The brown butter can be made up to a week in advance and stored in an airtight container in the refrigerator. Bring to room temperature before using.

PLACE the shrimp and scallops in a bowl and cover them with hot water to rehydrate. Let them sit for at least 1 hour. Drain, pat dry, and set aside.

IN A WOK or a medium, heavy, flat-bottomed skillet, heat the oil over medium-high heat until it shimmers. Add the rehydrated shrimp and scallops to the pan.

When they start to turn golden brown, about 1 minute, add the Chinese sausage, ginger, and whole dried chili. After another minute, add the garlic. When the mixture is a golden brown color, carefully strain out the oil and discard. Transfer the mixture to a food processor and process until finely chopped. (If you don't have a food processor, use a sharp chef's knife and chop as finely as possible, then transfer to a medium bowl. Work those knife skills!) Add the brown butter, vinegar, salt, and 1 tablespoon water to the food processor or the bowl. Pulse or whisk together until nicely blended. Some chunks are okay and it will be grainy. The XO Brown Butter can be made up to 3 weeks ahead and stored in an airtight container in the refrigerator or in the freezer for up to 2 months.

FAMILY MEAL

268 CHINESE CAESAR SALAD

270 ASIAN PIZZA

271 CONGEE WITH NIRVANA CHICKEN AND
     SCALLION SALSA

274 ASHLEY'S LEMONY GARLICKY
     CHICKEN SOUP

277 MOM'S STIR-FRIED SHRIMP AND
     SCALLIONS

278 SWEET SOY BACON AND EGG BANH MI

CHINESE CAESAR SALAD

SERVES 4

I love Caesar salad, and I order it wherever I can. I love it with anchovies or without. I love it with big croutons or small croutons. Most of all, I love to make it for staff meal. It is so out of our wheelhouse that the staff gets really excited for it. This version uses only ingredients that we have in house, mimicking the Parmigiano-Reggiano with garlic and tofu. It's a terrific side dish for dinner, or add roasted chicken for a full meal. The dressing makes about twice what you need for four servings, so use any remaining dressing for another salad, as a zesty sandwich spread, or as dip for crudités. *Bao* are also called *mantou*, and they are the Chinese Wonder bread. They are slightly sweet, very white, and found in bags in the frozen section of any Asian supermarket. *—Chef Karen*

¼ teaspoon whole Sichuan peppercorns

4 bao (also called mantou) or 4 slices soft white Italian bread

¼ cup extra-virgin olive oil

½ teaspoon kosher salt

4 small romaine lettuce hearts (about 1 pound)

½ bunch scallions (4 or 5), white and green parts finely chopped (about ½ cup)

1 cup fresh cilantro leaves (about ½ bunch)

½ cup Caesar Dressing (recipe follows)

Preheat the oven to 350°F and place a rack in the center of the oven.

In a small skillet, toast the Sichuan peppercorns over medium-low heat until they start to become fragrant and floral and pop a bit, 4 to 6 minutes. Use a spice grinder to grind them to a powder.Cut the bao into ½-inch cubes and toss them in a medium bowl with the olive oil, salt, and ground Sichuan peppercorns. Place on a baking sheet and bake until golden brown and crispy, 15 to 20 minutes. The bao croutons can be made up to 3 days in advance and stored in an airtight container at room temperature.

Cut or tear the romaine lettuce into bite-size pieces and put in a large bowl along with the scallions. Coarsely chop the fresh cilantro and add to the romaine. Toss well with the Caesar Dressing, using your hands to get the salad really well dressed. Serve family-style in a large bowl with the bao croutons on top, or divide among four bowls and top each evenly with the croutons.

Caesar Dressing

MAKES ABOUT 1 CUP

¾ teaspoon whole Sichuan peppercorns

2 ounces silky tofu (about ¼ cup)

4 medium garlic cloves

2 large egg yolks

2 tablespoons unseasoned rice vinegar

1 tablespoon Dijon mustard

1½ teaspoons kosher salt

1 teaspoon freshly ground black pepper

½ cup vegetable oil, such as canola

IN A SMALL skillet, toast the Sichuan peppercorns over medium-low heat until they start to become fragrant and floral and pop a bit, 4 to 6 minutes. Use a spice grinder, coffee grinder, or mortar and pestle to grind them to a powder.

IN A BLENDER, combine the tofu, garlic, egg yolks, vinegar, Dijon mustard, salt, black pepper, and ground Sichuan peppercorns until smooth. With the blender running on medium speed, slowly drizzle in the vegetable oil until the dressing emulsifies and comes together. The Caesar Dressing can be made up to 4 days in advance and stored in an airtight container in the refrigerator. Whisk vigorously before using.

ASIAN PIZZA

SERVES 4 TO 6

We get dough for our sloppy joe rolls and our scallion pancakes from our sister restaurant, Flour Bakery. Every now and then we leave the dough out too long in our warm kitchen, and they overproof and sort of meld together, becoming impossible to work with. I secretly love when this happens because it means I am making "pizza" for staff meal. I stretch out the dough, brush it with sesame oil and sprinkle with scallions, and top it with tomato-ginger jam and whatever we have from the stations on the line. On lucky days, we have feta cheese in house for a special treat for everyone, including me. —*Chef Karen*

2 cups chopped rapini (about 1 medium bunch) or regular broccoli

¼ cup fine or coarse cornmeal

1 pound pizza dough (see Note)

¼ cup toasted sesame oil

6 scallions, green parts only thinly sliced

1 cup Chili-Tomato Jam (page 310)

1 cup fresh Thai basil leaves (about ½ bunch)

1 cup crumbled feta cheese

Bring a large pot of water to a rolling boil, add the rapini, and cook for 2 minutes. Drain the rapini and set aside. The rapini can be blanched up to 2 days in advance and stored in an airtight container in the refrigerator.

Leave the pizza dough out at room temperature until it gets puffy, airy, and soft and is easy to work with, 2 to 3 hours in a warm room.

When ready to bake, preheat the oven to 450°F and place a rack in the center of the oven.

Sprinkle a handful of cornmeal over the bottom of a 13 x 18-inch baking pan and gently stretch and roll out the pizza dough to fill the pan. Brush the dough with the sesame oil and sprinkle evenly with the scallions. Bake for 6 minutes.

Pull the crust out of the oven and spread evenly with the Chili-Tomato Jam. Sprinkle the rapini, basil, and feta evenly over the jam. Bake until the cheese is melty and the dough is golden brown, 15 to 18 minutes. Serve immediately.

Note: Purchase pizza dough at your local pizza shop or bakery.

CONGEE WITH NIRVANA CHICKEN AND SCALLION SALSA

SERVES 4 TO 6

I grew up eating congee, or rice porridge. It's what Mom made for me whenever I was sick or cranky. In Chinese, it is known as *xifan*, which translates to "watery rice." Bland and soft, the congee gets its flavor from whatever you decide to put into it. My mom would fry a can of tuna fish (don't knock it till you've tried it) until crispy and spoon a few generous heaps into my congee. At the restaurant we have found it to be the perfect foil for one of our most flavorful dishes, Nirvana Chicken. I learned to make a soy-braised chicken from my sister-in-law, Kathy, and the first time I made it for Christopher, he said, "This is nirvana." The name stuck. You'll make it for this congee first and soon find other excuses to make it and have on hand all the time like we do.

½ bunch scallions (4 or 5), white and green parts thinly sliced (about ½ cup)

5 tablespoons soy sauce

¼ cup unseasoned rice vinegar

¼ teaspoon kosher salt

1 fresh Thai bird chili, sliced

1 recipe Nirvana Chicken (recipe follows)

2 cups Basic Chicken Stock (page 313) or canned low-sodium chicken broth

1 cup uncooked short-grain white rice

1 recipe Crispy Shallots (page 312)

In a small bowl, combine the scallions, soy sauce, vinegar, salt, and Thai bird chili. Stir well and set aside.

Remove the Nirvana Chicken from the braising liquid and set aside. (If you made the chicken in advance, rewarm the chicken and braising liquid until it warms up but is still cool enough to handle.) Strain the braising liquid through a fine-mesh strainer into a

medium saucepan to remove the solids. Spoon off the fat that rises to the top. Add the stock and 4 cups water to the strained liquid and bring it up to a simmer. Add the rice and simmer gently over low heat for 1 hour, stirring frequently so that the rice never sticks to the bottom. The congee should be loose and soupy, so if it starts to thicken, add more water to loosen it up.

continued
↓

CONGEE WITH
NIRVANA
CHICKEN AND
SCALLION
SALSA

—————

continued

While the rice is cooking, pull the meat off the bones of the chicken thighs. We think the skin is delicious and like to crisp it up in the oven, chop it, and add it to the congee, but you can discard it if you don't like it. When the rice is super soft and almost melty and the liquid has thickened, 60 to 90 minutes, add the pulled meat (and chicken skin!) to the pot and stir. Divide the congee among four to six bowls, top evenly with the scallion salsa and the shallots, and eat for breakfast, lunch, or dinner.

Nirvana Chicken

1 pound bone-in, skin-on chicken thighs

2 teaspoons kosher salt

½ teaspoon freshly ground black pepper

1 tablespoon vegetable oil, such as canola

2 cups Basic Chicken Stock (page 313) or canned low-sodium chicken broth

½ bunch scallions (4 or 5), white and green parts thinly sliced (about ½ cup)

One 2-inch knob fresh ginger, peeled and thinly sliced into coins

3 medium garlic cloves, sliced

½ cup low-sodium soy sauce

¼ cup michiu (rice cooking wine), dry sherry, or dry white wine

2 teaspoons sambal oelek

2 whole star anise

PREHEAT the oven to 350°F and place a rack in the center of the oven.

LAY OUT the chicken thighs and season both sides well with the salt and pepper. In a large braising dish or Dutch oven, heat the vegetable oil over high heat until it shimmers. Using tongs or very carefully by hand, add the chicken thighs to the barising dish and sear, turning them from time to time until they are deep golden brown, about 5 minutes. Remove the chicken, drain off the fat in the dish, and turn the heat down to medium. Add the stock to the dish and, using a wooden spoon, scrape up all the browned bits from the bottom of the dish. Add the scallions, ginger, garlic, soy sauce, michiu, sambal oelek, star anise, and ¼ cup water and bring to a simmer. Return the chicken thighs to the dish, skin-side up. Cover the dish tightly with aluminum foil (or cover with the lid if using a Dutch oven). Place in the oven and cook for 2 hours, or until the chicken is falling off the bone. The Nirvana Chicken can be made up to 3 days in advance and stored in the braising liquid in an airtight container in the refrigerator. The fat will solidify in the refrigerator; remove it before using.

ASHLEY'S LEMONY GARLICKY CHICKEN SOUP

SERVES 4 TO 6

Our sous chef, Ashley, made Filipino chicken *tinola* for a lunchtime special one week, and we couldn't stop eating it. It is garlicky, aromatic, and satisfying yet light. One bite of this and you will never open a can of soup again. *Tinola* is a soup served as an entrée in the Philippines. Traditionally, this dish is cooked with chicken, green papaya wedges, and leaves of chili peppers in broth flavored by ginger, onions, garlic, and fish sauce. When Ashley was growing up, her grandmother would make *tinola* for all her grandchildren because it is filling and easily feeds a large group of people. Grandma Lujares loves that her granddaughter now makes it for the Myers+Chang family.

6 ounces dried thin rice vermicelli noodles

3 tablespoons vegetable oil, such as canola

1 stalk lemongrass

3 quarts Basic Chicken Stock (page 313) or canned low-sodium chicken broth

12 medium garlic cloves, lightly smashed

One 3-inch knob fresh ginger, peeled and sliced thinly

¾ cup freshly squeezed lemon juice (from about 4 lemons)

2 tablespoons fish sauce

1 tablespoon plus 1 teaspoon kosher salt

1½ teaspoons freshly ground black pepper

1 small chayote, summer squash, or zucchini (about 1 pound)

1 tablespoon peeled and finely chopped fresh ginger (about 1-inch knob)

8 ounces boneless, skinless chicken breast, sliced into small strips about ¼ inch thick

1 bunch watercress

1 lime, cut into 4 to 6 wedges

Place the noodles in a large bowl and pour boiling water over them to cover. Help them soften by pushing them into the water with a wooden spoon or rubber spatula. Let sit for 4 minutes until soft, then drain. Toss with 1 tablespoon of the vegetable oil to keep the noodles from sticking together,

cover with plastic wrap to keep the noodles from drying out, and set aside.

Peel and discard the dry, papery outer layers of the lemongrass; trim off the top two-thirds of the stalk, which is also dry and papery, and the very base and discard. Finely chop the bottom third (5 to 6 inches) of the stalk, where the stem is pale and bendable. You should have about 2 tablespoons chopped lemongrass.

In a large stockpot, combine the lemongrass, stock, 10 of the garlic cloves, the sliced ginger, lemon juice, and fish sauce and bring to a boil over high heat. Reduce the heat to medium and simmer for about 30 minutes. You should be able to smell the broth from the next room. Season with 1 tablespoon of the salt and 1 teaspoon of the pepper and taste for seasoning. Does it need perking up? Add a pinch more salt. You know what you like and what tastes good. Trust yourself; we do! When it is delicious, strain it through a fine-mesh sieve, discard the solids, and place the broth back on the stove over low heat to keep it hot.

Using a vegetable peeler or a small sharp knife, peel the chayote. Cut it in half, use a spoon to dig out the pit, and cut each half in half. Slice each piece into ¼-inch half-moons and set aside. (If you don't have chayote, trim the squash, halve them lengthwise, slice the halves into ½-inch half-moons, and set aside.)

In a wok or a large, heavy, flat-bottomed skillet, heat the remaining 2 tablespoons vegetable oil over high heat until it shimmers, about 1 minute. Thinly slice the remaining 2 garlic cloves and add with the chopped ginger to the wok. Stir with a wooden spoon until golden, 1 to 2 minutes. Season the chicken breast strips with the remaining 1 teaspoon salt and ½ teaspoon pepper and add to the wok. Stir until the chicken turns opaque and starts to caramelize, 3 to 4 minutes. Add the chayote and about 2 cups of the chicken broth and simmer until the vegetables start to soften (you want them to have a little texture) and the chicken finishes cooking, 3 to 4 minutes.

Divide the rice vermicelli noodles among four to six deep soup bowls. Divide the chicken among the bowls. Tear up the watercress and add a handful to each bowl, using up all the watercress. Ladle the remaining broth into the bowls evenly. Right before serving, squeeze the lime wedges into the soup.

MOM'S STIR-FRIED SHRIMP AND SCALLIONS

SERVES 4

While most of my friends' moms were whipping up hamburgers and hot dogs (which I begged my mom to make) for fast easy dinners, my mom would make this homey shrimp stir-fry whenever she was strapped for time. She was a very busy working mom, and this was one of her signature go-tos. Years later, when I asked her for the recipe, she hemmed and hawed until finally she revealed her secret ingredient: ketchup. Use one you like a lot, since the recipe calls for a considerable amount. I love making and eating this; it reminds me of Mom every time.

1½ pounds large shrimp, peeled and deveined

2 tablespoons peeled and finely chopped fresh ginger (about 2-inch knob)

3 medium garlic cloves, thinly sliced

2 large egg whites

1½ teaspoons red pepper flakes

2 teaspoons cornstarch

¾ cup ketchup

½ cup Basic Chicken Stock (page 313) or canned low-sodium chicken broth

1 tablespoon sugar

1½ teaspoons kosher salt

1½ teaspoons freshly ground black pepper

⅓ cup vegetable oil, such as canola

½ bunch scallions (4 or 5), white and green parts finely chopped (about ½ cup)

½ cup chopped fresh cilantro stems and leaves (about ½ bunch)

Perfect White Rice (page 315) or Perfect Brown Rice (page 316)

In a large bowl, combine the shrimp, ginger, garlic, egg whites, red pepper flakes, and 1 teaspoon of the cornstarch and mix well with your hands. In a small bowl, whisk together the ketchup, stock, sugar, salt, pepper, and the remaining 1 teaspoon cornstarch until well combined.

In a wok or a large, heavy, flat-bottomed skillet, heat the vegetable oil over high heat until it shimmers, about 1 minute. Add the shrimp and cook, stirring continuously with a wooden spoon, until the shrimp start to turn pink and get a touch crispy on the edges, about 1 minute. Add the ketchup mixture and simmer until the shrimp are just cooked through, 3 to 4 minutes. Stir in the scallions and cilantro and serve immediately with rice.

SWEET SOY BACON AND EGG BANH MI

SERVES 4

The banh mi is a popular Vietnamese sandwich that is the direct by-product of French colonialism in Indochina. It combines ingredients from France such as baguettes, jalapeños, and mayonnaise with native Vietnamese ingredients such as cilantro, sriracha, pickled carrots, and daikon. Our version, made with bacon and eggs, is the star of our dim sum weekend brunch. We use a locally produced small-batch bacon and serve it open-faced with a serrated knife for sharing. It has been named the ultimate Sunday morning hangover cure by *Boston Magazine* (and many of our guests).

8 slices thick-cut applewood-smoked bacon

½ cup Indonesian sweet soy sauce (kecap manis; see Note, page 280)

One 20- to 24-inch French baguette

4 tablespoons Sriracha Aioli (page 308; see Note, page 280)

1 recipe Pickled Vegetables (recipe follows)

4 teaspoons unsalted butter

8 large eggs

1 cup fresh cilantro leaves (about ½ bunch)

Preheat the oven to 350°F and place a rack in the center of the oven.

On a baking sheet, lay out the bacon and brush evenly with the sweet soy sauce. Bake for 10 to 15 minutes, until just barely crisp. The soy sauce will caramelize and the bacon will become more amazing than bacon already is. Remove from the oven and set aside.

Divide the baguette into four equal portions and split each halfway through. Spread 1 tablespoon of the Sriracha Aioli on both sides of each baguette portion. Drain the pickled carrot and daikon from the Pickled Vegetables and divide them evenly over the bottom of each baguette portion. Drain the pickled jalapeños from the Pickled Vegetables and divide them evenly on top of the pickled

continued
↓

carrot and daikon. Arrange the cilantro on top of the jalapeños. Set aside while you cook the eggs.

In a large skillet, melt 2 teaspoons of the butter over medium-high heat. Carefully crack 4 of the eggs into the pan. Cook until the tops of the whites are set but the yolks are still runny, 2 to 3 minutes. If the butter starts to spit, it is a sign that the heat is too high. In this case, turn the heat down to low. When the sunny-side-up eggs are ready, remove the pan from the heat and use a spatula to remove them from the pan. Place the eggs on a plate and repeat with the remaining 4 eggs.

Note: If you can't find *kecap manis,* use ¼ cup soy sauce mixed with ¼ cup dark brown sugar.

If you don't have time to make the Sriracha Aioli, you can use ¼ cup mayonnaise mixed with 1 tablespoon sriracha.

Finish each baguette by placing 2 sunny-side-up eggs on top of the cilantro and 2 slices of the soy-glazed bacon on top of the eggs. Close the baguettes and serve.

Pickled Vegetables

½ cup unseasoned rice vinegar

½ cup champagne vinegar

2 tablespoons kosher salt

2 tablespoons sugar

2 medium garlic cloves, smashed

One 1-inch knob fresh ginger, smashed

2 medium carrots, shredded on the large holes of a box grater or using the grating blade of a food processor (about 1 cup)

½ medium daikon radish, shredded on the large holes of a box grater or using the grating blade of a food processor (about 1 cup), or 1 bunch red radishes, sliced

2 jalapeños, thinly sliced into rings

IN A SMALL POT, combine the rice vinegar, champagne vinegar, salt, sugar, garlic, ginger, and ½ cup water and bring to a boil, stirring until the sugar and salt have dissolved. Let cool completely. Place the carrot and daikon in a small, nonreactive bowl or container; place the jalapeño rings in a separate small, nonreactive bowl or container. Pour the pickling liquid over each to cover and let sit at room temperature for at least 4 hours. The Pickled Vegetables can be made up to 3 days in advance and stored in their pickling liquid in separate airtight containers in the refrigerator.

DESSERTS

287   VANILLA BEAN PARFAIT WITH
ORANGE GRANITA

289   CHOCOLATE TOFU MOUSSE WITH
BLACK-AND-WHITE SESAME BRITTLE

292   VIETNAMESE ESPRESSO ICE CREAM

293   RED BEAN SOUP

294   TOASTED-COCONUT MERINGUE CLOUDS

296   CORNMEAL-LIME SANDWICH COOKIES

299   HOMEMADE FORTUNE COOKIES

VANILLA BEAN PARFAIT WITH ORANGE GRANITA

SERVES 6

Over the years, we've probably gotten no fewer than one thousand comment cards singing the praises of this parfait as a "wicked good" interpretation of the Creamsicle. I didn't grow up eating typical Americana dessert fare and have never had a Creamsicle, but I remember seeing pictures of them painted on the side of the ice cream truck that would circle the block during hot summers when I was a kid. I pined for this treat—any treat, actually—while instead, a large plate of oranges was waiting for me at home. Oranges were also our nightly dessert. That wasn't going to fly at Myers+Chang (I have my pastry chef reputation to maintain, after all), so I married fresh orange ice with vanilla bean parfait (essentially an ice cream made without an ice cream maker). There are a gazillion ways to plate it to make it pretty, or fun, or whimsical. It is creamy and refreshing and a lovely way to end a big Asian feast.

½ fresh vanilla bean

6 large egg yolks

⅔ cup sugar

2 cups heavy cream

½ teaspoon kosher salt

1 recipe Orange Granita (recipe follows)

2 oranges, peeled and pith removed, sliced into thin rounds

6 to 8 fresh mint leaves

Line a 9 x 5-inch loaf pan with plastic wrap. Split the vanilla bean in half lengthwise with a sharp small knife and open it up. Use the knife to scrape out the seeds, where all the wonderful vanilla flavor is. In the bowl of a stand mixer fitted with the whisk attachment or in a medium bowl using a hand mixer, whip the egg yolks and vanilla bean seeds on medium speed until the yolks have lightened in color and become somewhat frothy, 3 to 4 minutes.

Meanwhile, in a small saucepan, combine the sugar and ½ cup water and stir to dissolve the sugar. Clip a candy thermometer to the side of the pan and cook the sugar syrup over high heat until it reaches soft ball stage, 238°F.

continued
↓

With the mixer running on low speed, drizzle the hot sugar syrup down the side of the mixer bowl into the yolks. When all the syrup has been incorporated, increase the mixer speed to medium. Whip for 8 to 10 minutes, until the mixture is light and fluffy and cool. Poke your finger in there to test the temperature.

Meanwhile, in a separate bowl, whip the heavy cream and salt together on medium speed until they hold stiff peaks (i.e., when you lift a spoonful of the cream, it holds its shape well). Gently fold the whipped cream into the cooled fluffy egg-sugar mixture. Scrape the mixture into the prepared pan and smooth and even out the top. Cover the pan entirely with plastic wrap and freeze for at least 24 hours or up to 1 week.

Remove the vanilla parfait from the freezer and remove the plastic wrap. Using a hot sharp knife, slice the parfait into six slices and place one on each of six dessert plates. Divide the granita evenly among the six plates. Arrange the orange slices evenly on top of the granita. Thinly slice the mint and sprinkle it evenly on top of all six dishes. Serve immediately.

Orange Granita

MAKES 4 CUPS

⅓ cup sugar
2½ cups fresh orange juice

IN A MEDIUM saucepan, combine the sugar and ½ cup water and bring to a boil. Add the orange juice and stir. Transfer to a metal or plastic container that fits in your freezer. Freeze for 3 to 4 hours. Every 30 minutes, use a fork to scrape and mix the granita so it does not freeze into a solid block. It should be completely frozen but still easily spoonable. The Orange Granita can be made up to 1 month in advance and stored, covered with plastic wrap, in the freezer.

CHOCOLATE TOFU MOUSSE WITH BLACK-AND-WHITE SESAME BRITTLE

SERVES 4 TO 6

We stirred up some controversy when we first put this dessert on our menu. We named it Ancient Chinese Secret Chocolate Mousse, a play on the 1970s TV commercial for Calgon laundry detergent in which the Chinese laundry man answers, "Ancient Chinese secret!" to the housewife's question about how the laundry got so clean. We simply wanted to hint at the fact that this mousse is not only fabulous but also entirely vegan. Not one speck of cream or a single egg yolk goes into this smooth, chocolaty mousse. If you don't tell your friends that it is made with tofu, none of them will guess. At the restaurant, I often wait till guests have licked the bowl clean before asking them if they like it and if they can guess what it is made out of. Invariably they are shocked that a dessert so rich and creamy is made out of tofu. Top the mousse with sparkly sesame brittle for an easy dessert that is just as good, if not better than, traditional chocolate mousse and a lot healthier, too.

8 ounces high-quality bittersweet chocolate	1 pound silken or extra-soft tofu, drained	¾ teaspoon kosher salt
¾ cup sugar	1 teaspoon vanilla extract	1 recipe Black-and-White Sesame Brittle (recipe follows)
¾ cup brewed hot coffee or hot water		

In a microwave or in the top of a double boiler, melt the chocolate and set aside. In a small bowl, combine the sugar and hot coffee and stir until the sugar has dissolved. Pour the syrup into a blender and add the melted chocolate, tofu, vanilla, and salt. Blend on medium speed until completely smooth, scraping down the sides of

the blender jar a few times as needed. Remove the mousse from the blender and divide it among four to six serving bowls. Refrigerate the mousse for at least an hour to firm up it up before serving. Break the sesame brittle into small bite-size pieces with your hands, place on top of the mousse to garnish, and serve. The mousse can be made

continued
↓

DESSERTS

CHOCOLATE
TOFU MOUSSE
WITH BLACK-
AND-WHITE
SESAME
BRITTLE

291

up to 4 days in advance. Instead of dividing it into serving bowls, store it in an airtight container in the refrigerator. When ready to serve, stir vigorously to loosen up the mousse for a smooth appearance before dividing it among four to six serving bowls.

continued

Black-and-White Sesame Brittle

MAKES ABOUT ⅔ CUP

⅓ cup sugar

3 tablespoons black sesame seeds

3 tablespoons white sesame seeds

LINE a baking sheet with parchment paper.

IN A SMALL saucepan, combine the sugar and 2 to 3 tablespoons water and bring to a boil over high heat. Use a wet pastry brush to remove any sugar crystals clinging to the side of the pan. Let the sugar boil undisturbed (jostling the pan or stirring the mixture could cause crystallization) until it starts to color and turn light brown. At this point, you can gently swirl the pan to even out the caramelization. Add the sesame seeds and swirl them around in the caramel until the caramel turns medium amber brown. (The caramel may foam a bit when you add the sesame seeds—this is normal, and once you swirl it around for a few seconds, the foaming will subside.) When the caramel is medium amber, immediately remove the pan from the heat and quickly pour the brittle mixture over the prepared baking sheet. Tilt the sheet back and forth to get the brittle to even out and flow into a thin layer. Be careful; the brittle is very hot! Let the brittle cool for 30 to 40 minutes until it is cool to the touch. Break it up into small pieces and store indefinitely in an airtight container at room temperature.

VIETNAMESE ESPRESSO ICE CREAM

MAKES ABOUT 2 QUARTS

Family meal is the meal we make for our staff every day around four thirty p.m. It's the last bit of food the servers and cooks inhale until dinner service ends around ten or eleven p.m. We put a lot of love into what we cook for the team. But admittedly, we rarely have time to make (or eat) dessert. For holidays, though, we always try to do something special. A few Thanksgivings ago, Chef roasted a few humongous turkeys, and our sous chef Gabriel whipped up some amazing chocolate ice cream. Not only was it deliciously smooth, but it was also particularly impressive because he made it without an ice cream maker. We quizzed him and he told us his secret: sweetened condensed milk. It's so creamy that when you freeze it, it stays super luscious like the most deluxe ice cream you can buy. We made our variation by adding espresso powder to the base recipe for an ice cream that is reminiscent of the syrupy espressos popular in Vietnam. Add more espresso powder if you want it super strong.

1 tablespoon plus 1 teaspoon instant espresso powder

1 tablespoon vanilla extract

¼ teaspoon kosher salt

2½ cups heavy cream

One 14-ounce can sweetened condensed milk

In a small bowl, whisk together the espresso powder, vanilla, salt, and 1 tablespoon warm water until the espresso powder has dissolved. Stir the espresso mixture into the heavy cream and whip either by hand or with a hand mixer or stand mixer fitted with the whisk attachment until it thickens to soft peaks (i.e., it holds a soft peak when you lift a spoon out of the mixture). Pour in the sweetened condensed milk and continue to whip until the mixture is thoroughly combined and at soft peak stage. The ice cream base will be billowing and will mound gently on a spoon when you dip into it. Transfer the ice cream to a storage container, place in the freezer, and freeze until solid, at least 8 hours. The ice cream can be stored in the freezer in an airtight container for up to 1 month.

RED BEAN SOUP

SERVES 4

I could eat this morning, noon, and night. It might not sound like much or look like much, but for me, this is the ultimate comfort food. My mom would make this on special occasions and serve a small bowlful at the end of big banquet dinners. I would wait patiently for her to serve it to her dinner guests and then ladle up a big cereal bowl for me. Red beans (also known as adzuki beans) are cooked with water and a bit of sugar until the beans are totally soft and sweet and the broth is rich and a bit creamy. Eaten warm, it's the best afternoon snack when it is cold and wintery outside. Chilled, it makes an awesome quick breakfast.

1 cup adzuki beans
½ cup sugar

In a large saucepan, combine the adzuki beans and 12 cups water and bring to a boil. Turn down the heat so the soup gently simmers. Stir in the sugar. Cook, stirring occasionally, until the beans are totally soft, about 2½ hours. If needed, add up to 2 cups more water to keep the soup from becoming too thick. The soup may be served hot or chilled and can be stored in an airtight container in the refrigerator for up to 1 week.

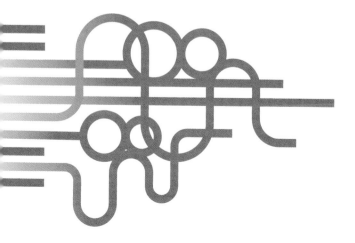

TOASTED-COCONUT MERINGUE CLOUDS

MAKES 8 LARGE CLOUDS

I love a little plastic-wrapped fortune cookie as much as the next person. But as a professional pastry chef, there was no way I was going to buy cases of packaged fortune cookies to pass out along with customers' checks. I couldn't bear the thought of the last thing you eat at our restaurant being a cookie mass produced in a factory a million miles away. Sadly, making homemade fortune cookies for every single guest proved to be too labor intensive. (Once you try the recipe on page 299, you'll see what I mean.) So we settled on a bite-size puff of sweet coconut meringue as our parting treat. Guests often ask for more, so we also make these big poufy clouds as well. If you prefer the smaller size, simply spoon them smaller, or use a pastry bag to pipe them into tiny bites.

1 cup sweetened shredded coconut

1 cup egg whites (from about 8 large eggs)

1 cup granulated sugar

1 cup confectioners' sugar, sifted

½ teaspoon kosher salt

Preheat the oven to 175°F and place a rack in the center of the oven.

Place the coconut on a baking sheet and toast in the oven for 10 to 12 minutes, until light golden brown. Remove from the oven and set aside.

In the bowl of a stand mixer fitted with the whisk attachment or in a large bowl using a hand mixer, beat the egg whites on medium speed until soft peaks form, 3 to 4 minutes. The whites will start to froth and turn into bubbles, and eventually the yellowy viscous part of the whites will disappear. Keep whipping until you can see the tines of your whisk leaving a slight trail in the whites. Test for soft peak stage by stopping the mixer and removing the whisk from the whites and lifting it up; the whites should peak and then droop.

With the mixer on medium speed, add the granulated sugar in three increments, mixing for 1 minute between additions. Once you've beaten all the sugar into the egg whites, increase the mixer speed to medium-high and beat for about 30 seconds more. Remove the bowl from the mixer. Sift the confectioners' sugar and salt together and fold the mixture into the beaten egg whites. Fold in the toasted coconut, reserving a few tablespoons to garnish the tops of the meringues.

Line a baking sheet with parchment paper. Use a large spoon to scoop large, baseball-size, billowing mounds of meringue onto the prepared baking sheet. You should get about eight meringue clouds. Sprinkle the remaining toasted coconut on top of the meringues. Bake for about 3 hours, until the meringues are firm to the touch and you can easily remove them from the baking sheet without having them fall apart. For meringues with a soft, chewy center, remove them from oven at this point and let them cool. For fully crisped meringues, turn off the oven and leave the meringues in it for at least 6 or up to 12 hours. The meringues can be stored in an airtight container at room temperature for up to 1 week.

CORNMEAL-LIME SANDWICH COOKIES

MAKES 10 TO 12 LARGE COOKIES

Our dear friend Chef Jamie Mammano, owner of most of Boston's best restaurants—Mistral, Ostra, Sorrelina, Mooo, and Teatro—and the Mi Niña tortilla chip company, is an accomplished, talented man of feisty opinions. He does not hand out compliments lightly. He says this is the best cookie in the world. Period. That's enough for us. Yes, this was a paid commercial announcement for Mistral, Ostra, Sorrelina, Mooo, Teatro, and the Mi Niña tortilla chip company. And our cornmeal-lime cookies.

1 cup (2 sticks) unsalted butter, at room temperatue

1 cup sugar

2 tablespoons grated lime zest (from about 4 limes)

2 large eggs

1 teaspoon vanilla extract

2 cups all-purpose flour

½ cup coarse yellow cornmeal

2 teaspoons baking powder

½ teaspoon kosher salt

1 recipe Creamy Lime Filling (recipe follows)

Preheat the oven to 350°F and place a rack in the center of the oven. Line a baking sheet with parchment paper.

In the bowl of a stand mixer fitted with the paddle attachment or in a large bowl using a wooden spoon or a hand mixer, beat the butter and sugar on medium speed until light and fluffy, about 5 minutes (at least 10 minutes if mixing by hand). Stop the mixer and use a rubber spatula to scrape down the sides, the bottom, and the paddle itself a few times during the mixing process; the sugar and butter love to collect there and stay unmixed. Add the lime zest and beat for about 1 minute on medium speed to release the lime flavor. Add the eggs and vanilla and beat on medium speed until thoroughly combined, 2 to 3 minutes. Scrape down the bowl and the paddle to make sure the eggs are thoroughly incorporated.

In a small bowl, mix together the flour, cornmeal, baking powder, and salt. With the mixer on low speed (or using a wooden spoon if mixing by hand), add the flour mixture in three or four additions and mix until the flour is completely incorporated and the dough is uniform.

Using a large spoon or an ice cream scoop, drop the dough in scant ¼-cup balls onto the prepared baking sheet about 2 inches apart. Flatten the dough with the palm of your hand into discs about 2 inches in diameter. (**Pro tip:** Dip your palm in flour or water to prevent it from sticking to the dough.) Bake until the cookies are pale brown on the edges, still pale in the center, and just firm to the touch in the center, 20 to 24 minutes. Be careful not to overbake or let the tops brown. Remove the cookies from the oven and let cool on the baking sheet for 15 to 20 minutes, then transfer them to a wire rack to cool to room temperature. When the cookies are entirely cool, turn over half of them so the flat side faces up. Spoon about 1 rounded tablespoon of the filling onto the center of each turned-over cookie and top with the other half of the cookies. Press down until the filling comes out to the edge of the cookie. The cookies can be stored in an airtight container at room temperature for up to 4 days or in the freezer for up to 3 weeks.

Creamy Lime Filling

MAKES ABOUT ¾ CUP

½ cup (1 stick) unsalted butter, at room temperature

1⅔ cups confectioners' sugar, sifted

1 teaspoon vanilla extract

2 tablespoons grated lime zest (from about 4 limes)

1 tablespoon freshly squeezed lime juice

Pinch of kosher salt

IN THE BOWL of a stand mixer fitted with the paddle attachment or in a large bowl using a hand mixer, beat the butter on low speed for about 30 seconds. Add the confectioners' sugar and vanilla and beat until totally smooth. Add the lime zest, lime juice, and salt and beat until smooth. The mixture will look like spackle and feel about the same. (You can also mix this together by hand. Make sure the butter is very soft and use your hands to mix and knead the confectioners' sugar into the butter. Add a few drops of water if needed to loosen up the dough.) The filling can be made up to 2 days in advance and stored in an airtight container at room temperature or in the refrigerator for up to 2 weeks. Bring to room temperature before using.

HOMEMADE FORTUNE COOKIES

MAKES 16 TO 18 COOKIES

Who thinks to make a homemade fortune cookie? A pastry chef who opens a Chinese restaurant, that's who. I am unabashedly a cookie snob. I want fresh and homemade and flavorful, all the things that pale packaged fortune cookies are not. Plus, I love the challenge of making something by hand that is typically machine-made. These are not hard to make, but they do require a bit of practice and Teflon fingers. Once you get the hang of it, they are really, really fun. Make personalized fortunes for special occasions and impress your guests (and yourself).

¾ cup sugar

3 large eggs whites

1 teaspoon almond extract or vanilla extract

½ cup vegetable oil, such as canola

½ cup all-purpose flour

⅛ teaspoon ground ginger

⅛ teaspoon kosher salt

In a medium bowl, whisk together the sugar, egg whites, and almond extract until combined. Whisk in the oil first, then the flour, ginger, and salt until well combined and free of lumps. Pour the batter into an airtight container and refrigerate for at least 4 hours or up to 1 week. The batter needs to sit for a bit to fully absorb the flour into the whites.

Preheat the oven to 325°F and place a rack in the center of the oven.

Line a very flat baking sheet with parchment paper and liberally spray with nonstick spray, or line the baking sheet with a silicone baking mat. (It will be infinitely easier with a silicone baking mat, but parchment does work.) Write out sixteen fortunes on little slips of paper (about ¼ x 2 inches). Fold the fortunes into teeny tiny squares. Set aside.

Spoon 1 rounded tablespoon of the batter onto the baking sheet and use the back of a small butter knife or an offset spatula to spread the batter evenly and as thinly as you can into a circle about 5 inches in diameter. It takes some practice to get the batter nice and thin. Do your best; if you need to, dip your fingers in water and use them to smear the batter a bit before spreading it with

continued ↓

the knife or offset spatula. Bake for 12 to 16 minutes, until the cookie is golden brown all over.

Okay, here is the fun part! Read these directions a few times before trying these to make sure you understand how to shape the cookies. You have about 10 seconds after the cookie has come out of the oven during which it is still pliable. This 10-second window coincides with when the cookie is at its hottest and is most difficult to handle. Try wearing latex or plastic gloves to shield your fingers from the heat. Moving quickly, remove the baking sheet from the oven and use an offset spatula to quickly remove the cookie from the baking sheet. The easiest way to do this is to swipe the spatula under the cookie very fast to loosen the whole thing. Time matters! Place one of the fortunes in the middle of the cookie, fold the cookie in half, hold the half-moon-shaped cookie in both hands with the rounded half facing up to the sky, and push the base of the half-moon with both thumbs upward to make the cookie bend in half into the characteristic fortune cookie shape. Hold the cookie until it cools and hardens into shape or put it pointed-side down into an empty egg carton, which is the perfect shape for holding the folded cookies. Whew! Take a deep breath and congratulate yourself.

Repeat until all of the batter has been used up. Once you are more adept with the technique, you can make three or four cookies at a time. The cookies can be made up to 3 days in advance and stored in an airtight container at room temperature.

Teach a m... ...sh and he'll still... ...gave him a fish.

When in doubt, order more.

Treat yourself with at least as much kindness as you treat your friends.

SAUCES, CONDIMENTS, AND BASICS

304   NUOC CHAM

304   CHINESE HOT MUSTARD SAUCE

305   DRAGON SAUCE (Homemade Sriracha)

306   FUN SAUCE

307   HOMEMADE RED CURRY PASTE

308   LEMON-GINGER DRESSING

308   SRIRACHA AIOLI

309   ROASTED-GARLIC WHIPPED TOFU

310   CHILI-TOMATO JAM

311   KHAO KOOR

312   PICKLED SHALLOTS

312   CRISPY SHALLOTS

313   BASIC CHICKEN STOCK

314   BRAISED SHORT RIBS

315   PERFECT WHITE RICE

316   PERFECT BROWN RICE

NUOC CHAM

MAKES 1 CUP

This essential staple Vietnamese dressing marries stinky fish sauce with enough lime and sugar and garlic to balance out the funk and turn it into something magical. We use it liberally in as many dishes as we can. A squirt of *nuoc cham* brightens up any stir-fry and makes every salad special.

½ cup freshly squeezed lime juice

¼ cup sugar

¼ cup fish sauce

1 fresh Thai bird chili, thinly sliced, or 1 jalapeño, minced

1 medium garlic clove, finely minced

In a medium bowl, whisk together all the ingredients. The Nuoc Cham can be stored in an airtight container in the refrigerator for up to 1 week.

CHINESE HOT MUSTARD SAUCE

MAKES ABOUT ½ CUP

If you are used to eating Chinese mustard out of a little packet, just stop. Right now. Find Chinese mustard powder (either in Asian grocery stores or online) and make and keep this sauce forever. It's spicy and punchy and super easy to make.

2 tablespoons unseasoned rice vinegar

2 tablespoons soy sauce

2 tablespoons sugar

1 tablespoon toasted sesame oil

4 teaspoons Chinese mustard powder

2 tablespoons vegetable oil, such as canola

In a small bowl, whisk together the vinegar, soy sauce, sugar, and sesame oil. Add the mustard powder and whisk vigorously until thoroughly mixed in. While whisking vigorously, slowly drizzle in the sesame oil to emulsify the sauce. It will be beautiful, thick, and shiny. The Chinese Hot Mustard Sauce can be stored in an airtight container in the refrigerator for up to 2 months.

DRAGON SAUCE (HOMEMADE SRIRACHA)

MAKES ABOUT 2 CUPS

Making sriracha is like making ketchup. So many great varieties already exist that you may wonder, Why delve into making a homemade version? It's really fun, for one, and you get to boast that you have made a condiment that most people have never thought to make themselves. We only thought to do so after reading about our friends Diane and Todd's Sriracha-making adventure in their excellent blog *White on Rice*. This makes the freshest chili sauce you'll ever try.

1 tablespoon vegetable oil, such as canola

3 medium garlic cloves, minced

1 medium shallot, minced

1 cup tomato sauce

1 cup fresh whole red Thai bird chilies, stemmed and coarsely chopped

⅓ cup unseasoned rice vinegar

1 tablespoon fish sauce (or substitute soy sauce for a vegetarian version)

1 tablespoon sugar

1 teaspoon kosher salt

In a small saucepan, heat the vegetable oil over medium heat. Add the garlic and shallot and cook, stirring frequently, until light brown and fragrant, 3 to 4 minutes. (Don't let the garlic get black and burned or the sauce will be bitter.) Add the tomato sauce and the chilies. Bring the mixture to a boil and cook for 1 minute. Add the vinegar, fish sauce, sugar, and salt and reduce the heat to a low, happy simmer. Simmer the sauce for about 5 minutes; this will break down the chilies so when you puree the sauce, it will be perfectly smooth. Remove from the heat and let cool completely. Transfer the sauce to a blender and blend on high speed until smooth and most of the chili skins have broken down. Push the sauce through a fine sieve to remove any seeds and remaining skin for a silky smooth finish. The Dragon Sauce can be stored in an airtight container in the refrigerator for up to 3 weeks.

FUN SAUCE

MAKES 1½ CUPS

This basic stir-fry sauce started off as the sauce for our Beef and Chinese Broccoli Chow Fun (page 223)—hence the name. It's extremely versatile, so we use it in many of our dishes, not just the beef and broccoli. You can take most of our stir-fry dishes, omit the meat and substitute tofu, and use this vegetarian sauce to bind everything together. We make it by the gallons and store it in our walk-in refrigerator for weeks.

1 cup low-sodium soy sauce

2 tablespoons black Chinkiang vinegar

2 tablespoons toasted sesame oil

1½ teaspoons freshly ground black pepper

1 tablespoon cornstarch

In large saucepan, whisk together the soy sauce, vinegar, sesame oil, pepper, and ¼ cup water and bring to a boil. Reduce the heat to low. In a small bowl, whisk together the cornstarch and 1 tablespoon cold water until smooth to form a slurry (see Note, page 195). Slowly add it to the soy mixture on the stove, whisking all the while. Bring the heat back up to medium-high and whisk until the mixture thickens, 1 to 2 minutes. It should be shiny and coat the back of a spoon. Remove the sauce from the heat and pour it into a bowl or container and refrigerate until cool. The Fun Sauce can be stored in an airtight container in the refrigerator for up to 2 months.

HOMEMADE RED CURRY PASTE

MAKES ABOUT 2 CUPS

2 cups dried red Thai chilies

¼ cup peeled and chopped fresh galangal root (see Note)

¼ cup chopped garlic (8 to 10 large cloves)

2 tablespoons coriander seeds, toasted and ground

2 tablespoons finely minced fresh cilantro root, or 4 tablespoons finely minced fresh cilantro stems

2 makrut lime leaves, sliced super thin, or grated zest of 2 limes

2 teaspoons cumin seeds, toasted and ground

½ cup vegetable oil, such as canola

Place the dried chilies in a large bowl. Pour 4 cups boiling water over the chilies and cover with plastic wrap. Let the chilies sit for 1 hour and then blend them in a blender on medium speed with ½ cup of the soaking water to make the paste move. Add the galangal, garlic, coriander, cilantro, lime leaves, and cumin. With the blender running, slowly drizzle in the vegetable oil to allow the machine to do its work. Once all the oil has been incorporated, increase the blender speed to high and blend until very smooth. The paste should be thick and free of lumps. The Red Curry Paste can be stored in an airtight container in the refrigerator for up to 2 weeks or in the freezer for up to 2 months.

Note: You can find galangal at Asian markets, or substitute 2 tablespoons peeled and chopped fresh ginger if you can't find galangal.

LEMON-GINGER DRESSING

MAKES ABOUT 1¼ CUPS

A quick, zesty, bright dressing that is great on pretty much everything. Make it in big batches and use it all month long.

½ cup low-sodium soy sauce

⅓ cup unseasoned rice vinegar

3 tablespoons extra-virgin olive oil

3 tablespoons toasted sesame oil

2 tablespoons grated lemon zest (from 2 or 3 lemons)

2 tablespoons freshly squeezed lemon juice

1 tablespoon plus 1 teaspoon honey

1 tablespoon peeled and finely chopped fresh ginger (about 1-inch knob)

½ teaspoon cayenne pepper

In a small bowl, whisk together all the ingredients until well combined. Another nice way to make it is to combine all the ingredients in a ball jar, screw the lid on tight, and shake, shake, shake! The Lemon-Ginger Dressing can be stored in an airtight container in the refrigerator for up to 1 month.

SRIRACHA AIOLI

MAKES ABOUT ⅔ CUP

The fast way to make this is to simply stir together ½ cup mayonnaise with 2 tablespoons sriracha. But try making it from scratch and you'll be rewarded with ultra-creamy and luxurious aioli that you'll want to dunk everything in. Plus, it is fun to tell people you made mayonnaise from scratch.

1 large egg yolk

1 tablespoon plus 2 teaspoons sriracha

1 tablespoon freshly squeezed lemon juice

1 teaspoon Dijon mustard

1 teaspoon kosher salt

½ cup vegetable oil, such as canola

In a food processor or in a small bowl using a whisk, blend or whisk together the egg yolk, sriracha, lemon juice, mustard, and salt. Process on high or whisk vigorously until the mixture is homogenous. With the food processor running or while whisking, gradually add the vegetable oil, starting with a few drops at a time, until the mixture is emulsified. If the aioli is too thick, add 1 or 2 drops of water. The Sriracha Aioli can be stored in an airtight container in the refrigerator for up to 4 days.

ROASTED-GARLIC WHIPPED TOFU

MAKES 1¼ CUPS

My secret is that I am lactose-intolerant. (A sad fact for someone who loves cheese, especially a chef!) So any time I can substitute tofu for dairy and make something delicious and creamy with no dairy, I get really excited. This dip is an excellent substitute for ranch dressing or for sour cream and onion dip; it's a lot healthier, and it also happens to be vegan. It is ideal for parties or just snacking. Serve it with pickles, chips, or crudités, or as a condiment alongside grilled steak or chicken. In a pinch, it is also a great salad dressing! —*Chef Karen*

8 medium garlic cloves	1 cup silken tofu (about 8 ounces)	1 teaspoon freshly ground black pepper
1 cup extra-virgin olive oil	2 teaspoons kosher salt	

Preheat the oven to 350°F and place a rack in the center of the oven.

Place the garlic cloves in a heavy, sturdy ovensafe dish or pan and pour in the olive oil to cover the garlic cloves. Place in the oven for 25 to 30 minutes, until the garlic is toasted to pale golden brown. Carefully remove from the oven and let cool until cool enough to handle, about 1 hour. (The oil is very hot when it comes out of the oven, so be very careful.) When cool enough to handle, transfer the garlic and about half the olive oil to a blender. (Use the remaining oil to make garlic bread or to sauté vegetables.) Add the tofu, salt, and pepper. Puree until the mixture is totally smooth, creamy, and shiny. The Roasted-Garlic Whipped Tofu can be made up to 3 days in advance and stored in an airtight container in the refrigerator. Whipped tofu will firm up when chilled, so give it a vigorous stir to loosen before serving.

CHILI-TOMATO JAM

MAKES ABOUT 2 CUPS

This is a pungent and punchy condiment that relies on slow cooking and some honey to make it nice and jammy. We use it in our Rainbow Trout (page 133) and as part of our Asian Pizza (page 270). It's fabulous to have on hand for grilled and roasted fish and roasted chicken.

¼ cup extra-virgin olive oil

1 medium yellow onion, diced

2 medium garlic cloves, sliced

2 tablespoons peeled and finely chopped fresh ginger (about 2-inch knob)

One 14.5- to 16-ounce can crushed tomatoes (San Marzano really are the most lovely)

2 tablespoons honey

1 tablespoon Madras curry powder

1 tablespoon sambal oelek

1 tablespoon ground ginger

1 tablespoon Chinese five-spice powder

1 tablespoon kosher salt

In a medium flat-bottomed saucepan, heat the olive oil over medium heat. Add the onion, garlic, and fresh ginger and cook, stirring occasionally, until the onion softens and becomes shiny and translucent, 2 to 3 minutes. Add the tomatoes, honey, curry powder, sambal oelek, ground ginger, five-spice powder, and salt. Simmer, stirring frequently, until it becomes jam-like and thick, 30 to 40 minutes. The Chili-Tomato Jam can be stored in an airtight container in the refrigerator for up to 5 days or in the freezer for up to 1 month. Reheat until hot before serving, adding a little water as needed to loosen.

MYERS+
CHANG
AT HOME

KHAO KOOR

MAKES ABOUT ¼ CUP

Khao koor (pronounced "cow-core") is uncooked Thai sweet rice ground to a coarse powder. We call it the Asian crouton. It doesn't get soggy in dressing, and it adds nice crunch to your salad. We toast ours with aromatics to add color and citrusy fragrance to our dishes. If you don't have lemongrass or lime leaf, you can use lemon and lime zest or simply omit both and make plain *khao koor*, which is still a great crunchy garnish.

| 1 stalk lemongrass or grated zest of 1 lemon | ¼ cup uncooked sweet rice (we like Three Ladies brand) | 1 makrut lime leaf or grated zest of 1 lime |

<u>Preheat the oven</u> to 250°F and place a rack in the center of the oven.

<u>Peel and discard</u> the dry, papery outer layers of the lemongrass; trim off the top two-thirds of the stalk, which is also dry and papery, along with the very base and discard. Slice the bottom third into small thin rounds. Toss the rice with the lime leaf and lemongrass and spread on a baking sheet. Bake for 1½ hours. Remove from the oven, let cool, and grind in a blender or spice grinder. Your coffee grinder will work, too. If you have a mortar and pestle, try that! You want to grind it to a rough, sandlike texture. If you grind it too fine, it is just powdery dust; if it is too coarse, it will hurt your teeth. The Khao Koor can be stored indefinitely in an airtight container at room temperature.

PICKLED SHALLOTS

MAKES ABOUT ¼ CUP

¼ cup unseasoned rice vinegar

1 tablespoon sugar

2 teaspoons kosher salt

1 medium garlic clove, smashed

2 large shallots, very thinly sliced into rings

In a small saucepan, combine the vinegar, sugar, salt, and garlic and heat over medium-high heat until the sugar and salt have dissolved. Let cool completely and transfer to a bowl or storage container. Add the shallots and soak in the pickling liquid in the refrigerator for at least 4 hours or up to 1 week. The Pickled Shallots can be stored in an airtight container in the refrigerator for up to 1 week. Strain and remove the garlic clove before using.

CRISPY SHALLOTS

MAKES ABOUT ¼ CUP

These are hard not to snack on or put on top of pretty much everything. You sometimes find crispy shallots sold in prepackaged bags at the Asian grocery. Don't take that shortcut. They don't hold a candle to these.

4 medium shallots

2 cups vegetable oil, such as canola, for frying (see Note, page 92)

¼ teaspoon kosher salt

Thinly slice the shallots on a mandoline or with a very sharp knife; they must be super-duper thin and as evenly sliced as possible. In a small saucepan, stir together the shallots and the oil and place over medium heat. Stir the shallots until the oil barely starts to simmer, then cook until the shallots turn golden brown, stirring occasionally, 6 to 8 minutes. Remove from the oil with a slotted spoon and place on a paper towel–lined plate. It will take 15 to 18 minutes total from cold oil to finished. Dust the shallots with the salt and let cool. The Crispy Shallots can be stored in an airtight container at room temperature for up to 5 days.

BASIC CHICKEN STOCK

MAKES ABOUT 2 QUARTS

Sure, it's easy to buy a can of chicken broth in the grocery store. But it's just as easy to throw all of the ingredients below on the stove and have homemade chicken stock two hours later. Store it in your freezer and use it to make everything taste better.

3 pounds chicken wings and/or bones

1 medium yellow onion, coarsely chopped

1 bunch scallions (8 or 9), coarsely chopped

2 celery stalks, coarsely chopped

1 large carrot, coarsely chopped

Three 1-inch knobs fresh ginger, unpeeled, sliced

6 whole dried red Thai chilies

Place the wings and/or bones in a large stockpot. Cover with about 12 cups water and bring to a boil. Skim the foamy impurities off the top and reduce the heat to maintain a simmer. Add the onion, scallions, celery, carrot, ginger, and chilies to the stock. Simmer gently for about 2 hours. Strain. Skim off the top layer of fat that rises to top of the stock. The Basic Chicken Stock can be stored in an airtight container in the refrigerator for up to 1 week or in the freezer for up to 1 month.

BRAISED SHORT RIBS

MAKES JUST OVER 1 QUART SHREDDED MEAT

We make this versatile short rib meat for banh mi sandwiches, bao buns, tacos, and dumplings. It stores well in the freezer and is great to have on hand for last-minute dinners.

½ Asian pear, cored and roughly chopped

1 quart Basic Chicken Stock (page 313) or canned low-sodium chicken broth

½ medium yellow onion, coarsely chopped

2 scallions, white and green parts coarsely chopped

1 medium garlic clove, smashed

One 1-inch knob fresh ginger, peeled and sliced

2 whole star anise

2 tablespoons soy sauce

1 tablespoon sugar

1 tablespoon honey

1 tablespoon sesame oil

2 tablespoons vegetable oil, such as canola

1½ pounds boneless English-style short ribs, trimmed and cut into 2-inch medallions

2 teaspoons kosher salt

1 teaspoon freshly ground black pepper

Preheat the oven to 350°F and place a rack in the center of the oven.

In a large bowl, mix together the pear, stock, onion, scallions, garlic, ginger, star anise, soy sauce, sugar, honey, and sesame oil. Set aside. The braising mixture can be made up to 1 day in advance and stored in an airtight container in the refrigerator.

In a large braising dish or Dutch oven, heat the vegetable oil over medium-high heat until hot. Season the short ribs all over with the salt and pepper. Carefully place them in the braising dish and turn the heat down to medium. Sear for 3 to 4 minutes on each side until well browned and caramelized. Pour the braising mixture over the ribs and bring to a boil. Cover the dish tightly with aluminum foil (or cover with the lid if using a Dutch oven). Place in the oven and braise for 2 to 2½ hours, or until the meat is tender enough to pierce with a fork.

Remove from the oven and let cool to room temperature. When cool enough to handle, shred the meat with your hands into a large bowl, discarding any fat. Strain the braising liquid into the bowl to cover the meat, discarding the solids. The Braised Short Ribs can be stored in an airtight container in the refrigerator for 3 days or in the freezer for 2 weeks.

314

PERFECT WHITE RICE

MAKES 3 CUPS

If you don't have a rice cooker, cooking rice on the stovetop couldn't be easier. Rinse the rice a few times before cooking to remove any excess starch (which could make your rice too sticky), and make sure you let it sit and absorb the last of the water so that it comes out fluffy and perfect. There is nothing quite as comforting as a pot of rice cooking on the stove. It's my favorite smell in the world.

1 cup medium-grain white rice

<u>Wash the rice</u> by submerging it in 1 quart water, stirring it with your hands, and draining well. Repeat twice more. When the rice is submerged and mixed with your hands the first time, the water turns so cloudy you can't see the rice anymore. The second time, the water clouds a little less, and by the third time, the water is still cloudy but you can see the rice. In a medium saucepan, combine the rice and 2 cups water and bring to a boil over high heat. Stir the rice with a wooden spoon, reduce the heat to medium-low, and cook until the rice starts to absorb the water, about 4 minutes. Cover the pot and cook over low heat for 6 to 8 minutes, stirring the rice from time to time. Turn off the heat and cover the pot. Let the rice sit for about 15 minutes to absorb the last of the water. Fluff with a fork. Cover tightly until ready to serve.

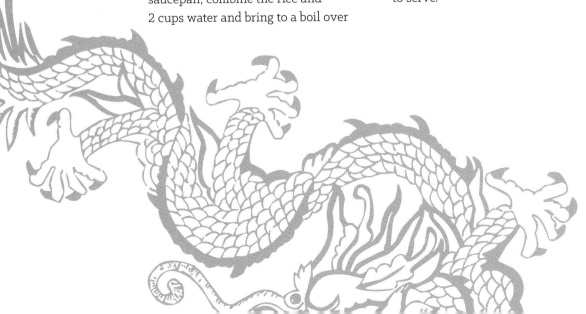

PERFECT BROWN RICE

MAKES 3 CUPS

Making brown rice is the same as making white rice, except that it takes a touch more water and steams for a lot longer. As with all rice, you may need to add more water depending on the age of your rice.

1 cup medium-grain brown rice

<u>Wash the rice</u> by submerging it in 1 quart water, stirring it with your hands, and draining well. Repeat twice more. When the rice is submerged and mixed with your hands the first time, the water turns so cloudy you can't see the rice anymore. The second time, the water clouds a little less, and by the third time, the water is still cloudy but you can see the rice. In medium saucepan, combine the rice and 2¼ cups water and bring to a boil over high heat. Stir the rice with a wooden spoon, reduce the heat to medium-low, and cook until the rice starts to absorb the water, about 4 minutes. Cover the pot and cook over low heat for 30 minutes, stirring the rice from time to time. Turn off the heat and cover the pot. Let the rice sit for about 15 minutes to absorb the last of the water. Fluff with a fork. Cover tightly until ready to serve.

INDEX

Page numbers in *italics* indicate illustrations

A

Aioli, Sriracha, 308–309
Apricot Dipping Sauce, Spicy, 103
Arctic Char Rolls with Housemade Chinese Hot Mustard, 91–92

B

Bacon
    and Calamari Pad Thai, 214–216, *215*
    and Egg Banh Mi, Sweet Soy, 278–281, *279*
    Lamb Belly, 222
    Mushu Stir-Fry, Triple Pork, 194–195
Banh Mi, Sweet Soy Bacon and Egg, 278–281, *279*
BBQ Sauce, Korean, 150
Beef. *See also* Short Rib(s), Braised
    Bulgogi BBQ Sloppy "Jo", 148–150, *149*
    and Chinese Broccoli Chow Fun, 223–224, *225*

Kimchi Quinoa *Bokkeumbap*, 240–241, *241*
Rainbow, 196–197
Shanghai Noodles, Surf and Turf Black Pepper, 210–213, *212*
Tiger's Tears, 126–127
Black Bean Sauce, 188
Black Pepper Sauce, 213
    –Scallion, *175*, 175
Black Vinegar–Wasabi Dipping Sauce, 163
Bok Choy
    and Chicken with Udon Noodles, Wok-Charred, *206*, 207–209, *209*
    Ginger-Scallion, 252–253
Brittle, Black-and-White Sesame, *290*, 291
Broccoli, Chinese, and Beef Chow Fun, 223–224, *225*
Brussels Sprouts, Sweet-and-Sour, 247–248, *248*

Bulgogi BBQ Sloppy "Jo", 148–150, *149*
Butter
    Honey-Sesame, 143
    Sriracha, *84*, 85
    Tamarind, 138
    XO Brown, 264

C

Caesar Salad, Chinese, 268–269
Calamari and Bacon Pad Thai, 214–216, *215*
Carrots, Red Miso-Glazed, 250, *251*
Cauliflower with Tofu, Red Curry, 182–183
Cellophane Noodles, Slippery, Twice-Cooked Lamb Belly Stir-Fry with, 220–222
Chicken
    and Bok Choy with Udon Noodles, Wok-Charred, *206*, 207–209, *209*
    Fried, and Ginger-Sesame Waffles, Indonesian, 139–144, *140–141*

Chicken, *continued*
    Lemon, Panko-Crusted, 145–147, *146*
    Nirvana, 272
    and Rapini Stir-Fry, *184*, 185–186
    Salad, Chinese, Christopher's, *120*, 121–122, *122*
    Salad, Thai Ginger, 123–124, *125*
    Soup, Lemony Garlicky, Ashley's, 274–275
    Stock, Basic, 313
    velveting, 65–66, 185–186, 208
    Wings, Garlicky Spicy Coal Black, 96–97
Chickpeas, Kung Pao, 254–255, *255*
Chili(es)
    Dragon Sauce, 305
    Jam, Thai, 261
    -Tomato Jam, 310
Chili Oil, Sichuan, 178, *179*
Chimichurri, Thai Basil, 113
Chocolate Tofu Mousse with Black-and-White Sesame Brittle, 289–291, *290*
Chow Fun, Beef and Chinese Broccoli, 223–225, *226*
Clams in Chinese Black Bean Sauce, 187–188
Coconut
    and Corn Soup, 81–82, *82*
    Meringue Clouds, Toasted-, 294–295
    Rice, 135
Cod, Tamarind-Glazed, with Vietnamese Mint, Jicama, and Grapefruit Slaw, 136–138
Congee with Nirvana Chicken and Scallion Salsa, 271–272, *273*
Cookies
    Cornmeal-Lime Sandwich, 296–297
    Fortune, Homemade, *298*, 299–300, *301*

Corn
    and Coconut Soup, 81–82, *82*
    Grilled, with Sriracha Butter, 84, 85
Crab, Ginger-Scallion, and Crispy Vermicelli Stir-Fry, 202–203, *204–205*
Cucumber(s)
    Kimchi, 150
    Salad, Cool, Pan-Roasted Soy-Glazed Salmon with, 130–132, *131*
    Sesame, Taiwanese, 78
Curry(ied)
    Duck and Wheat Berries, 233–235
    Madras, 44
    Red, Cauliflower with Tofu, 182–183
    Red, Ginger Squash Soup, 79–80
    Sauce, 235
    Sauce, Vegetarian, 183
Curry Paste, Red, Homemade, 307

D
Dan Dan Noodle(s)
    Salad, Taiwanese, *108*, 109–111
    Sichuan, 217–219, *218*
Desserts, 284–301
Dim sum dishes, 74–103
Dip, Whipped Tofu, Roasted-Garlic, 309
Dipping Sauce(s)
    Apricot, Spicy, 103
    Black Pepper–Scallion, *175*, 175
    Black Vinegar–Wasabi, 163
    Dumpling, Classic, 160
    Kimchi-Yogurt, 166
Dragon Sauce, 305
Dressing(s)
    Caesar, 269
    Ginger Goddess, 107
    Lemon-Ginger, 308
    Nuoc Cham, 304
    Sichuan, 95, 257
    Vietnamese, 138
    Whipped Tofu, Roasted-Garlic, 309

Duck
    Braised, 234
    and Ginger Dumplings, Juicy, 167–170, *169*, *170*
    and Wheat Berries, Curried, 233–235
Duck Sauce, Rhubarb, *89*, 90
Dumplings, 66–69, 156–179
Dumpling Sauce, Classic, 160

E
Edamame, Wasabi, and Mustard Green Dumplings with Black Vinegar–Wasabi Dipping Sauce, 161–163
Egg(s)
    Deviled, Soy Sauce, with Five-Spice, 74, 76–77, *77*
    and Sweet Soy Bacon Banh Mi, 278–281, *279*
Eggplant, Hakka, 244–246, *245*
Egg Roll, Kevin's Old-School, 101–103
Equipment and tools, 58–62, *60–61*

F
Farro, in The Green Monster, *230*, 231–232
Fennel and Kale Salad with Fuyu Persimmons, 112–113
Fingerling Potatoes, Smashed, with Thai Chili Jam, *258*, 259–261, *260*
Fortune Cookies, Homemade, *298*, 299–300, *301*
Fritters, Chinese Sausage and Sweet Potato, 98–100, *99*
Fun Sauce, 306

G
Ginger
    Chicken Salad, Thai, 123–124, *125*
    and Duck Dumplings, Juicy, 167–170, *169*, *170*
    Goddess Dressing, 107
    -Lemon Dressing, 308
    Red Curry Squash Soup, 79–80
    -Scallion Bok Choy, 252–253

MYERS+
CHANG
AT HOME

-Scallion Crab and Crispy
Vermicelli Stir-Fry, 202–203,
204–205
-Sesame Waffles, *141*, 143
Granita, Orange, 288
Grapefruit, Mint, and Jicama Slaw,
Vietnamese, 136–138
Green Monster, The, *230*, 231–232

H, I, J
Hakka Eggplant, 244–246, *245*
Hot and Sour Soup, Esti's, 83–84

Ice Cream, Espresso, Vietnamese, 292
Ingredients, 32–57

Jicama, Mint, and Grapefruit Slaw,
Vietnamese, 136–138

K
Kale and Fennel Salad with Fuyu
Persimmons, 112–113
Khao Koor, 311
Kimchi
Cucumbers, 150
Quinoa *Bokkeumbap*, 240–241, *241*
-Sesame Salsa, 152
in Tofu, Spicy Silky, *192*, 193
-Yogurt Dipping Sauce, 166
Kung Pao Chickpeas, 254–255, *255*

L
Lamb Belly Stir-Fry with Slippery
Cellophane Noodles, Twice-
Cooked, 220–222
Lemon
Chicken, Panko-Crusted, 145–147,
146
-Ginger Dressing, 308
Sauce, Candied, 147
Lemongrass Pesto, 232
Lo Mein, Wild Mushroom, 200–201
Long Beans, Amandine, with
Homemade XO Butter, 262–264

M
Meringue Clouds, Toasted-Coconut,
294–295

Mousse, Chocolate Tofu, with Black-
and-White Sesame Brittle,
289–291, *290*
Mushroom
Shiitake, and Spinach Dumplings
with Classic Dumpling Sauce,
158–160
Wild, Lo Mein, 200–201
Mushu Stir-Fry, Triple Pork, 194–195
Mussels, Wok-Roasted Lemongrass,
with Garlic Toast, 189–190, *191*
Mustard Green, Edamame, and
Wasabi Dumplings with Black
Vinegar–Wasabi Dipping Sauce,
161–163
Mustard Sauce, Chinese Hot, 304

N
Nam Prik Pao, 261
Nasi Goreng, 236–239, *237*
Noodles, 198–224
Nuoc Cham, 304

O
Orange Granita, 288

P
Pad Thai, Bacon and Calamari,
214–216, *215*
Papaya Slaw, Green, 118–119
Parfait, Vanilla Bean, with Orange
Granita, *286*, 287–288
Peanut Satay Sauce, 115
Pesto, Lemongrass, 232
Pickled Shallots, 312
Pickled Vegetables, 281
Pizza, Asian, 270
Pork. *See also* Bacon; Sausage,
Chinese
and Chive Dumplings,
Mama Chang's, with Black
Pepper–Scallion Sauce, 171–175,
172–173
in Dan Dan Noodles, Sichuan,
217–219, *218*
Mushu Stir-Fry, Triple, 194–195
Ragu, 219

Spare Ribs, Tea-Smoked,
153–154, *155*
in Tofu, Spicy Silky, *192*, 193

Q
Quinoa Kimchi *Bokkeumbap*,
240–241, *241*

R
Rainbow Sauce, 197
Rainbow Trout with Coconut Rice and
Chili-Tomato Jam, 133–135, *134*
Red Bean Soup, 293
Rhubarb Duck Sauce, *89*, 90
Rice, 47
Brown, Perfect, 316
Coconut, 135
Congee with Nirvana Chicken and
Scallion Salsa, 271–272, *273*
Fried, Genmai, 228–229
Fried, Indonesian, 236–239, *237*,
238
Khao Koor, 311
White, Perfect, 315

S
Salad Dressing. *See* Dressing(s)
Salads, 104–127, 130, 268
Salmon, Pan-Roasted Soy-Glazed,
with Cool Cucumber Salad,
130–132, *131*
Satay Sauce, Peanut, 115
Sauce(s). *See also* Dipping Sauce(s);
Dressing(s)
Aioli, Sriracha, 308–309
Black Bean, 188
Black Pepper, 213
Chicken Stir-Fry, 186
Chimichurri, Thai Basil, 113
Curry, 235
Curry, Vegetarian, 183
Dan Dan, 111
Dragon (Homemade Sriracha), 305
Fun, 306
Ginger-Scallion, 253
Hakka, 246
Korean BBQ, 150
Kung Pao, 255

Sauce(s), *continued*
    Lemon, Candied, 147
    Lemongrass Pesto, 232
    Mushu, 195
    Mustard, Hot, Chinese, 304
    Pad Thai, 216
    Peanut Satay, 115
    Rainbow, 197
    Rhubarb Duck, *89*, 90
    Salmon, 132
    Scallion, 203
    Surprising, 144
    Udon, 209
Sausage, Chinese
    Mushu Stir-Fry, Triple Pork,
      194–195
    and Sweet Potato Fritters,
      98–100, *99*
Sesame
    Brittle, Black-and-White, *290*, 291
    Cucumbers, Taiwanese, 78
    -Ginger Waffles, *141*, 143
    -Honey Butter, 143
    -Kimchi Salsa, 152
Shallots
    Crispy, 312
    Pickled, 312
Shanghai Noodles, Surf and Turf
    Black Pepper, 210–213, *212*
Shiitake Mushroom and Spinach
    Dumplings with Classic
    Dumpling Sauce, 158–160
Short Rib(s), Braised, 314
    Dumplings with Sichuan Chili Oil,
      176–178, *177*, *179*
    Korean-, Tacos with Kimchi-
      Sesame Salsa, 151–152
Shrimp
    Dumplings, Lemony, with Kimchi-
      Yogurt Dipping Sauce, 164–166,
      165
    Fried Rice, Indonesian, 236–239,
      237, *238*

Lettuce Wraps, Sichuan, 93–95, *94*
and Scallions, Mom's Stir-Fried,
    276, 277
Shanghai Noodles, Surf and Turf
    Black Pepper, 210–213, *212*
Slaw
    Green Papaya, 118–119
    Mint, Jicama, and Grapefruit,
      Vietnamese, 136–138
Sloppy "Jo", Bulgogi BBQ, 148–150, *149*
Soba Noodles, Buckwheat, with
    Fresh Tofu and Lemon-Ginger
    Dressing, 116–117, *117*
Soup(s)
    Chicken, Lemony Garlicky,
      Ashley's, 274–275
    Corn and Coconut, 81–82, *82*
    Hot and Sour, Esti's, 83–84
    Red Bean, 293
    Squash, Red Curry Ginger, 79–80
Spare Ribs, Tea-Smoked Pork,
    153–154, *155*
Spinach
    Chinese Water, with Fermented
      Tofu, 249
    and Shiitake Mushroom
      Dumplings with Classic
      Dumpling Sauce, 158–160
Spring Rolls, Auntie Mia's, *86*,
    86–88, *89*
Squash Soup, Red Curry Ginger,
    79–80
Sriracha
    Aioli, 308–309
    Butter, 85
    Homemade, 305
Stock, Chicken, Basic, 313
Sugar Snap Peas with Ginger Goddess
    Dressing, 106–107, *107*
Summer Squash and Zucchini,
    Sichuan, 256–257
Surprising Sauce, 144
Sweet Potato and Chinese Sausage
    Fritters, 98–100, *99*

T
Tacos, Korean Braised Short Rib, with
    Kimchi-Sesame Salsa, 151–152
Tamarind Butter, 138
Terasi, 239
Tiger's Tears, 126–127
Tofu
    with Cauliflower, Red Curry,
      182–183
    and Chinese Broccoli Chow Fun,
      224
    Chocolate Mousse with Black-and-
      White Sesame Brittle, 289–291,
      290
    Fermented, Chinese Water Spinach
      with, 249
    Fresh, Buckwheat Soba Noodles
      with Lemon-Ginger Dressing
      and, 116–117, *117*
    Fresh Rolls with Herbs, Lettuce
      and, Vietnamese, 114–115
    Spicy Silky, *192*, 193
    Whipped, Roasted-Garlic, 309
Tomato-Chili Jam, 310
Trout, Rainbow, with Coconut Rice
    and Chili-Tomato Jam,
    133–135, *134*

U, V
Udon Noodles with Chicken and
    Bok-Choy, Wok-Charred, *206*,
    207–209, *209*

Velveting meats, 65–66, 185–186, 208
Vermicelli, Crispy, and Ginger-
    Scallion Crab Stir-Fry, 202–203,
    204–205

W, X, Z
Waffles, Ginger-Sesame, *141*, 143
Wheat Berries and Duck, Curried,
    233–235
Wok cooking, 62–64, 180–197

XO Brown Butter, 264

Zucchini and Summer Squash,
    Sichuan, 256–257

MYERS+
CHANG
AT HOME